Now My Eye Sees You

Hebrew Bible Monographs, 24

Series Editors
David J.A. Clines, J. Cheryl Exum, Keith W. Whitelam

Editorial Board
A. Graeme Auld, Marc Brettler, Francis Landy,
Hugh S. Pyper, Stuart D.E. Weeks

Now my Eye Sees You

Unveiling an Apocalyptic Job

Timothy Jay Johnson

Sheffield Phoenix Press

2013

Copyright © 2009, 2013 Sheffield Phoenix Press

First published in hardback, 2009
First published in paperback, 2013

Published by Sheffield Phoenix Press
Department of Biblical Studies, University of Sheffield
45 Victoria Street, Sheffield S3 7QB England

www.sheffieldphoenix.com

All rights reserved.
No part of this publication may be reproduced or transmitted in any form or by any means, electronic or mechanical, including photocopying, recording or any information storage or retrieval system, without the publisher's permission in writing.

A CIP catalogue record for this book
is available from the British Library

Typeset by CA Typesetting Ltd
Printed by Lightning Source

ISBN 978-1-909697-19-5 (paperback)
ISBN 978-1-906055-73-8 (hardback)

ISSN 1747-9614

Contents

Preface	vii
Abbreviations	ix
INTRODUCTION	1
Genre and the Book of Job	1
A Brief Discussion of Genre	3
Methodological Assumptions Concerning Genre	10
The Plan of This Book	11

Chapter 1
TRADITIONAL AND CRITICAL EVALUATIONS
OF JOB'S GOVERNING GENRE   15
   Introduction   15
   Wisdom as Genre for Job   15
   Alternative Genres for Job   23
   Conclusion   38

Chapter 2
COMPARING JOB TO APOCALYPSE   39
   Introduction   39
   Master Paradigm   43
   Comparing Job to the Master Paradigm   47
   Paolo Sacchi   65
   Job as Apocalyptic Compared to Koch and Sacchi   67
   Job as an Apocalyptic Chronoscope   71
   Conclusion   75

Chapter 3
TRADITION'S ESCHATOLOGICAL INTERPRETATIONS OF JOB   78
   Introduction   78
   Earliest Job   79
   Ezekiel's References   81
   LXX Job   84
   Paleo-Hebrew Job   86
   The Targums of Job at Qumran   88
   Rabbinic Targum   90

The *Testament of Job*	92
Letter of James	95
Apocalypse of Paul	99
Medieval References	100
Lawrence L. Besserman	101
The LXX in the Early Christian Church	101
Conclusion	104

Chapter 4
READING JOB THROUGH APOCALYPTIC EYES

	106
Introduction	106
Job 1.1–4.11: Job's Demise and Challenge	107
Job 4.12–28.22: Revelation of Humanity's Unrighteousness—Job Persecuted	116
Job 28.23–37.24: God's Revelation of Wisdom—Job Encouraged	136
Job 38.1–42.7: God's Revelation of Divine Prerogative—Job Submits	146
Job 42.7-17: Job's Reward for Persevering	156
Conclusion	158

Chapter 5
IMPLICATIONS FOR APOCALYPTIC JOB ON THEMES AND SETTINGS

	159
Introduction	159
The Themes of Job	161
The Setting of Job	166
Wisdom and Apocalypse	170
Conclusion	175

CONCLUSION	177
Bibliography	181
Index of References	191
Index of Authors	196

Preface

My interest in researching Job as a nascent form of apocalypse was first piqued in 1998 by Duane Garrett's provocative lectures at Bethel Seminary in St Paul, Minnesota. Upon discovering that scholars such as John J. Collins and Christopher Rowland had also intimated Job's affinities with apocalypse, I began the long journey that has culminated in this effort to flesh out Job's association with apocalyptic literature. This book is based on my doctoral dissertation, which was completed at Marquette University in May 2004.

I wish to thank especially my wife for her willingness to allow me the luxury of study. Over the years, she has labored in a variety of vocational settings far beneath her talents in order to support my studies. She has at times single-handedly raised our three children—once again, in complete support of my research. She is an extraordinary, compassionate and patient gift from God, and she has endured no small amount of personal disruption for my sake. I both thank her and love her dearly. I hope one day to return just a portion of the favor.

I am exceedingly grateful for my dissertation director, John J. Schmitt. Not only was he willing to take on my rather curious project, but he did so with a patient and endearing spirit. His cheerfulness and encouragement has always been a wonderful model for me to follow in my own teaching career. Like him, my remaining committee members, Deirdre Dempsey, Sharon Pace, Michel Barnes and Fr William Kurz encouraged me to pursue publication of this project, and for that I am very grateful. Special thanks are also due to Duncan Burns for both his work on the indexes and his careful readings of this manuscript, which is vastly improved as a result. Finally, I owe a great debt of gratitude to Professor D.J.A. Clines and his colleagues at Sheffield Phoenix Press for their willingness to publish my work.

Timothy Jay Johnson
Oconomowoc, WI
March 2009

ABBREVIATIONS

ABD	David Noel Freedman (ed.), *The Anchor Bible Dictionary* (New York: Doubleday, 1992)
AB	Anchor Bible Series
ACCS	Ancient Christian Commentary on Scripture
ANET	James B. Pritchard (ed.), *Ancient Near Eastern Texts Relating to the Old Testament* (Princeton: Princeton University Press, 1950; 2nd edn, 1975)
BAGD	Walter Bauer, William F. Arndt, F. William Gingrich and Frederick W. Danker, *A Greek–English Lexicon of the New Testament and Other Early Christian Literature* (Chicago: University of Chicago Press, 2nd edn, 1958)
BDB	F. Brown, S. Driver, and C. Briggs (eds.), *Hebrew and English Lexicon of the Old Testament* (Oxford: Clarendon, 1907)
BIOSCS	*Bulletin of the International Organization for Septuagint and Cognate Studies*
BZAW	*Beihefte zur Zeitschrift für die alttestamentliche Wissenschaft*
CBQ	*Catholic Biblical Quarterly*
CBQMS	Catholic Biblical Quarterly Monograph Series
DJD	The Discoveries in the Judean Desert
FOTL	The Forms of the Old Testament Literature Series
HBT	*Horizons in Biblical Theology*
HTR	*Harvard Theological Review*
HUCA	*Hebrew Union College Annual*
ICC	*The International Critical Commentary*
IDB	G.A. Buttrick (ed.), *The Interpreter's Dictionary of the Bible* (New York: Abingdon, 1962)
IDBSup	*IDB*, Supplementary Volume
JAOS	*Journal of the American Oriental Society*
JBL	*Journal of Biblical Literature*
JJS	*Journal of Jewish Studies*
JNES	*Journal of Near Eastern Studies*
JSJ	*Journal for the Study of Judaism*
JSNT	*Journal for the Study of the New Testament*
JSOT	*Journal for the Study of the Old Testament*
JSOTSS	*Journal for the Study of the Old Testament Supplement Series*
JSP	*Journal for the Study of the Pseudepigrapha*
JTC	*Journal for Theology and the Church*
JTS	*Journal of Theological Studies*
LXX	Septuagint
MT	Masoretic text

NCB	The New Century Bible Commentary
NETS	A. Pietersma and B. Wright (eds.), *A New English Translation of the Septuagint* (New York: Oxford University Press, 2007)
NICNT	The New International Commentary on the New Testament
NICOT	The New International Commentary on the Old Testament
NTS	New Testament Studies
OG	Old Greek
OTL	Old Testament Library
OTP	James Charlesworth (ed.), *Old Testament Pseudepigrapha*
SBLDS	SBL Dissertation Series
SBLSP	SBL Seminar Papers
SBLSS	SBL Supplement Series
TNTC	Tyndale New Testament Commentaries
TOTC	Tyndale Old Testament Commentaries
TUMSR	Trinity University Monograph Series in Religion
VT	*Vetus Testamentum*
WBC	Word Biblical Commentary
WTJ	*The Westminster Theological Journal*
ZAW	*Zeitschrift für die alttestamentliche Wissenschaft*

INTRODUCTION

Genre and the Book of Job

For over two millennia the book of Job has confounded interpreters. The book's multiple literary, thematic and theological layers seem to resist a coherently unified interpretation. For example, and most notable among many enigmas in Job, scholars have long puzzled over how to integrate the framing sections of Job that are written in prose with the lengthy dialogue speeches that are written in poetry. Their mere presence has led many to assume that more than one author crafted the book of Job. They may be right. However, the presence of more than one hand does not necessarily deny that a final hand wove all the pieces together in a deliberately unified manner. Such a unified vision would imply purpose, which further implies that some kind of intentional genre or classification of writing was incorporated into the work's final shape. However, scholarship has labored unsuccessfully to discern the seemingly elusive governing genre. The purpose of my project is to propose such an over-arching genre for the book of Job that runs counter to conventional wisdom.

It is axiomatic in the academy that the book of Job is part of the Wisdom Literature. The natural implication, correctly or incorrectly, is that 'wisdom' is the literary genre governing Job. As evidence, scholars point to wisdom terms such as 'sage' and 'wisdom' that surface throughout the book. Seemingly more compelling are the presence of the mysterious search for wisdom as found in ch. 28, the challenge to a theology of retribution, and numerous connections between Job and what scholars have termed wisdom documents of the ancient Near East. All one must do is consult any introductory work on the Hebrew Bible or Wisdom Literature to see that Job as wisdom is one of the 'assured results' of scholarship.[1]

Despite this apparent unanimity, numerous scholars have challenged wisdom's privileged status as Job's literary genre, and one could say that the number of alternative proposals offered over the years is sufficient testimony to an ongoing dissatisfaction that wisdom governs Job. As I will show later, the wide variety of alternative suggestions has been even less convincing than that of wisdom itself. Consequently, no one hypothesis has been able to unseat wisdom from its throne as Job's governing genre.

---

1. Generally accepted as wisdom are: Proverbs, Ecclesiastes and Job. In the Deuterocanonicals, Sirach and the Wisdom of Solomon are also considered wisdom books.

A common weakness shared by all of these proposals is that none of the alternatives is able to subsume satisfactorily all of the diverse features of Job in a coherent fashion. My study adds to the list of dissenters and instead proposes that Job is more akin to a nascent form of 'apocalypse'. The amount of evidence supporting my contention seems too great to dismiss without a thorough investigation.

I am indebted to Duane Garrett for his stimulating lectures on the topic, which provided the motivation for this research. Fortunately, a handful of scholars who either support or intimate various agreements with my view have put their ideas in print, even if only in brief. Most notable among these are John J. Collins,[2] Christopher Rowland,[3] Frank Moore Cross[4] and Ithamar Gruenwald.[5] Each of these briefly points to the affinities shared between Job and apocalypse, though none has developed the connections fully. I will undertake the daunting task of investigating what these scholars have hitherto only suggested.

I understand that if the reader has a difficult time conceiving of Job as apocalypse, it may be due, in part, to the hegemonic grip 'wisdom' has on Job. However, one needs look no further than William Blake's pictorial descriptions of Job for evidence that Job elicits imagery close to apocalypse.[6] Blake's celestial forms portray otherworldly, distorted, rapturous, surreal and demonic scenery.[7] As an artist and biblical scholar, his own drawings may very well testify to an apocalyptic motif, which is perhaps more telling than is first thought, for they portend a feature of Job that has yet to be readily discussed in scholarship.[8]

---

2. John J. Collins, 'Cosmos and Salvation: Jewish Wisdom and Apocalyptic in the Hellenistic Age', *History of Religions* 17 (1977), pp. 121-42 (140); see n. 74 where Collins states, 'The Hebrew wisdom book which has the greatest affinities with apocalyptic, the Book of Job...'

3. Christopher Rowland, *The Open Heaven: A Study of Apocalyptic in Judaism and Early Christianity* (New York: Crossroad, 1982), pp. 206-207.

4. F. Moore Cross, 'New Directions in the Study of Apocalyptic', *JTC* 6 (1969), pp. 157-65 (163).

5. Ithamar Gruenwald, *Apocalyptic and Merkavah Mysticism* (Leiden: E.J. Brill, 1980), especially Chapter 1 (pp. 3-28).

6. See S. Foster Damon, *Blake's Job: William Blake's Illustrations of the Book of Job* (Hanover: University Press of New England, 1982). Illustration II, 14, reveals such an apocalyptic scene. One particular feature of this illustration is the centrality of the Satan figure with both Job and his wife dimly cast under his two arms.

7. Robert N. Essick, *William Blake, Printmaker* (Princeton: Princeton University Press, 1980), dedicates an entire chapter (Chapter 18) to a discussion of Blake's Job; see pp. 234-49.

8. Damon notes that Blake considered the book of Job as a spiritual, internal battle between Job's God and the Satan. Indeed, 'Job's prime error was admitting this Accuser into his heaven' (p. 7).

It is worth noting that the search for Job's overall genre is no mere exercise in intellectual gymnastics. Indeed, determining the governing genre in Job 'is an essential clue to the book's meaning'.[9] All too often Job's literary units are dismembered, which may simply reduce the reader's ability to comprehend the overarching message. To be sure, the text lends itself to such dissection. However, Leo Perdue and W. Clark Gilpin lament that 'few efforts to relate the stages and provide a uniform interpretation of the entire book have been undertaken'.[10] Carole Fontaine concurs, noting that, 'While current trends in exegesis show considerable interest in dealing with the whole text as a literary unit, no one interpretive scheme seems to account adequately for the symbiotic relationship existing between the prose and poetry in Job'.[11] I hope to make a small contribution to such an assembly of Job's seemingly disparate phases and genres and in so doing offer a unique interpretation of Job that may foster further research and interest in one of the Bible's most challenging and profitable books.

Before advancing further, it is important to say a word or two about genre. While I am not interested in reviewing all that has been said about genre, my reader needs to know that the voluminous research dedicated to issues of genre has failed to produce any consensus concerning the nature and use of the term 'genre'. Still, my own biases will surely influence this project, and a brief review of the research will at least contribute to the defense of my own appropriation of the term. This is particularly important for my work, because, in classifying Job, I am arguing away from the designation 'wisdom' and moving toward the notion of 'apocalypse', both of which are considered biblical genres.

A Brief Discussion of Genre

David Duff suggests that the modern period has not treated the term 'genre' with particular favor, instead preferring 'to dispense altogether with the doctrine of literary kinds or genres'. He goes on to lament that, 'If the death of the author has been a familiar refrain of modern literary theory, so too has the dissolution of genres'.[12] Duff acknowledges that one of the 'enduring

---

9. W.S. LaSor, D.A. Hubbard and F.W. Bush (eds.), *Old Testament Survey: The Message, Form, and Background of the Old Testament* (Grand Rapids: Eerdmans, 2nd edn, 1996), p. 487.

10. Leo G. Perdue and W. Clark Gilpin (eds.), *The Voice from the Whirlwind: Interpreting the Book of Job* (Nashville: Abingdon Press, 1992), p. 16.

11. Carole Fontaine, 'Folktale Structure in the Book of Job: A Formalist Reading', in E. Follis (ed.), *Directions in Biblical Hebrew Poetry* (JSOTSup, 40; Sheffield: JSOT Press, 1987), pp. 205-32 (205).

12. David Duff, *Modern Genre Theory* (Harlow, Essex: Longman, 2000), p. 1.

problems of genre theory' is 'confusion of terminology', which 'no modern language seems to have solved'.[13] No consensus seems to exist with respect to nomenclature. For example, and particularly relevant for biblical scholars, Duff wonders whether there is a distinction between the terms 'form' and 'genre'.[14] More will be said on this specific distinction shortly, but the point is clear. If literary critics are unable to speak with one voice, how much more difficult is it for biblical scholars, who significantly depend on those very literary critics, to speak consistently about issues of genre? Despite his pessimism, Duff is convinced that recent trends suggest a recovery of genre's value.

The SBL's recent monograph, *Bakhtin and Genre Theory in Biblical Studies*, seems to confirm Duff's optimism in general, and Carol Newsom's recent work on Job, which advocates a 'recuperation of genre as a critical category for understanding the book of Job' and is particularly valuable for my study, is further testimony that biblical scholars, at least, value continued research into genre.[15]

Newsom's selective chronicling of the history of genre studies in biblical disciplines is a useful starting point for lightly unpacking the nature of genre as it relates particularly to biblical studies. For better or worse, biblical scholars owe their genre-heritage in large measure to Gunkel's development of form criticism. In the biblical studies guild, genre is the fundamental component involved in form-critical studies whose task is to analyze small compositional units and recover pre-literary oral forms in order to discover the social setting (*Sitz im Leben*) from which these units emerged. There are two stages to this method of study, each bearing on the identification of genre. The first considers the specific form of an individual passage but does not concern itself with the passage's content. Once several of these are studied, the second stage attempts to classify them into a particular *Gattung* or 'genre'.[16] Newsom argues that due to such a concentration on the *Sitz im Leben* of these early speech forms, form criticism contributed greatly to the 'sociology of genres'.[17] Such an approach concentrated on classification over against interpretation of the meaning communicated via the form.

13. Duff, *Modern Genre Theory*, p. 17.
14. Duff, *Modern Genre Theory*, p. 17.
15. Roland Boer (ed.), *Bakhtin and Genre Theory in Biblical Studies* (SBL Semeia Studies, 63; Atlanta: SBL, 2007); Carol Newsom, *The Book of Job: A Contest of Moral Imaginations* (Oxford: Oxford University Press, 2003), pp. 3-11 (11).
16. John Barton, 'Form Criticism: Old Testament', in *ABD*, II, pp. 838-41.
17. Carol Newsom, 'Spying Out the Land: A Report from Genology', in Boer (ed.), *Bakhtin*, pp. 19-30 (19).

Katharine Dell points out that a genre differs from a form in that form, content, and context (*Sitz im Leben*) need to correspond in a genre.[18] Thus, several forms may be categorized as a lament, for example, implying that these forms conform to certain norms shared among all laments. A particular psalm may be a lament, or a lament may reside within a larger unit of work whose overall genre is not necessarily that of lament. Tremper Longman argues similarly, reserving 'form' for 'smaller units' and genre for 'larger units', though he acknowledges that 'principles apply to both'.[19] Thus, when a lament emerges in a work, no matter how frequently, its mere existence does not necessarily imply that the overall work is governed by the genre of lament. On the other hand, Dell cautions that it is just as wrong to predetermine the overall genre of a work and then assert that the forms found in that work correspond to this designated genre.[20]

Those who identify a book's governing genre based on form-critical analysis are open to the criticism that it is difficult to ascertain the broad literary parameters of an entire book based on the smaller, isolated forms leading to those conclusions. Such a criticism is leveled against Westermann's study of Job, but, as will be shown later, the same assessment is just as easily leveled against wisdom as the governing genre of Job.[21]

Over time, scholars concluded that deductive applications were too inflexible because form-critical scholars tended to equate given forms as content-laden genres, which seemed to suggest that genres exist as rigid, set forms. Instead, many were seeing that genre went beyond forms alone.[22] A re-examination was called for and emerged in the SBL Genres Project of the 1970s, which has produced much fruit, the most notable perhaps being the work on apocalypses published in *Semeia* 14. Despite this interest and energy, a uniformly accepted definition of genre has seemingly yet to surface.

Rightfully identifying genre as a 'slippery word', Newsom helpfully suggests the following definition of genre: 'Patterns of similarity and dissimilarity, that is, the recognition that the text at hand is like these and not those, establish the reader's sense of genre'.[23] As seen earlier, it is not surprising to

---

18. Katharine Dell, *The Book of Job as Sceptical Literature* (BZAW, 197; Berlin: Walter de Gruyter, 1991), p. 88.
19. Tremper Longman III, 'Form Criticism, Recent Developments in Genre Theory, and the Evangelical', *WTJ* 47 (1985), pp. 46-67 (50).
20. Dell, *Job as Sceptical Literature*, p. 89.
21. Roland Murphy, *Wisdom Literature: Job, Proverbs, Ruth, Canticles, Ecclesiastes, and Esther* (FOTL, 13; Grand Rapids: Eerdmans, 1981), p. 17.
22. Christine Mitchell, 'Power, *Eros*, and Biblical Genres', in Boer (ed.), *Bakhtin*, pp. 31-42 (31).
23. Newsom, *Book of Job*, pp. 4, 11.

see that Newsom regards social expectations as more determinant classifiers than form. However, she clearly argues that classification is important. While less driven by social expectations, Duff also concurs that the act of classification is an important aspect of genre, which he defines as: 'A recurring type or category of text, as defined by structural, thematic and/or functional criteria'.[24]

Not all embrace a classificatory approach. For example, while Alastair Fowler claims that every work of literature belongs to at least one genre, he insists that genre's value lies within communication rather than categorization. As such, genre reflects meaning and is a 'goal-directed "program" of interpretation, which shapes both local information and hermeneutic instruction'.[25] Newsom and many others recognize scholarship's increasing interest in genre's communicative features over against their classificatory function. Nevertheless, advocates of classification, such as Adena Rosmarin, claim that 'classification enables criticism to begin'.[26] Jean Molino more explicitly states that one of the deficiencies of genre studies is that they are not descriptive or classificatory enough.[27] Such a classificatory approach was taken by the authors appearing in *Semeia* 14. Given her own definition of genre, Newsom unsurprisingly acknowledges that 'some sort of mental grouping of texts on the basis of perceived similarity' naturally occurs.[28] In my view, the two are easily reconciled by the fact that classification improves the possibility of clearer communication, which I take to be a product of coherent understanding.

It therefore seems that the act of classifying genres represents a natural and needed element in the critical task of interpretation. Neglecting classification undermines the goal orientation of an author/redactor and also underequips the reader, who, though he/she may intuitively perceive similarities and differences in various works, will be simultaneously unable to exploit those instincts unless categories are available.

Towards the possibility of a more nuanced classificatory activity, Newsom champions recent work engaging cognitive science and the process of categorizing literature, suggesting that members of a particular category exist because they reflect varying degrees of conformity to a 'prototypical' example, which serves as a template for comparing all potential claims to membership. Thus, instead of defining membership via particular characteristics that are shared by each member, members are treated as more or

---

24. Duff, *Modern Genre Theory*, p. xiii.
25. Alastair Fowler, *Kinds of Literature: An Introduction to the Theory of Genres and Modes* (Cambridge, MA: Harvard University Press, 1982), pp. 20-23.
26. Adena Rosmarin, as quoted in Newsom, 'Spying', p. 21.
27. Jean Molino, 'Les genres littéraires', *Poétique* 24 (1993), pp. 3-28 (17).
28. Newsom, 'Spying', p. 22.

less 'central and peripheral' varying one from another simply by a 'matter of degree'.[29]

This 'prototype' theory seems like a more sophisticated restatement of the strategies instituted by the Apocalypse Group's work found in *Semeia* 14, which also identified several candidates as exemplars. However, Newsom insists that the prototype theory differs in that the distinctive features alone are insufficient for determining membership into one genre or the other. Instead, it is the 'way in which they are related to one another in a *Gestalt* structure that serves as an idealized cognitive model. Thus the elements only make sense in relation to the whole.'[30] The striking benefit of the prototype theory is its flexibility; as long as the *Gestalt* is preserved, 'default and optional elements' of a work can exist without impinging on that work's credible place within the genre.[31]

Unfortunately, Newsom does not offer guidelines for what delimits the so-called *Gestalt* structure of any particular work, let alone apocalypse, but she does acknowledge that the Apocalypse Group 'anticipated something like the *Gestalt* notion as essential to genre recognition' by arguing that 'transcendence' contributed to the coherence of apocalypses.[32] Admittedly, it is difficult to discern a particular advantage that the prototype theory wields over the work of the Apocalypse Group. While Newsom clearly respects their influential work, her ultimate concern seems to be that the kind of classification seen in the group's efforts ultimately funnels one's decision-making into a 'binary logic' that asks, Does a text belong or not?[33] But is not this the goal of any kind of classification, nuanced or otherwise? Eventually, one has to make a judgment. In my view, Newsom's prototype theory simply extends the life of the analysis, seemingly hoping to avoid some kind of 'binary' judgment. Yet Newsom's work also raises a question: Would anyone pursue any kind of classification if the critic cannot ultimately make a judgment?

A further feature of Newsom's prototype theory and what the Apocalypse Group accomplished is the shared interest in ahistorical concerns. Neither project conducts a detailed diachronic analysis concerning how genres evolve over time. Thus, it appears that the prototype theory does not offer anything more substantial than what has already been produced by the Apocalypse Group. It would be interesting to see how the prototype theory would be applied to other generic areas of interest, for example, the loose congregation of so-called Wisdom Literature. In the end, the most valuable

---

29. Newsom, 'Spying', p. 24.
30. Newsom, 'Spying', p. 25.
31. Newsom, 'Spying', p. 25.
32. Newsom, 'Spying', p. 25.
33. Newsom, 'Spying', p. 26.

insight stemming from Newsom's discussion of the prototype theory is that its inability to produce anything distinctly novel from the categorical tendencies of the Apocalypse Groups offers further proof of the Apocalypse Group's enduring value to scholarship. Categorization is therefore a needed stage in the process of genre analysis.

Aside from the prototype theory, Newsom also seems to represent those sharing more recent interest with the evolutionary or diachronic aspects of genre. The fundamental question stemming from this discussion is whether or not genres change over time. This aspect of genre analysis is particularly important in my own work on Job as presented later.

Drawing from Fowler, Duff and Bakhtin, Newsom is able to substantiate that genres do, in fact, change. In particular, Bakhtin uniquely merges the diachronic and synchronic aspects of genre morphology: 'A genre lives in the present, but always remembers its past, its beginning'. And again Bakhtin states: 'a genre is always the same and yet not the same, always old and new simultaneously'.[34] Molino also seems to recognize that genres change, noting that when smaller 'microgenres' confront each other, an intermediate 'mesogenre' is birthed from the womb of the same tradition.[35] Thus, if Bakhtin and others are correct, then one would expect that classification of genres may reach beyond the normal chronological windows imposed by synchronic examinations. In the case of apocalypses, for example, most argue that apocalypses emerged from prophetic literature, but some others have suggested that they grew out of Wisdom Literature. More will be said on this later, but the point is that many see a pre-apocalypse stage of one sort or another. Thus, one may be able to discern apocalyptic inferences before or after the typical window dating from roughly the third century BCE to the second century CE. As I will suggest, this is exactly the case with Job. While some key defining characteristics typically associated with 'classic' apocalyptic works fitting in the chronological window are not readily obvious in Job, the *Gestalt* of Job seems to accord with that which defines apocalyptic.

With respect to the value of diachronic approaches to genre studies, Newsom also suggests that the internal dynamics of late Christian and Gnostic works can be better understood because these apocalypses have absorbed a variety of other genres into the broader apocalyptic work.[36] In other words, we can see how they have modified and made use of other genres. While Newsom chooses so-called 'late' manifestations of apocalyptic, I see a similar compositional integration of sub-genres occurring in Job, where an overarching genre binds the multiple 'forms' present in the work.

34. Newsom, 'Spying', p. 28
35. Molino, 'Les genres', p. 18.
36. Newsom, 'Spying', p. 28.

Introduction 9

However, some question whether it is possible to retrieve the one genre governing any particular book. Mary Gerhart feels that one cannot claim to find the 'original genre' of a work any more than one can discover the author's intent.[37] For her, individual readers' 'generic competence' varies from person to person, thereby militating against any original intention. Her concerns revolve around a reader's ability to 'construct, identify, compare, test, retrieve, and critique genres'.[38] Subsequently, any given text is capable of revealing differing genres.

In my view, such a privileging of the reader's role in interpretation invites the kind of subjective individualized interpretations of a text that leads to the very need for some degree of categorizing biblical books into appropriate genres in the first place. In the dynamic relationship of author, reader and the text, how can the reader expect to retrieve accurately what an author seeks to convey if the reader is able to 'construct' the genre for a particular work? I am more inclined to follow the lead of E.D. Hirsch (and others) who claims that verbal meaning is genre-bound.[39] As is well-known, Hirsch privileges the author's intent over against the reader's.

Still, Gerhart elevates the importance that genre plays in the reader's participation in interpretation because any interpretation involves some level of assumption about the class of literature being studied. I will not interpret a love letter from my wife in the same way that I read a newspaper; the two are different classes of writing. The assumptions readers make directly influence their understanding of the function of the text they are interpreting, the goals it can fulfill and what its intentions may be.[40] This is especially keen in the case of Job where a generic assumption is much more difficult to establish, especially as one proceeds through the book. However, since readers either consciously or subconsciously assume a governing genre at the outset, such an expectation will surely impact one's interpretation of Job. Westermann recognized this and astutely observed regarding Job that 'the whole question of literary form would become significant only if the judgment concerning literary classification were to have a decisive effect upon the exegesis of the book'.[41]

---

37. Mary Gerhart, 'Generic Competence in Biblical Hermeneutics', *Semeia* 43 (1988), pp. 29-44 (33).

38. Gerhart, 'Generic', p. 33.

39. E.D. Hirsch, *Validity in Interpretation* (New Haven: Yale University Press, 1967), pp. 71-77.

40. George W. Coats, 'Genres: Why Should They Be Important for Exegesis?', in *Saga, Legend, Tale, Novella, Fable: Narrative Forms in Old Testament Literature* (JSOTSup, 35; Sheffield: JSOT Press, 1985), pp. 7-15 (10).

41. Westermann, *The Structure of the Book of Job: A Form-Critical Analysis* (trans. Charles A. Muenchow; Philadelphia: Fortress Press, 1981), p. 1.

George Coats argues similarly, suggesting that knowing the genre of a work 'in advance' makes an important difference in interpretation.[42] I share his observation that classifying a particular work according to some genre will naturally occur during interpretation, thereby raising that process 'to a conscious level so that it might be carefully controlled'. In such a controlled environment, the interpreter 'will be in a much better position to make an accurate judgment about the object of interest'.[43] Coats concludes that when a genre of literature is accurately identified, one of the clarifying features will be that the genre fulfills a typical function, which serves as 'particular intention'.[44] Thus, classifying the genre of a work is necessary for interpretation because it assists in the process of discerning the author's intention behind the conscious decision to use a particular genre by design.

Much more could be said concerning genre. My goal here has been simply to review some of the key questions concerning this field of study and demonstrate that many unresolved questions remain. Grant Osborne puts it most aptly: 'Any attempt to grasp easily this complex topic is indeed doomed to disappointment'.[45] However, given the number of outstanding problems, and at the risk of oversimplifying the maze of issues concerning genre, it is necessary to delineate my own approach to understanding and assessing issues of genre.

Methodological Assumptions Concerning Genre

It should be obvious by now that my primary interest in studying the genre of Job lies in how such a study can advance a coherent and useful interpretation of the book. Like Coats and Hirsch, I maintain that the most likely source of meaning is found in the author's intention. An author or redactor fashions a work within a conscious generic framework for a particular communicative purpose. While a work may be comprised of numerous genres, there still exists an intrinsic genre, which Hirsch defines as 'that sense of the whole by means of which an interpreter can correctly understand any part in its determinacy'.[46] In short, I maintain that meaning is genre-bound and that in order to interpret as correctly as possible the interpreter needs consciously to identify a genre that holds all of the pieces of a work together.

I take Hirsch's notion of 'intrinsic genre' to be distinct from the smaller features of a work, which can be labeled 'forms'. Forms can be isolated, but

---

42. Coats, 'Genres', pp. 7-8.
43. Coats, 'Genres', pp. 9-10.
44. Coats, 'Genres', p. 13.
45. Grant Osborne, 'Genre Criticism—Sensus Literalis', *Trinity Journal* 4 (1983), pp. 1-27 (3).
46. Hirsch, *Validity*, p. 86.

Introduction 11

they do not typically function as the governing intrinsic genre that binds the entire work together. The book of Job represents one of the most spectacular mixtures of forms in the Bible, but my project concentrates on the forest instead of the several intriguing trees that reside within it. Thus, I am less concerned with investigating all of the forms contained in Job, and instead am more fascinated by the prospect of revealing the intrinsic genre, which I claim is a rudimentary phase of apocalypse.

In order to make such a claim, I am forced to re-classify Job away from wisdom and into the realm of apocalypse. Thus, I concur that classification is a necessary exercise towards correctly identifying a genre for a particular work. In Chapter 2 I will rely heavily on the excellent work of the Apocalypse Group in order to demonstrate that Job has more family resemblances with apocalypse than has been hitherto recognized within scholarship. By contrast, my task in Chapter 1 is to raise questions in my readers' mind regarding the long association that Job has had with wisdom. However, my work there will be even more difficult than trying to demonstrate Job's affinities with apocalypse because, to my knowledge, no classificatory research on a par with that carried out by the Apocalypse Group has yet been accomplished within wisdom circles. This is a rather massive lacuna in the field of generic studies that needs to be corrected. Thus, in Chapter 1 I will be left to create my own set of criteria for arguing that Job is peripheral enough to pure wisdom that the very suggestion of another classification is warranted.

Finally, I assume with Newsom and others that genres change over time. With respect to Job, I will touch on this issue in Chapter 3 and, to a lesser degree, Chapter 5. In brief, since I date the final compilation of Job to a period prior to the generally accepted chronological window during which apocalyptic writing seemed to have flourished, I maintain that Job contains core, or intrinsic, literary traits of apocalypses that evolved and expanded into the more robustly eschatological and otherworldly features so typical of paradigmatic apocalypses. Yet Job is marked by such core apocalyptic features as revelation, plot, heavenly conflict, perseverance in the midst of persecution, an otherworldly mediator and reward due to faithfulness. It seems that Job was a grandfather whose generic literary DNA belies the family resemblance of apocalypse.

The Plan of This Book

Gerhart usefully suggests that 'genric analysis at its best is always in service of an hypothesis'.[47] In this way, alternative readings can be made of a text simply by testing various genres on the text itself. This testing of hypotheses

---

47. Gerhart, 'Generic', p. 34.

is what has emerged in generic studies of Job; yet, as mentioned earlier, none of the hypotheses offered to date has met with the same level of agreement among scholars as has wisdom. My aim is to test the hypothesis that Job can produce meaningful results if read as a nascent apocalypse and that the disparate nature of the text can be adequately harmonized under this rubric.

David Penchansky, however, cautions against attempts to harmonize Job's disparate texts. At the same time, he has bemoaned that scholarship tends to concentrate on the middle of Job and relegates the frame story as a later irrelevant addition. By contrast, popular and religious readings appreciate the piety found in the framework while neglecting the defiant Job of the poetic sections.[48] Penchansky also laments the lack of a desire 'to examine the effects of juxtaposition' found in Job.[49] I seek to do just that, and in so doing hope to accomplish what David Robertson has challenged students of Job to seek: 'the superior interpretation is the one that best accounts for all the data in the most consistent, uncomplicated fashion'.[50]

In the process of pursuing this literary dimension, historical issues will inevitably arise. If Job is considered nascent apocalypse, surely important questions regarding setting, author, or date of the composition will follow. Furthermore, an entirely new theological trajectory will be established. For example, how will the place of suffering be viewed from a proto-apocalyptic Job? While my intention is not to discuss these important areas of study at length in this work, I certainly acknowledge and accept that my proposal will necessarily impact their investigation.

I am most interested in working with the Masoretic text (MT) of Job as found in its final form.[51] This does not discount the important results of the historical-critical work that hypothesizes the existence of multiple textual additions and disruptions throughout the course of Job's transmission. Indeed, the beauty of my approach is its appeal to both proponents of narrative methods and to those accepting the findings of historical-critical research, though I recognize that the two approaches are not mutually exclusive. I do not consider them mutually exclusive. In either case, whether I am addressing an original author or a final redactor, my purpose is to demonstrate how the various components of Job ultimately come together as one amazing literary unit.

---

48. David Penchansky, *The Betrayal of God: Ideological Conflict in Job* (Louisville: Westminster/John Knox Press, 1991), pp. 28-30.

49. Penchansky, *Betrayal*, p. 26.

50. David A. Robertson, 'The Comedy of Job: A Response', in R. Polzin and D.A. Robertson (eds.), *Studies in the Book of Job* (Semeia, 7; Missoula, MT: Scholars Press, 1977), pp. 41-44 (42).

51. I will make exclusive use of *BHS*, unless otherwise noted.

Introduction

My approach also does not necessarily endorse the theological implications associated with a canonical methodology, which also treats the text in its final form. For example, I do not intend to interpret Job as part of a larger unity between the Christian Old and New Testaments. Instead, I wish to limit my analysis and brief interpretation to the text within the Jewish library without recourse to such issues. At this point, my effort is not intended to be theological, that is, systematically speaking. Rather, it is designed to focus solely on the literary characteristics woven throughout the book of Job with the goal of revealing a new foundation upon which interpretation, and later theological reflection might profit.

The plan of the book proceeds in the following manner. Chapter 1 delineates the present status of the problem in two parts. The first part prepares the way for my perspective by pointing out the weaknesses inherent with the literary classification of wisdom for Job. Included in this discussion is a conventional listing for what constitutes a wisdom genre and why wisdom is an inadequate label for Job. The second part reviews and critiques those works serving as alternatives to wisdom. Some, notably Westermann and Dell, commit entire monographs to the problem, while others, such as J.W. Whedbee[52] and Luis Alonso Schökel,[53] offer less ambitious articles and essays.

Chapter 2 formally introduces the genre of apocalypse and outlines the important Master Paradigm resulting from the Apocalypse Group's Genres Project. This list enumerates the fundamental features attributed to any apocalypse.[54] A simple comparison of this list with the content and forms found in Job serves to offer convincing proof that Job can be at least associated with apocalypse. Though the outcome of this comparison is persuasive, a crucial element commonly expected in any apocalypse is missing from Job, namely, overt eschatology.

Chapter 3 seeks to combat this perceived problem by tracing important stages of the history of the interpretation of the Job tradition and displaying those several instances where eschatology is either explicitly or implicitly revealed. Here critical studies offer several helpful options for disclosing the theoretical stages at which Job developed. And yet, for me, it is the Hellenistic impression left on both the Greek translation (LXX) and the pseudepigraphical *Testament of Job* that are most interesting. A brief excursus regarding the authority of the LXX seeks to elevate the status of these

---

52. J.W. Whedbee, 'The Comedy of Job', in Polzin and Robertson (eds.), *Studies in the Book of Job*, pp. 1-39.

53. L. Alonso Schökel, 'Toward a Dramatic Reading of the Book of Job', in Polzin and Robertson (eds.), *Studies in the Book of Job*, pp. 45-61.

54. J. Collins, 'Introduction: Towards the Morphology of a Genre', *Semeia* 14 (1979), pp. 1-20 (5-8).

instances where eschatology is present in the Joban tradition. Additional study of other translations and the place of Job at both Qumran and in the New Testament community further establish the importance of eschatology in the Joban tradition.

Chapter 4 seeks to broaden the application of apocalypse to Job by treating the entire book according to a unique structural framework that comports to an apocalyptic approach. In this section the proposal will be manifested in full and will disclose how all the various sections found in Job are literarily connected.

Chapter 5 briefly advances the theory to non-literary dimensions of Joban studies. For example, the chapter probes a possible setting for the final form of Job. Establishing the setting for the apocalyptists has been as troubling as the attempts to locate the scribes of wisdom. I suggest that Job as proto-apocalypse could reopen Gerhard von Rad's suggestion that apocalypse grew out of wisdom. Using my suggested paradigm, Job might actually strengthen von Rad's argument. Naturally, discussion of date, setting and purpose are necessarily impacted.

The student of Job will certainly want to know how traditionally sensitive issues of suffering and the problem of evil are impacted by this proposal. Both of these will receive treatment, though not exhaustively, in an attempt to underscore the validity of my thesis and to acknowledge that the material elements of Job are not removed from view.

1

TRADITIONAL AND CRITICAL EVALUATIONS OF JOB'S GOVERNING GENRE

Introduction

This chapter surveys an assortment of past research related to the genre of Job on two levels. The first level focuses on the traditional understanding that Job is part of Wisdom Literature and the second reviews several studies that pose alternatives to wisdom as the genre that controls Job. Katharine Dell's recent and valuable summary of influential research on the genre of Job informs much of this first level.[1] In the second part of this chapter, I pay particular attention to the alternative paradigms' ability to incorporate the historically troubling sections of Job: the Wisdom chapter (ch. 28) and the Elihu speeches (chs. 32–37).

Wisdom as Genre for Job

Job and Ancient Near Eastern Texts
Dell points out that much of modern scholarship was consumed with probing deeply into the question of unjust suffering in Job. This question was considered a 'wisdom question' that coincided with an increasing interest in parallel ancient Near Eastern materials. Except for a small minority, one which includes Giorgio Buccellati, most scholars accepted the notion that the ancient Near Eastern parallels exhibited traits commonly identified as wisdom.[2] Since issues of form and social setting appeared to be shared

---

1. Dell's first two chapters do this admirably and indeed serve as a point of departure for this discussion. Also valuable is the concise treatment of significant works by Roland Murphy, *Wisdom Literature: Job, Proverbs, Ruth, Canticles, Ecclesiastes, and Esther* (FOTL, 13; Grand Rapids: Eerdmans, 1981). Of considerable value for the entirety of Joban research is David J.A. Clines's *Job 1–20* (WBC, 17; Dallas: Word Books, 1989).

2. Giorgio Buccellati, 'Wisdom and Not: The Case of Mesopotamia', *JAOS* 101 (1981), pp. 35-47. Stuart Weeks (*Early Israelite Wisdom* [OTM; Oxford: Clarendon Press, 1994], p. 7) also cautions against associating a genre with 'wisdom literature' since the identification of either a 'wisdom school' in ancient Israel, Egypt or Mesopotamia is impossible.

with the ancient Near Eastern parallels, Job's status of wisdom was further solidified.³

Buccellati, however, argues that wisdom themes are too diffused throughout a variety of literary forms to constitute a distinctive set of formal characteristics. Literary genres such as hymns, myths or epics do not usually contain wisdom themes, but when they do, the wisdom element is only a feature and not often a prevalent one at that. Likewise, wisdom themes are distributed throughout such a wide range of environments that it seems unlikely that one single intellectual or spiritual movement can claim ownership of them. Buccellati questions whether scholarship can legitimately speak of a 'wisdom literature' in a literary sense at all since it seems to be entirely too restrictive, and subsequently recommends that wisdom and literature be altogether separated.⁴ Bruce Zuckerman agrees, arguing that 'Wisdom is better grasped in terms of a cultural phenomenon that had an effect on a broad range of literatures, even including texts not normally thought to be Wisdom works'.⁵

Yet, it seems hard to ignore conventional thinking, which accepts that many of the ancient Near East's documents conform to the fluid classification of Wisdom Literature. Several of these ancient stories pertain to a righteous sufferer and naturally have drawn comparisons to the story of Job.⁶ As a result, the scholarly community, both consciously and unconsciously, treats Job as a piece of Wisdom Literature. Even David Penchansky's iconoclastic study on the dissonance found in Job is unable to avoid this supposed 'assured result'. Without substantiation, he places the tension-filled text in the 'sapiential movement' of Ancient Israel.⁷ More than anything else, this simply reflects how the consensus view has infiltrated scholarship's treatment of Job.

3. Dell, *Job as Sceptical Literature*, pp. 35, 38-39.
4. Buccellati, 'Wisdom and Not', p. 44.
5. Bruce Zuckerman, *Job the Silent: A Study in Historical Counterpoint* (New York: Oxford University Press, 1991), p. 243 n. 259.
6. See John Gray, 'The Book of Job in the Context of Near Eastern Literature', *ZAW* 82 (1970), pp. 251-69, and Moshe Weinfeld, 'Job and its Mesopotamian Parallels: A Typological Analysis', in W. Claassen (ed.), *Text and Context: Old Testament and Semitic Studies for F.C. Fensham* (JSOTSup, 48; Sheffield: JSOT Press, 1988), pp. 217-26. See also Marvin Pope, *Job* (AB, 15; Garden City: Doubleday, 1965), pp. l-lxvi. For the texts of 'Man and his God', 'Ludlul Bêl Nêmeqi', and 'The Babylonian Theodicy', see James B. Pritchard (ed.), *The Ancient Near East: A New Anthology of Texts and Pictures* (Princeton: Princeton University Press, 1975), II. See also Victor H. Matthews and Don C. Benjamin (eds.), *Old Testament Parallels: Laws and Stories From the Ancient Near East* (New York: Paulist Press, 2nd edn, 1997), pp. 203-28, which contains similar but different parallels to the story.
7. David Penchansky, *The Betrayal of God: Ideological Conflict in Job* (Louisville, KY: Westminster/John Knox Press, 1990), pp. 25, 35.

Job as Wisdom Literature

In addition to Job's association with several similar ancient Near East stories of a righteous sufferer, scholarship points to several features within the story itself that indicate it is part of the Wisdom Literature. Roland Murphy and James Crenshaw are leading representatives who point to, among other things, wisdom indicators such as the personification of wisdom in ch. 28, the presentation of a theology of retribution and occasional occurrences of the term 'wisdom'.[8]

However, Dell has forcefully challenged this entrenched position. She observes that one could argue that wisdom themes emerge in every book in the Old Testament. Thus, like Buccellati, she notes that the term 'wisdom' is used in a very general sense, which has resulted in such a diverse set of criteria for distinguishing wisdom texts that perhaps a wisdom classification cannot be established at all.[9] Claus Westermann echoes these sentiments when he suggests that one cannot develop a precise definition of wisdom if Proverbs, Job, Qohelet, Sirach and the Wisdom of Solomon are all considered wisdom, as they have traditionally been.[10]

With respect to Job, Dell finds the absence of explicit instruction telling since she considers didacticism critical to biblical wisdom.[11] In fact, Murphy notes the common presence of the 'didactic (or learned) saying' in wisdom, but this is in the context of proverbial sayings.[12] R.N. Whybray has suggested that Job is clearly not didactic in this way,[13] as does Joseph Blenkinsopp, who also questions whether Job is truly 'wisdom'.[14]

Thus, the question of whether Job genuinely conforms to a literary notion of wisdom seems to require a more refined definition of what constitutes

---

8. See James Crenshaw, *Old Testament Wisdom: An Introduction* (Atlanta: John Knox Press, 1981), p. 123; Roland Murphy both in *The Tree of Life: An Exploration of Biblical Wisdom Literature* (Grand Rapids: Eerdmans, 2nd edn, 1996), p. 33, and in his *Wisdom Literature*, pp. 16-20.

9. Dell, *Job as Sceptical Literature*, p. 61.

10. Claus Westermann, *Roots of Wisdom: The Oldest Proverbs of Israel and Other Peoples* (Louisville, KY: Westminster Press, 1995), p. 2.

11. Dell, *Job as Sceptical Literature*, p. 61.

12. Murphy, *Wisdom*, p. 5.

13. R.N. Whybray, *The Intellectual Tradition in the Old Testament* (BZAW, 135; Berlin: Walter de Gruyter, 1974), p. 62. Otto Kaiser (*Introduction to the Old Testament: A Presentation of its Results and Problems* [trans. John Sturdy; Minneapolis: Augsburg, 1975], p. 391) concurs that if Job is described as a didactic poem, 'little advance is made in understanding', though he concedes the book contains a special kind of wisdom.

14. Joseph Blenkinsopp, *Wisdom and the Law in the Old Testament: The Ordering of Life in Israel and in Early Judaism* (OBS; Oxford: Oxford University Press, 1983), p. 1. He suggests that Job may 'perhaps' be considered a part of the wisdom corpus.

Wisdom Literature. While the search for a practical definition of 'wisdom' lies outside the boundaries of this work, some general observations must be made, especially since they will inform my own work. That the term is used widely in scholarly circles cannot be denied, nor, in my mind, should it be wholly challenged because, as Roland Murphy states, 'it is merely a term of convenience'.[15] To my knowledge, no classificatory work on the boundaries of Wisdom Literature on par with the Apocalypse Group's research and publication in *Semeia* 14 has yet to be done. It is sorely needed. Due to that neglect, scholars are forced essentially to create their own set of criteria for what constitutes Wisdom Literature and, naturally, the results can vary widely, leading to anything but a satisfactory standard from which to begin.

For example, Walter Brueggemann's most developed treatment of wisdom focuses on Proverbs.[16] For Brueggemann, the themes emerging from wisdom are the affirmation of the world, the celebration of culture and an affirmation of human responsibility and capability.[17] These traits are surely present in Sirach and the Wisdom of Solomon as well, are less evident in Ecclesiastes, while distinctly remote in Job.

To that end, most scholars identify central or core books that most exemplify a notion of a wisdom genre and then use those books as exemplars. Such an approach was part of the Apocalypse Group's investigation, and is called for in part by Carol Newsom's allegiance to a 'prototype' model addressed earlier. Still, for my own research, what is at stake is how 'convenient' the term wisdom is for identifying Job's literary genre. In my view, the sheer number of attempts aimed at finding a more suitable genre speaks to the need for more precision with respect to classifying Job.

In the end, given that secular literary critics are unable to contribute to objective demarcations, establishing such precision requires some understanding of which books constitute biblical wisdom. Dell accuses Crenshaw of circularity because he devises such a definition based on the pool of books considered 'wisdom'.[18] Dell is surely correct, but then she too falls prey to this schema by assuming that Job is not wisdom, and by basing a definition on the traditional wisdom corpus *sans* Job.[19] However, the

---

15. Murphy, *Wisdom*, p. 3.
16. Walter Brueggemann, *In Man We Trust: The Neglected Side of Biblical Faith* (Atlanta: John Knox Press, 1972).
17. Brueggemann, *In Man We Trust*, p. 7.
18. Dell, *Job as Sceptical Literature*, p. 62 n. 23.
19. Dell, *Job as Sceptical Literature*, p. 63. In her more recent work, *'Get Wisdom, Get Insight': An Introduction to Israel's Wisdom Literature* (Macon, GA: Smyth & Helwys, 2000), p. 14, Dell limits her definition of wisdom to Proverbs, which is no less circular. She states: 'Furthermore, the basic form of wisdom is the proverb of which the book chiefly consists. If we characterise the forms, content and context so far as it can be known of the book of Proverbs and then compare other books to it, we shall be well on

identification of several features that are shared by the remaining four wisdom books, though less detectable or simply lacking in Job, can be instructive in casting further doubt on the designation that Job is wisdom while simultaneously intimating a notion of wisdom.

First, at the core of Proverbs, Sirach and the Wisdom of Solomon is the formal proverb itself. While these can be found in Qoheleth and Job, they are certainly not the dominant forms of composition in either case. On the other hand, Crenshaw regards Qoheleth's thought as 'aphoristic', and this seems to be borne out by the use of pithy forms of truth sayings and popular maxims.[20]

Second, the author of Proverbs addresses the reader directly. This too can be said of Sirach, the Wisdom of Solomon and Ecclesiastes, but it is not the case with Job. Dell notes that this phenomenon further enhances the presence of a narrative framework in Job, which is not a feature common to the remaining four books. Von Rad and Garrett have also remarked on Job's indirect mode of communicating to the reader.[21]

Third, and related to both of these two prior points, is the aspect of explicit instruction. Of the four books, each directs itself to training or teaching the reader. Job makes no such commitment. It is true that the friends seek to teach Job, but this is limited to the internal context of the story and is not directed to the reader.

Fourth, the anonymity of Job stands in stark contrast to the place of Solomon in Proverbs, Ecclesiastes, the Wisdom of Solomon and to the namesake in Sirach.

Fifth, James Crenshaw intimates that some suggest wisdom does not contain divine speech.[22] This holds with the four non-Joban books, but the great Yahweh speeches of Job 38–41 certainly place Job outside of this criterion.

Alastair Hunter's recent work on Wisdom Literature shares a similar frustration to Dell in attempting to tame the nature of a wisdom genre. He insightfully notes that no comparable genre exists in current secular literary theory.[23] Given the already discussed disarray concerning genre in literary circles and its impact on biblical scholars, the absence of shared wisdom

---

the way to defining the nature of wisdom as a genre and will have a starting point from which to clarify the extent of wisdom literature.'

20. James Crenshaw, *Story and Faith: A Guide to the Old Testament* (New York: Macmillan, 1986), pp. 345-46.

21. Gerhard von Rad, *Wisdom in Israel* (trans. James D. Martin; Nashville: Abingdon, 1972), p. 46, and D. Garrett, Lectures at Bethel Seminary, 1998 (unpublished). Garrett considers this device consonant with apocalypse.

22. James Crenshaw, 'Wisdom', in J.H. Hayes (ed.), *Old Testament Form Criticism* (TUMSR, 2; San Antonio: Trinity University Press, 1974), pp. 225-64 (226).

23. Alastair Hunter, *Wisdom Literature* (London: SCM Press, 2006), p. 3.

paradigms only exacerbates the disadvantage within which biblical scholars find themselves simply because they are left to their own definitions with seemingly little to no precedent or adjudicating references.

Hunter notes that von Rad's *Wisdom in Israel* takes notice of this problem and ultimately concludes that wisdom concentrates on a '*human* process of understanding and a quest'.[24] As alluded to earlier, Crenshaw would characterize wisdom as non-revelatory speech, yet Hunter is rightly dissatisfied with Crenshaw's ultimate designations that wisdom is concerned with 'attitude and intention' and later with 'character' because such designations tell us nothing about what wisdom looked like with respect to formal features.[25]

Still, Hunter is unable to escape recourse to the 'classic' wisdom books that most accept; Job, Proverbs and Ecclesiastes. However, he does seek to establish five objective criteria for establishing a list of wisdom books. He begins by centering on the Hebrew term for wisdom, חכמה. Noting that together Proverbs and Ecclesiastes account for nearly half of the term's usages in the Hebrew Bible, Hunter seems to consider them core wisdom texts. Building on them, Hunter asserts that the 'didactic imperative' as seen in ancient Near Eastern 'instruction literature' is a second objective category.[26] Hunter's third criterion is the existence of parallelism found in Hebrew poetry, particularly the couplet employed in wise sayings. These three seemingly function as the most purely formal boundaries for establishing wisdom texts. The remaining two are not exclusive to wisdom, but are still worth mentioning. They are 'first person deliberation on life experience' and 'reflective poems'.[27]

Accordingly, Proverbs and Ecclesiastes best conform to these five specifications, and while Sirach should be 'unequivocally' included in the collection, the Wisdom of Solomon should also be received, but with less enthusiasm.[28] Based on these five principles, Hunter observes that the book of Job is a 'glaring omission'.[29] To overcome this, Hunter is forced to propose 'another kind of characteristic' that would satisfy the 'intuitive urge to include Job' in the Wisdom corpus.[30] Four 'underlying perspectives which emerge from a consideration in broader terms of what these books are concerned with' are served up as the final safety net securing Job's membership

---

24. Hunter, *Wisdom Literature*, p. 5.
25. Hunter, *Wisdom Literature*, pp. 5-6.
26. Hunter, *Wisdom Literature*, pp. 21-22.
27. Hunter, *Wisdom Literature*, p. 22.
28. Hunter, *Wisdom Literature*, p. 22.
29. Hunter, *Wisdom Literature*, p. 23.
30. Hunter, *Wisdom Literature*, p. 23.

into the Wisdom corpus. Such extreme efforts to justify Job's place in the Wisdom Literature belie the reality that Job is not easily received within the most pure benchmarks of biblical חכמה.[31]

Finally, mention should be made of an ingenious attempt to associate Job with wisdom by Donald Gowan. His study proposes that Job belongs to an ancient 'wisdom script'.[32] Gowan recognized that several stories concerning wisdom seem to contain a certain pattern of repeating features that constitute what he calls a 'wisdom script'. Four key components comprise this script: the explicit and prominent mention of wisdom, a king as central figure, a serious dilemma as the main plot feature and the resolution of the dilemma on a purely intellectual level by means of something the story identifies as 'wisdom'.[33]

Gowan maintains that the author of the story had this script in mind and that he intentionally conformed the ancient tale of Job to it. By recognizing this design, Gowan hopes both to reveal how the poet may have wished that readers would understand the speeches, and to offer a novel explanation for the Elihu speeches.[34]

According to Gowan, the ancient audience would have been very familiar with the wisdom script. Therefore, as the story of Job develops through ch. 31, the readers would have been anticipating a type of wise figure who would solve the dilemma through some intellectual insight. They would not be surprised to encounter the Elihu figure; indeed, they would have identified him as the anticipated sage.

However, Gowan acknowledges that this is where the poet 'shatters the pattern of the wisdom script', since Elihu does not become the anticipated hero.[35] While Gowan does not state why the poet chose to break the pattern, it is surmised that he has done so for literary effect. One is left wondering how Gowan can claim that Job indeed conforms to the alleged 'wisdom script' since the fundamental element of the script does not play itself out. Such a lacuna calls into question Gowan's proposal.

Gowan's intriguing suggestion that Job may have been viewed as a king is unpersuasive because Job is nowhere portrayed as such in the MT. Gowan could bolster this particular point if he appealed to the OG of Job where Job is, in fact, considered a king. In addition, Gowan never makes a case for the 'explicit and prominent mention of wisdom'—he simply seems to assume that it exists.

---

31. Hunter, *Wisdom Literature*, p. 23.
32. Donald Gowan, 'Reading Job as "Wisdom Script"', *JSOT* 55 (1992), pp. 85-96.
33. Gowan, 'Reading Job', p. 85.
34. Gowan, 'Reading Job', pp. 89-90.
35. Gowan, 'Reading Job', p. 94.

Thus, it seems that Gowan's attempt to 'fit' Job into a wisdom script fails in three out of four tenets emerging from the pattern he has extrapolated from the ancient Near East texts. Yet this may be expected given that Gowan is short on examples from the ancient Near East. And, while he includes an interesting appendix of wisdom stories that conform, more or less, to the 'script', the vast majority of these stories (11 out of 13) are biblical.[36]

Gowan is no more convincing in his attempt to incorporate ch. 28 into his paradigm. Here Gowan considers the search for the allusive wisdom as merely an important interlude that completes the futile dialogue on wisdom. But ch. 28, much more than the Elihu speeches, provides the necessary solution to the dilemma of the speeches. Yet, the unnamed figure of ch. 28 cannot be considered the hero since most assume that the author interjected this chapter himself.[37] If this more natural approach to ch. 28 was accepted, and I believe this would be convincing, one would still be left with the question of how the Elihu and then the Yahweh speeches fit into the pattern, and it is this final set of speeches (chs. 38–41) that is most damaging to Gowan's proposal. He himself admits that, 'there is no place for a personal appearance of God in the wisdom script'.[38] This acknowledgement resonates with Crenshaw's contention that God does not speak in wisdom.[39]

In the end, Gowan does not claim to solidify Job's tenuous position in the wisdom corpus by his assertion that Job conforms to a 'wisdom script'. However, he has offered perhaps the best job of systematically applying a wisdom motif to the book of Job, even though it falls short. Its strength is the signaling of a meaningful role for the Wisdom chapter, but its critical weakness is that the 'wisdom script' cannot account for the language of the theophany, which represents the apex of the story.

In the end, it seems that Dell is likely correct when she states that Job should only be considered wisdom if it displays strong evidence of wisdom forms, content and overall didactic purpose or context in wisdom circles.[40] In my view, no one has effectively positioned Job as wisdom by considering those or similar criteria. Even Murphy acknowledges that 'the author of the

---

36. The two ancient Near Eastern stories are Ahikar and Apophis to Seqnen-Re in Gowan, 'Reading Job', p. 96.

37. Gowan, 'Reading Job', p. 92.

38. Gowan, 'Reading Job', p. 94. Importantly, Gowan notes that both Norman C. Habel, *The Book of Job* (OTL; Philadelphia: Westminster Press, 1985), pp. 36-37, and J.C.L. Gibson, *Job* (The Daily Study Bible; Philadelphia: Westminster Press, 1985), pp. 222, 226, state that nothing in the wisdom tradition has prepared for the personal appearance of God.

39. See n. 20.

40. Dell, *Job as Sceptical Literature*, pp. 58-63. This position is also held by E. Gerstenberger, 'Psalms', in J.H. Hayes (ed.), *Old Testament Form Criticism*, pp. 179-224 (218-21), with regard to classifying Psalms as wisdom.

book of Job moved outside of strict wisdom genres...'[41] Thus, at the very least, this presentation has demonstrated that Job does not convincingly conform to some wisdom rubric, regardless of how that rubric is constructed. It is no wonder that so many have tried to establish alternative genres that most readily control Job's literary disposition. The following section reviews several important investigations that have introduced alternatives to wisdom as the overarching genre for Job. Again, these numerous and diverse proposals are testimony enough that Job is an unlikely member of the so-called Wisdom corpus.

Alternative Genres for Job

Job as Dramatized Lament

Perhaps the most celebrated challenge to Job as wisdom comes from Claus Westermann. Westermann is most concerned with 'the underlying structures of Job' and concludes on the basis of a form-critical analysis that Job is a book of dramatized lamentation.[42] Westermann mourns that modern study of Job has been preoccupied with the search for the elusive 'problem' of Job; a search that he maintains inevitably presupposes that Job constitutes a book of wisdom.

Westermann argues that Job is not an abstract pursuit of the question on the 'problem of suffering'. Instead, Job represents an existential *reactio* to a prior *actio*, namely, Job's suffering, which results in his response, 'Why must I suffer?'[43]

Westermann, however, is quick to point out that the lament does not apply to the whole book of Job.[44] The presence of the forensic disputation speeches between the friends seems to argue against an overall lament structure. And yet, significantly for Westermann, these disputation speeches between Job and the friends (chs. 4–27) are sandwiched between Job's laments (chs. 3 and 29–31). The Yahweh speeches then serve as a response to Job's lament and appeal. Thus, Westermann concludes that the entirety of

---

41. Murphy, *Wisdom*, p. 3.
42. Westermann, *Structure*, p. vii. Westermann notes himself that he is not the first to suggest that Job reflects characteristics of lamentation. See p. 13 n. 1 of Westermann's study for a list of studies preceding Westermann. See also Dell, *Job as Sceptical Literature*, p. 100 n. 152, who observes that the increased treatment of laments prior to Westermann's work emerged from a lack of investigation into their significance at that time. Examples of these works are P. Volz, *Das Buch Hiob* (Göttingen: Vandenhoeck & Ruprecht, 1911), and Artur Weiser, *Das Buch Hiob übersetzt und erklärt* (Göttingen: Vandenhoeck & Ruprecht, 1951).
43. Westermann, *Structure*, p. 2.
44. Westermann, *Structure*, p. 3.

Job is not solely a disputation, but is more akin to drama.[45] From here Westermann leaps to the characterization of Job as a 'dramatized lament'.[46]

Two methodological issues cast doubt on Westermann's proposal. The first is his initial commitment to the centrality of suffering in Job. Westermann never explains why or how he concludes this, but the assumption appears at the outset and is pervasive throughout his argument.[47] Indeed, it seems that Westermann has an answer for the very question that he so decisively refutes, namely, 'What is the key "problem" in the book of Job?' In the end, he too seems to be controlled by the question!

Secondly, his conclusion that Job represents a dramatized lament is influenced by Aage Bentzen, who characterizes Job as a dramatized lament based on Job's similarities with the Babylonian poem, 'I will serve the Lord of Wisdom'.[48] However, this poem does not contain the narrative elements so crucial to Job and, as such, does not seem to be a valid source from which to draw conclusive comparisons.[49] Furthermore, Bentzen appeals to Psalms 41 and 51 as evidence for similar constructions.[50] Again, the narrative components are lacking and one must question whether or not Westermann's masterful works on the Psalms have been inappropriately superimposed on the book of Job.[51]

Murphy seems to resonate with this critique, suggesting that Westermann's form-critical approach does not account for the whole of the book and that the 'dramatized lament' is not a genre at all.[52] In contrast, Dell also considers the 'dramatized lament' inadequate, though she comes to this conclusion because she feels it is simply too broad.[53] I concur fully with Murphy, and hold that the 'dramatized lament' is not broad enough to

45. Westermann, *Structure*, p. 6.
46. Westermann, *Structure*, p. 11.
47. Westermann, *Structure*, pp. vii, ix.
48. Westermann, *Structure*, p. 8. Westermann cites Aage Bentzen, *Introduction to the Old Testament*, II (Copenhagen: G.E.C. Gad, 1952), p. 182. Murphy, *Wisdom*, p. 17, notes too that H. Gese, also comparing Job to the major ancient Near Eastern counterparts, concluded on similar grounds that Job was a 'paradigm of answered lament'. Murphy is not convinced and feels that Gese has overrated the role of the epilogue in his construction.
49. See *ANET* (2nd edn), pp. 148-60, for the text of *Ludlul Bel Nemeqi*, 'I Will Praise the Lord of Wisdom'.
50. Westermann, *Structure*, p. 11.
51. See, for example, his *Praise and Lament in the Psalms* (Atlanta: John Knox Press, 1981) and *The Psalms: Structure, Content, and Message* (Minneapolis: Fortress Press, 1980).
52. Murphy, *Wisdom Literature*, p. 17. Murphy states, 'Westermann is quite correct in underscoring the role of the complaint in Job... But the "dramatization of lament" is not a literary genre... The phrase has the virtue of emphasis, but that is its only strength.'
53. Dell, *Job as Sceptical Literature*, p. 90.

account adequately for the Wisdom chapter (ch. 28) or the Elihu speeches (chs. 32–37). Perhaps not surprisingly, Westermann treats these two sections at the very end of his study.

Westermann considers ch. 28 an 'intermezzo in the pause between the first and second acts of the drama'.[54] While this appears a plausible option, Westermann does not address the foundational role of an intermezzo within dramatized laments. Surely nothing in 'I will serve the Lord of Wisdom' corresponds to this. In short, it simply appears that Westermann is unable satisfactorily to fuse this chapter into his overall dramatized lament schema.

The Elihu speeches suffer a similar critique. The best Westermann can do with these chapters is relegate them to the status of a 'subsequent addition'. The implication is, perhaps, that they do not belong properly to the story, or at least to the story as conceived by the original redactor, that is, the one who intended the dramatized lament.[55] Meaningfully, Westermann ends his study by noting that it is the Elihu speeches that serve as the greatest obstacles to those seeking to solve 'the problem' within Job. As noted earlier, Westermann unknowingly assumes 'the problem', answers the problem, and then, ironically, falls prey to it in both the Wisdom chapter and the Elihu speeches.

While it is true that Job contains significant evidence of lament, and while Westermann has done scholarship a great service in elevating its formal presence, he has gone too far by absolutizing the genre with respect to the overall structure of Job.

Job as Rechtsleben
Murphy's critique of Westermann's form-critical approach is similarly leveled at Heinz Richter's proposal, which states that Job's genre is more forensic since it displays many legal characteristics.[56] Ludwig Köhler also suggested that the speeches of Job were, 'like those which were delivered by the parties before the legal assembly'.[57] Yet Köhler's limited discussion made no effort to encapsulate the entire story under a legal design. Richter, on the other hand, argued that identifying the forensic form of Job served as the way to the solution of discerning which genre governed Job.[58] Central to

---

54. Westermann, *Structure*, p. 137.
55. Westermann, *Structure*, p. 139.
56. Richter states, 'Der alles tragende Grund des Hiobdramas sind die Gattungen des Rechtslebens', in *Studien zu Hiob: Der Aufbau des Hiobbuches, dargestellt an den Gattungen des Rechtslebens* (Theologische Arbeiten, 11; Berlin: Evangelische Verlagsanstalt, 1959), pp. 131-32.
57. Ludwig Köhler, *Hebrew Man* (trans. Peter R. Ackroyd; New York: Abingdon Press, 1956), pp. 136, 137-39.
58. Richter, *Studien zu Hiob*, p. 132.

Richter's argument is the frequent occurrence of this forensic form (*Rechtsleben*). These forms contain legal language such as Job's assertion that God has breached his contract (Job 9.13-24; 19.1-12). Chapter 31 serves as Job's oath of innocence, one which also exudes legalistic overtones. The legal language appears in 444 verses of Job compared to the only 346 verses of Job related to wisdom (*Weisheit*).[59] The overall scheme for Richter is that chs. 4–14 are an attempt at a preliminary settlement between the friends and Job, chs. 15–31 represent the settlement itself and Job's prayer for a divine settlement, and 38.1–42.6 is the secular lawsuit itself.[60]

The obvious lacunae from Richter's hypothesis are treatments of the Elihu speeches and the Wisdom chapter, though the latter appears to be included in the proposed settlement. Yet, in Richter's analysis of chs. 15–31, he does not once engage with ch. 28, nor does he explain why he has avoided it. In fact, apart from his one brief allusion to its wisdom motif, Richter simply avoids ch. 28 altogether.[61] Given such a dearth of analysis, it is difficult to speculate even how this exceptionally important chapter fits into Richter's framework. I can only conclude that ch. 28 simply bedeviled Richter and was intentionally ignored, and that this omission in turn severely damages his proposal.

As is often the case, the Elihu passages are merely dismissed as a later addition, which seems to excuse their seeming inability to conform to the proposed program.[62] On the other hand, Richter does dedicate a brief chapter to the speeches, even considering them a resumption of the forensic speeches (*Wiederaufnahme*), though Elihu is a jurist, not a friend.[63] In my view, Richter does not consider them an organic element of the overall plot.[64]

In the end, Dell, like Murphy, correctly determines that the evidence for Richter's proposal, which heavily relies on the alleged commonplace of one small genre in Job, is 'rather too sparse to support his conclusions'.[65]

---

59. Richter, *Studien zu Hiob*, p. 16. By my own count, there are 1070 verses in Job.
60. Murphy, *Wisdom Literature*, p. 17.
61. Richter, *Studien zu Hiob*, p. 11.
62. Richter, *Studien zu Hiob*, p. 105. Richter states, 'Und die Elihureden – mögen sie auch ein Einschub aus späterer Zeit sein'.
63. Richter, *Studien zu Hiob*, p. 119.
64. Richter (*Studien zu Hiob*, p. 119) states, 'Die Elihureden sind für den Aufbau der Handlung also nicht nur zu entbehren, sondern sie bilden in ihr ein störendes Element, das ohne weiteres die fremde Hand erkennen läßt'. Dell, *Job as Sceptical Literature*, p. 91, considers Richter's treatment of the Elihu speeches more favorably, referring to them as an 'appeal'. However, I am not convinced that Richter sought to incorporate them into his paradigm as significantly and coherently as the term 'appeal' might suggest.
65. Dell, *Job as Sceptical Literature*, p. 91.

Job as Greek Tragedy

It may be that Job as tragedy has the longest period of advocacy.[66] As early as 428 CE, Theodore of Mopsuestia (d. 428 CE) declared Job an imitation of a Greek tragedy, though the idea as such or some aspect of that interpretation was condemned at Constantinople in 553 CE.[67] However, in 1587 Theodore Beza lectured on Job by dividing the book into acts and scenes, thereby carrying on the tradition that Job could be seen in a dramatic fashion. Horace Kallen is the most celebrated and recent proponent of Job as tragedy. For him, Job is so obviously influenced by Hellenism and in particular by Euripides that it can be seen to have been transformed into 'a Hebraized form of the Greek tragedy'.[68]

Kallen's hypothesis has the advantage of including all of the features of Job. Elihu serves as a messenger, which is consonant with Greek plays. His purpose in the setting of the tragedy is to explain what has happened, something his friends have failed to do, and to anticipate what is to come, Yahweh will speak for himself.[69] Chapter 28, so problematic for others, is considered the second of three choruses, three choruses being necessary in Greek tragedies.[70] In this manner, Westermann's proposal that ch. 28 is an 'intermezzo' is similar to Kallen's choruses.

Like Westermann's ideas, however, these 'choruses' seem somewhat contrived and tailored to the package of tragedy. Kallen notes that choruses mark off different 'acts' in Greek tragedies. Thus, he admits, we should expect the choruses to occur at the end of each of the three rounds of speeches, thereby separating the book into four acts; Round 1, chorus; Round 2, chorus; Round 3, chorus; Yahweh speeches. Kallen declares Job a play in four acts.[71] However, Kallen then acknowledges that these three choruses do not emerge in the natural breaks in Job. Instead, the first occurs within the dialogues themselves (ch. 24), the second is the Wisdom chapter (ch. 28), and the third is found in the midst of the Yahweh speeches during the description of Behemoth and Leviathan (40.15–41.26). These breaks are determined by a change in meter, theme or both.[72]

The identification of ch. 28 as a 'chorus' has tremendous appeal. It can explain why no particular voice from the known characters is discernable.

---

66. In what follows, I make use of George F. Moore's 'Introduction', in H. Kallen, *The Book of Job as a Greek Tragedy* (New York: Moffat, Yard & Company, 1918), pp. xxi-xxvi.
67. Moore, 'Introduction', p. xxiii.
68. Kallen, *Job as Greek Tragedy*, p. 7.
69. Kallen, *Job as Greek Tragedy*, p. 32.
70. Kallen, *Job as Greek Tragedy*, p. 35.
71. Kallen, *Job as Greek Tragedy*, p. 35.
72. Kallen, *Job as Greek Tragedy*, pp. 35-36.

The difficulty of this breakdown, however, lies in separating out two seemingly coherent literary units, the dialogue speeches and the Yahweh speeches. This is further amplified when reading Kallen's final product; significantly, he omits 19.26-27 because these verses contradict 'both the spirit and the letter of the rest of the chapter'.[73] So much for retaining the text as it stands.

This final point deals a severe blow to Kallen's theory. Reading through the tragedy as he has analyzed Job reveals several instances where Kallen has taken great license to add and subtract verses as he deems appropriate. His is a virtual reconstruction. As examples, both Elihu and ch. 28 appear in the tragedy long before the dialogue speeches are concluded, which completely violates the integrity of the book as it has existed. If Job is so clearly written as a tragedy, why is so much reconstructive surgery necessary to make it comprehensible?

Preceding Kallen's work by two centuries, it is worth noting that Robert Lowth also determined that Job was not a tragedy, though he recognized that it contained many elements akin to it. Lowth observed that Job lacked the one crucial characteristic required in a tragedy—action.[74] Richard Sewall agrees in an inductive study dedicated to the analysis of various tragedies, stating, 'the book as a whole is a religious book and not a formal tragedy'.[75] Finally, George Steiner argues that Job cannot be considered a tragedy because Job promotes hope, something wholly lacking in tragedies.[76] Nonetheless, others have continued to advance the idea that Job is tragedy and still others have developed ideas associated with features of drama.[77]

Job as Drama and Comedy
In the 1977 issue of *Semeia* entitled 'Studies in the Book of Job', major essays considered the legitimacy of Job as drama.[78] Luis Alonso Schökel invites the reader to 'project a mental picture of the book as drama', for through drama Job becomes 'intelligible and comprehensible in its unity'.[79]

73. Kallen, *Job as Greek Tragedy*, p. 82.
74. Moore, 'Introduction', p. xxi.
75. Richard B. Sewall, *The Vision of Tragedy* (New Haven: Yale University Press, enlarged edn, 1980), p. 21. Of particular interest, Sewall arrives at this conclusion only after accepting that the final phase of the story of Job, the Elihu speeches and onward, 'is swallowed up in mystical revelation or orthodox piety', which, 'carries him beyond the tragic domain'. Additionally, he assumes, without defense, that Job is the speaker of ch. 28, an assertion not generally accepted in scholarship.
76. George Steiner, 'Tragedy: Remorse and Justice', *The Listener* 18 (1979), pp. 508-11.
77. See Dell, *Job as Sceptical Literature*, pp. 98-101, and Whedbee, 'The Comedy of Job', pp. 2-3, for discussions on this.
78. See Polzin and Robertson (eds.), *Studies in the Book of Job*, pp. 1-154.
79. Alonso Schökel, 'Dramatic Reading of Job', p. 46.

For Alonso Schökel, Job was composed for the purpose of transforming the audience into the cast, thus the book is not one to be read but one to be encountered.[80] Alonso Schökel appeals to Archibald MacLeish's play in verse, *J.B.*,[81] to portray God on stage at a second level, fully in view of the audience, but not to the actors. The triangulated perspective forces the audience (reader) to participate and depicts God as a spectator and judge of the audience, who are now considered characters. In Job, Elihu serves as the personification of the observing audience (reader) who can no longer restrain themselves but who are compelled to engage Job, and it is this component of the genre of drama that provides the theological significance.[82]

Crenshaw questions the validity of drama as genre because it lacks the 'action' typically associated with drama. For him, Alonso Schökel 'yields to the temptation' of exchanging the lack of action for intellectual drama.[83] William Urbrock, however, recognizes the existential value to Job as drama, since it may lead to 'spiritual healing'.[84]

Both Alonso Schökel and MacLeish share a common weakness in their treatment of Job, namely, ch. 28. Neither is able to absorb this mysterious chapter into a dramatic rendering of Job. In contrast, *J.B.*, on several occasions, incorporates an unknown voice into the play,[85] which would allow for the 'unknown' voice of ch. 28 to speak from a mist produced by dry ice complemented by the sound of mining activity in the background.

Nevertheless, Alonso Schökel has produced a unique and plausible way of involving Elihu into the genre of drama. In doing so, he has advanced the value of this character, who is wholly absent in *J.B.* Thus, while drama provides an appealing and creative prism through which to interpret Job, it is unable to account for significant segments of the book of Job.

In the same collection of articles, William Whedbee offers a unique proposal to the discussion of genre classification of Job by proposing that Job should be considered a comedy.[86] Perhaps recognizing anticipated resistance to an apparently counterintuitive approach, Whedbee draws a distinction between laughter and comedy and defends his thesis by stating

---

80. So William J. Urbrock, 'Job as Tragedy or Comedy?', *Currents in Theology and Mission* 8 (1981), pp. 35-40 (38).

81. See Archibald MacLeish, *J.B.* (Boston: Houghton Mifflin, 1958).

82. Alonso Schökel, 'Dramatic Reading of Job', pp. 47-48.

83. Crenshaw, 'The Twofold Search: A Response to Luis Alonso Schökel', in Polzin and Robertson (eds.), *Studies in the Book of Job*, pp. 63-69 (63).

84. Urbrock, 'Reconciliation of Opposites in the Dramatic Ordeal of Job', in Polzin and Robertson (eds.), *Studies in the Book of Job*, pp. 147-53 (153).

85. Characterized as 'The Distant Voice'; see for example, MacLeish, *J.B.*, pp. 24, 130. The voice speaks the biblical lines of God from Job, but a character, 'Mr Zuss', has already been assigned the 'God' character.

86. Whedbee, 'The Comedy of Job'.

that, 'comedy can be profoundly serious; in fact, it has often served as one of the most compelling strategies for dealing with chaos and suffering'.[87] Early on, he delimits comedy with two characteristics: '(1) its perception of incongruity and irony; and (2) its basic plotline that leads ultimately to the happiness of the hero and his restoration to a harmonious society'.[88]

For Whedbee, incongruity stands at the center of the dialogue speeches. For example, Eliphaz encourages Job to confess his guilt and promises that in doing so Job will be restored (5.24-26). Job is restored at the end of the book, but not by means of repentance from his guilt.[89] The friends, throughout the speeches, come across as buffoons and thus resemble the classic comical figure of the *alazon*, which serves as the imposter or offender.[90] This role is also played by Elihu later on.[91]

Whedbee cites several similar examples both within the speeches and outside of them. Yet they all seem to be more ironic, or serve as parodies more than anything else. While irony and parody are certainly part of comedy, in and of themselves, they do not seem to constitute the essence of comedy. Thus, the 'happy ending' truly solidifies Whedbee's appeal to comedy as the overarching genre. He states, 'the happy ending, in my view, demonstrates the ultimate irony and comedy of Job'.[92]

James G. Williams points out that both Alonso Schökel and Whedbee have made impressive contributions to the importance of 'poetic imagination', which falls under the realm of structural analysis and literary criticism.[93] Both proposals are of exceptional heuristic value. Still, Williams correctly cautions that neither Job nor any book in Scripture will fit easily into comedy since it is a genre derived from outside the biblical tradition.[94]

I concur with this critique and suggest that it can be legitimately leveled against the genres of tragedy and drama. Whedbee seems to overemphasize the presence of the 'happy ending', though its presence cannot be denied. More damaging to Whedbee's thesis is that he does not treat ch. 28. This is significant because Whedbee is critical of those who apply genre labels to various developmental stages of Job, and not to its entirety.[95] Neither

---

87. Whedbee, 'The Comedy of Job', p. 4.
88. Whedbee, 'The Comedy of Job', p. 1.
89. Whedbee, 'The Comedy of Job', p. 11.
90. Whedbee, 'The Comedy of Job', p. 13.
91. Whedbee, 'The Comedy of Job', p. 20.
92. Whedbee, 'The Comedy of Job', p. 30.
93. James G. Williams, 'Comedy, Irony, Intercession: A Few Notes in Response', in Polzin and Robertson (eds.), *Studies in the Book of Job*, pp. 135-45 (135).
94. Williams, 'Comedy, Irony, Intercession', p. 136.
95. Whedbee, 'The Comedy of Job', p. 2. Whedbee (p. 3) can be seen to critical of the proposal that Job is a Greek tragedy. In particular, he is sympathetic towards the work

Whedbee nor Alonso Schökel addresses critical issues regarding ch. 28, nor do they explain why ch. 28 does not conform to their proposals. I can only assume that this very important, though enigmatic, chapter could not conform easily to their paradigms.

Job as Parody
One important point of intersection shared by Alonso Schökel and Whedbee is their recognition of the influence that parody has on Job. Neither, however, suggests that parody is the overall genre for Job. However, both Bruce Zuckerman and Katherine Dell have promoted parody as the genre controlling Job.

Dell and Zuckerman offered similar proposals nearly simultaneously. Each produced an entire study suggesting that the genre of Job is parody, and each takes an approach different from the other. Both attempts result in fruitful findings for those seeking to pin down the genre of Job, though in my view neither is able to consolidate all of Job's cleavages under the rubric.

As noted earlier, Dell feels that traditional and critical approaches to Job have failed to reach a consensus regarding the book's message due in part to the incorrect assumption that Job is part of the 'wisdom literature'. Instead, she proposes that the 'whole book is characterized by a deliberate *misuse*, or improper use of genre...the overall genre of the book is one which misuses various genres in order to enhance this impression'.[96] Somewhat surprisingly, she then proposes a new form-critical approach that 'breaks the whole book down into smaller genres and gradually builds up a complete picture'.[97] In the end, her method seems to be similar to the proposals she critiques, only adorned in new garb. Nevertheless, her analysis helpfully identifies several instances of the 'misuse' of forms. These numerous occasions lead her to conclude that parody is a more 'suitable genre' for Job.[98] The intentional use of parody by the author of Job indicates that Job should be characterized as 'skeptical literature' since the author sought to break from traditional use of the forms and therefore sought to break from the traditional message associated with them.

Yet, Dell does not clearly explain her intentions. On the one hand, she does not seem to find value in identifying an overall genre for Job, seemingly fearing that such an attempt might enhance the efforts of those

---

of Terrien in this area, but is critical of his proposal because it is limited to the poetic sections of Job.

    96. Dell, *Job as Sceptical Literature*, p. 148. In her more recent work, *'Get Wisdom, Get Insight'*, pp. 46-48, Dell nicely condenses her thesis, though she acknowledges that her approach is most appropriate for the dialogue section of Job only.
    97. Dell, *Job as Sceptical Literature*, p. 102.
    98. Dell, *Job as Sceptical Literature*, pp. 214-15.

advocating wisdom's supremacy in Job. She says, 'One aim of this detailed study of smaller genres is to show that *Job* is not so typical a wisdom book as scholars have assumed'.[99] On the other hand, she contends that parody is the genre that best covers Job (see above). In the end, it appears that she has undermined her own cause.

Her point, however, is well taken, and is one also made by Westermann. The mere existence of a form does not necessarily constitute a governing genre. However, even this is not clear when Dell says, '*Job* defies exclusive classification as only one of these (genres), since none is dominant'.[100] It appears that if a form does in fact emerge more often than other forms, a genre can be more accurately assigned. Further, nowhere does she state that a majority of forms constitutes the prerequisite for genre classification. This is probably because she has already correctly pointed out that a genre requires form, content and context, not simply a majority of forms.

Fortunately, Dell leaves the door open for the reader by finding continued value in the pursuit of an overall genre. She admits, 'either *Job* as a whole has no genre and is an accidental jumble of small genres; or its various sections can be characterized in terms of genre, but the whole belongs to a genre that has not yet been isolated and identified'.[101] To complete the perplexity, she concludes that both Pope and Habel's resistance to an overall genre (both of which she earlier considered) are 'unsatisfactory', and announces that she intends to explore the possibility of an existing pattern.[102]

Dell's inference that Job is best considered a parody, like all prior form-critical attempts, is simply unable to incorporate the panoply of forms into her schema. She is forced to admit this with respect to Job 28 and the Elihu speeches:

> Whilst I have argued above for a possible misuse of forms in chapter 38, the technique cannot be found in sections which are often seen as late additions—for example the speeches of Elihu and the hymn to wisdom (chapter 28). This factor might provide support for arguments in favor of their being later additions...[103]

Like Westermann, she too can only dismiss these troubling sections to the status of 'later additions'. Furthermore, her argument that these sections are later additions, based on the fact that they do not accord with her hypothesis, is circular.

---

99. Dell, *Job as Sceptical Literature*, p. 103.
100. Dell, *Job as Sceptical Literature*, p. 105.
101. Dell, *Job as Sceptical Literature*, p. 107.
102. Dell, *Job as Sceptical Literature*, p. 107.
103. Dell, *Job as Sceptical Literature*, pp. 138, 196.

1. Traditional and Critical Evaluations 33

Like Westermann and others, Murphy cautions against form-critical studies that seek to identify one overall genre. He states, 'the most exact and careful analysis of forms and motifs must be carried out with a sense for the broad perspective. The mere occurrence of certain genres is not enough to determine the literary genre of the work.'[104]

In contrast to Dell, Zuckerman is less concerned with the emergence of parody via form-criticism, and more interested in counterpoint, that is, 'the playing off of distinct but related themes, one against the other', via a tradition-critical approach.[105] The central theme under Zuckerman's scrutiny is the patience of Job.[106] Zuckerman wonders how this tradition of Job has remained so influential given the obvious centrality of the impatience of Job in the speeches (chs. 4–27). The key for his interpretation of Job lies in the late nineteenth-century Yiddish story, 'Bontsye Shvag', in which parody serves as the regnant element. 'Bontsye Shvag', like Job, exhibits the essential element for a successful parody; the prior existence of known material shared between author and reader.[107]

'Bontsye Shvag' is the story of an exceptionally pious man who passively absorbs all of life's difficulties without making a complaint. At the end of the story, long after the reader has determined that the story is extolling this pious figure, the author reveals that the story is instead a devastating parody of piety by humiliating the character before the heavenly court. The author, Y.L. Perets, wishes to state that anyone who does not complain in the midst of suffering is simply a fool, not pious.[108]

In like manner, Zuckerman suggests that the most ancient story of Job contained the idea of a patient Job, which served as the object of ire for the author of the disputation speeches. This author was not content with the pious Job and instead introduced the more restless Job found in the speeches and later laments. However, at an even later stage in the development of Job, a redactor re-established the presence of the patient and pious Job by inserting the prose narrative sections found in the prologue and epilogue. Thus, the book of James is able to speak of the patient (enduring) Job, even though the text depicts a character anything but.[109] In the end, the final (authorized) version of Job is a parody of the more ancient tale where the author of Job parodied the patient Job and instead depicted him as impatient.

---

104. Murphy, *Wisdom*, p. 17.
105. Bruce Zuckerman, *Job the Silent: A Study in Historical Counterpoint* (New York: Oxford University Press, 1991), p. 4.
106. Zuckerman, *Job the Silent*, p. 3.
107. Zuckerman, *Job the Silent*, p. 44
108. Zuckerman, *Job the Silent*, p. 65
109. Zuckerman, *Job the Silent*, p. 14.

Of particular importance, Zuckerman asserts that parodies are meant to be timely, not timeless. Thus, it is important not to avoid isolating the literary works from their historical and cultural environments if interpreters are to identify correctly the dynamics of the story's development.[110] While Zuckerman rightly observes the difficulty in recovering the historical impetus behind the various traditions layered onto Job, he posits times of distress as the background for the final compilation of Job.

Even though Zuckerman recognizes problems with various genre designations for Job, he, unlike Dell, readily considers Job part of the Wisdom Literature.[111] Nevertheless, parody serves as the structural foundation.[112] Still, Zuckerman's treatment of the problematic sections; the Wisdom chapter (ch. 28) and the Elihu speeches (chs. 32–37), is unconvincing.

The Wisdom chapter is considered a redundant later addition, one that merely prepares the reader for an amplification of God's nature later in the Theophany. Zuckerman suggests that the poem may have been added to 'soften the blow' in preparation for the ruthless presentation God makes of himself later. The substantive parody of ch. 28 occurs in the pietistic depiction of wisdom in v. 28: 'Truly, the fear of the Lord, that is wisdom; and to depart from evil is understanding'. This verse contrasts the futility of humanity's search for wisdom. Thus, instead of parodying the pietism of the ancient tale, as is the case with the majority of the story, ch. 28 ultimately serves as the reverse. While the proposal is ingenious, the lack of consistency seems questionable, if not contrived.

Even if Zuckerman's attempt to incorporate ch. 28 is deemed successful, he fully retreats from any such attempt with the Elihu speeches. He states, 'To put it simply: the Elihu speeches, taken as satire, do not fit very well within the parodistic design presented above'.[113] Zuckerman later wonders why the author of the Elihu speeches was compelled to 'violate the integrity of such a great work of literature'.[114] Finally, Zuckerman concludes, 'the author of Elihu sees no hint of parody in the Poem of Job'.[115]

Zuckerman is unable to sustain his schema over the canonical form of Job. The fact that he employs a late nineteenth-century phenomenon to interpret Job should also not go unnoticed. Such an anachronistically established methodology can only suggest difficulties, especially given the disparate structural relationship between the two objects of comparison. 'Bontsye Shvayg' simply does not contain the complex literary characteristics evident

110. Zuckerman, *Job the Silent*, p. 87.
111. Zuckerman, *Job the Silent*, p. 104.
112. Zuckerman, *Job the Silent*, p. 137.
113. Zuckerman, *Job the Silent*, p. 146.
114. Zuckerman, *Job the Silent*, p. 153.
115. Zuckerman, *Job the Silent*, p. 157.

in Job. It is therefore not too surprising to discover that Zuckerman's paradigm fails to account for all of the literary features of Job.

Zuckerman and Dell each make valuable contributions to scholarship's understanding of how the form of parody may have been employed by the author of Job. However, just as other proposals, including wisdom, cannot encapsulate all the major literary structures into their schemes, neither is parody in either Zuckerman's or Dell's presentation able to either.

Job as Polyphonic
Seeking to stake out a position somewhere between the extremes of historical-criticism and postmodernity, Carol Newsom argues for a 'recuperation of genre as a critical category for understanding the book of Job', which 'is based neither on the modernist assumptions of historical criticism and New Critical literary approaches nor on the assumptions of deconstruction'.[116]

Newsom recounts the centuries-old struggle to reconcile the seemingly contradictory genres contained in Job; most importantly, the narratives of the prologue and the epilogue, and the poetry that constitutes Job 3.1–42.7. The challenge has been to integrate these and other seemingly disparate features, such as the Wisdom hymn of ch. 28, into a coherence. It has yet to be resolved, and influential interpreters abiding in either the tent of New Criticism, such as Norman Habel, or the tent of Deconstruction, such as David Clines, neglect genre, because they are suspicious of investigations into genre, which are the domain of the fragmentary tendencies of historical-criticism.

However, Newsom's solution seems just as postmodern as Derrida's rejection of genre. Leaning heavily on the work of Mikhail Bakhtin, Newsom identifies Job as 'polyphonic', listing his four characteristics designating a polyphonic text: (1) it embodies a dialogic sense of truth; (2) the author's position, although represented in the text, is not privileged; (3) the polyphonic text ends without finalizing closure; and (4) it is always open, that is, it exhibits 'unfinalizability'.[117]

Bakhtin's agenda is to 'challenge the dominant conception of truth as systemic and monological'.[118] Monologic systems, as opposed to dialogic systems, are seemingly defective because they are propositional and closed and therefore limit the number of participants. Bakhtin's polyphonic appreciation requires that 'the author gives up the type of control exercised in monologic works...'[119] This obviously departs from my own earlier-stated

---

116. Newsom, *The Book of Job: A Contest of Moral Imaginations* (Oxford: Oxford University Press, 2003), p. 11.
117. Newsom, *Moral Imaginations*, p. 21.
118. Newsom, *Moral Imaginations*, p. 22.
119. Newsom, *Moral Imaginations*, p. 23.

commitment to the centrality of an author's intention, the removal of which naturally jeopardizes access to an intended governing genre. Furthermore, denying a systematic approach to interpreting Job logically permits the kind of 'unfinalizability' that eliminates the goal of bringing Job to some degree of closure.[120]

Fortunately, Newsom recognizes the limitations that Bakhtin's model would have on a biblical text that naturally resists such open-ended boundaries. In a manner not too dissimilar from Zuckerman's and Dell's own work with Job's genres, Newsom is more interested in discerning the interplay between the competing genres. However, the most unfortunate aspect for Newsom's polyphonic approach, at least in terms of establishing a governing genre is concerned, is that she cannot, or will not, subsume the Elihu speeches into her interpretive matrix. On the one hand, she argues that aside from the Elihu speeches, Job is the product of one author.[121] On the other hand, she teases the reader by coyly suggesting that her polyphonic approach 'could accommodate either an analysis of the Elihu speeches as original or secondary'.[122] She ultimately chooses the latter because she is 'persuaded by the classic arguments', which, interestingly, are based on historical-critical grounds.[123]

Newsom's commitment to Bakhtin's methodology cannot allow for a systemic, finalized interpretation that assumes authorial intention, which means that no overarching genre can be legitimately established. In imposing Bakhtin's program, Newsom has preserved and repackaged a remnant of the modern world, one which argues that Job's genre is simply 'sui generis', in order to advance a postmodern interpretation for the purpose of reading Job 'as a book of our age'.[124]

Job as Poeticized Folktale
On final but important work is that of Carole Fontaine's less ambitious, though very persuasive essay, which seeks to identify Job as 'poeticized folktale'.[125] Applying a formalist grid that is heavily informed by Vladimir

---

120. Newsom, *Moral Imaginations*, p. 24.
121. Newsom, *Moral Imaginations*, p. 16.
122. Newsom, *Moral Imaginations*, p. 201.
123. Newsom, *Moral Imaginations*, p. 201.
124. Newsom, *Moral Imaginations*, p. 261.
125. Carole Fontaine, 'Folktale Structure in the Book of Job: A Formalist Reading', in E. Follis (ed.), *Directions in Biblical Hebrew Poetry* (JSOTSup, 40; Sheffield: JSOT Press, 1987), pp. 205-32. See also her discussion in 'Wounded Hero on a Shaman's Quest', in Perdue and Gilpin (eds.), *The Voice from the Whirlwind*, pp. 70-85 (71-80). This essay could be retitled, in my view, since the large majority of the essay is dedicated to her earlier work on Job as a folktale without any clear transition from it to the role of

Propp's research on Russian fairy tales, Fontaine argues that the poetic sections of Job contribute to the structures characterized by folktales, which are most apparent in the narrative prologue and epilogue.[126]

The model seems to work extremely well until the Elihu speeches, at which point Fontaine concedes that the speeches essentially intrude on Propp's model. At the moment in the story where Propp's analysis anticipates a struggle between the hero and villain, the story of Job presents another antagonist who cannot be considered the villain any more than any of the three friends.[127] Fontaine is forced to label these speeches as the 'reduplication' of a sequence that has already occurred in the story, which constitutes a 'new "move"'.[128]

While such a new move is not 'beyond the bounds' of the folk tale structure, which even Propp acknowledged is fairly fluid, the designation of Elihu as both magical agent and helper is not overly convincing. Furthermore, Fontaine concludes that 'almost all of the *dramatis personae* expected in the tale are present in Job'.[129] That is, not all of the expected characters that Propp identifies emerge.

While it is impossible to ascertain whether the author(s) had such a structure as Propp proposes in mind, the various evidence of infidelity to the model warrants caution rather than outright acceptance. Furthermore, it is hard to imagine that even if the author(s) did consciously incorporate a certain 'folk tale pattern', they would designate God as the 'imposter', which Fontaine seems to suggest.[130]

Still, Fontaine's work is extraordinarily valuable to my own efforts because, as will later be seen, she advances the notion that the mysterious figure of ch. 28 may be a 'magical agent' that is designed to assist Job. Such a relationship is consonant with the role of a mediator in an apocalypse, who offers a revelation to the 'hero'. In addition, Fontaine indicates that the purpose of ch. 28 and the Yahweh speeches is to assist Job in 'completing his mission'.[131] This too aligns with the function of apocalyptic revelations to their respective heroes.

---

the Shaman for Job. In this essay, Fontaine presents some natural cautions to her folktale approach, the most damaging of which is that it is likely improper to apply a twentieth-century model of Russian fairy tales to an ancient work like Job.
   126.   Fontaine, 'Folktale', p. 206.
   127.   Fontaine, 'Folktale', p. 220.
   128.   Fontaine, 'Folktale', p. 220.
   129.   Fontaine, 'Folktale', p. 226.
   130.   Fontaine, 'Shaman', p. 76. I must confess a degree of personal resistance to the idea of God as 'imposter'.
   131.   Fontaine, 'Folktale', p. 77.

Conclusion

The ability of a given paradigm to account satisfactorily for all of the seemingly disparate literary phenomena contained in Job serves as the litmus test that either validates or denies an alternative genre. If one or more of the major sections of Job cannot accommodate the proposal, it clearly was not intended by an original author, or, more likely, by a redactor, either of which must have had a clear literary agenda in mind.

I have sought to highlight several of the most important and more recent attempts and to show that all of them fail to integrate seamlessly all of the literary strands evident in Job. I have also tried to show that these efforts still have yielded much fruit for studying Job's genre and interpretation.

Given the difficulties encountered by these and other attempts to 'hedge' in Job's genre, most scholars have come to agree with Norman Habel that the creative literary work of Job simply does not conform to any single traditional genre.[132] Marvin Pope offered a similar sentiment, suggesting that Job be classified as *sui generis*.[133] However, as noted repeatedly, it is hard to conceive of a book void of some formal governing genre as though the author or redactor simply wrote without any program. The mere fact that the book of Job has been considered a classic for centuries seems to speak against the idea that the author of Job simply haphazardly combined the various elements. Recognizing the subsequent apathy associated with such an attitude, it is again worth quoting Westermann who correctly noted that 'the whole question of literary form would become significant only if the judgement concerning literary classification were to have a decisive effect upon the exegesis of the book'.[134]

I maintain that pursuit of a given work's genre is essential if one is to interpret responsibly. I contend that the author(s)/redactor(s) had an agenda and that the coagulation of the seemingly disparate sections of Job was crafted along the lines of an early, undeveloped form of apocalypse. To argue that the author(s) had a specific, formalized apocalyptic framework in mind during the story's compilation would be anachronistic, and I attempt to avoid such an assertion. However, it seems that a structure related to apocalypse was in view, and that the textual witness bears this suggestion out. I now turn to a more formal analysis of this hypothesis in order to establish more firmly the basis for an exciting new interpretive framework from which to understand the book of Job.

---

132. Habel, *The Book of Job*, p. 160. Robert Gordis (*Poets, Prophets, and Sages: Essays in Biblical Interpretation* [Bloomington: Indiana University Press, 1971], p. 281) concurs, stating that Job 'is as unique in form as it is profound in content'.

133. Pope, *Job*, p. xxx. See also Crenshaw, 'Wisdom', p. 253. See also Dell, *Job as Sceptical Literature*, p. 102 n. 162, for a list of those concurring.

134. Westermann, *Structure*, p. 1.

2

COMPARING JOB TO APOCALYPSE

Introduction

As Chapter 1 demonstrated, attempts to identify the overarching genre of Job failed, in part, because these attempts were unable to incorporate all of Job's diverse forms and contents into their proposed paradigms. E.D. Hirsch recognized, however, that such failures still produce an important heuristic function in interpretation. He says, 'The central role of genre concepts in interpretation is most easily grasped when the process of interpretation is going badly or when it has to undergo revision'.[1] John Collins has also recognized the value of investigating genres, stating:

> An interpreter always begins with an assumption about the genre of a text. If our expectations are fulfilled, the assumptions will need no revision. If they are not fulfilled, we must revise our idea of the genre or relinquish the attempt to understand. There can be no understanding without at least an implicit notion of genre.[2]

I therefore take the shortcomings of all attempts to classify Job's genre as my point of departure in revising previous assumptions regarding Job's genre. Scholarship is not willing to relinquish the attempt to understand the book of Job, nor am I. However, scholarship has all too easily contented itself with labeling Job as *sui generis*, which I consider a content-less formulation for Job's genre that ultimately privileges the reader over against the author.

Perhaps what is most needed is to step back and consider how all of the competing genres and disparate features within Job might coalesce. Fohrer expresses a similar sentiment:

---

1. E.D. Hirsch Jr, *Validity in Interpretation* (New Haven: Yale University Press, 1967), p. 71.
2. J.J. Collins, *The Apocalyptic Imagination: An Introduction to Jewish Apocalyptic Literature* (Grand Rapids: Eerdmans, 2nd edn, 1998), p. 8.

> Differences between form and function show that the form which is used does not always correspond to the content, or enable one to decide what this must be. This must be borne in mind in attempting to grasp the book of Job as a formal whole. It is certainly true that the book does not amount either to an epic or a drama, and equally it is not a pure wisdom book or didactic poem. But nor can it be classified as a trial or a dramatized lament, by one-sidedly stressing a single formal sphere, and paying no attention to the way forms are used.[3]

This chapter seeks to unveil evidence for Job's apocalyptic DNA in three parts. The first part will briefly survey formal issues of Apocalyptic Literature. I do not intend to be exhaustive in this overview of the literary genre of apocalypse—other specialists have accomplished this admirably.[4] However, in order to make the case that Job is akin to apocalypse, it is important to outline the substantive features associated with the genre. As mentioned in the Introduction, I fully support classificatory analyses, for it is only these kinds of investigation that one can move toward any degree of objective clarification regarding a hypothesis. Thus, I will draw heavily from the Apocalypse Group's 'Master Paradigm', which is the product of the efforts of many scholars who sought to provide some uniformity to the term 'apocalyptic' under the auspices of the SBL's Genres Project.

In the second part, I compare the story of Job to the proposed 'Master Paradigm' in order to demonstrate that Job easily conforms in many ways to an apocalyptic profile. The Master Paradigm is, however, a predominantly American approach that some European scholars criticize for failing to account for the evolution of apocalypse itself.[5] Therefore, the third and final section of this chapter will interact with Paolo Sacchi's important work on apocalypse, which generally represents a European perspective on apocalypses, as well as with Michael E. Vines's very recent effort to forge a

---

3. G. Fohrer, *Das Buch Hiob* (Kommentar zum Alten Testament; Gütersloh: Gerd Mohn, 1963), p. 53: 'Der Unterschied zwischen Form und Funktion zeigt, daß die verwendete Form nicht immer dem Inhalt entspricht oder auf ihn schließen läßt. Dies ist für das formale Gesamtverständnis des Buches Hiob zu bedenken. Gewiß stellt das Buch weder ein Epos noch ein Drama dar, ebensowenig ein reines Weisheitsbuch oder eine reine Lehrdichtung. Man kann es aber auch nicht als Verhandlung einer Rechtssache oder dramatisierte Klage bezeichnen, indem man einseitig einen einzigen Formbereich ohne Berücksichtigung der funktionellen Verwendung heranzieht.'

4. See Collins, *The Apocalyptic Imagination*.

5. Leo G. Perdue (*Wisdom in Revolt: Metaphorical Theology in the Book of Job* [JSOTSup, 112; Sheffield: JSOT Press, 1991], p. 77) concurs, stating, 'Much of the disagreement over the form of the book results in part from a failure to recognize the evolving morphology of the Joban tradition which culminates in the coalescence of three separate genres: didactic narrative, lament, and disputation'. While I would consider these final three as parts of an even larger whole, Perdue recognizes the need to consider diachronic strategies for grasping Job's governing genre.

working definition of apocalypse that is informed by Mikhail Bakhtin's research on genres. Since both Sacchi and Vines are generally critical of the Apocalypse Group's work, my reader will be exposed to three different approaches to defining apocalypse. At the same time, my intention in both the second and third parts of the present chapter is to demonstrate the validity of my claim that the governing genre of Job should be considered some nascent form of apocalypse instead of 'wisdom'. In my view, all three descriptions of apocalypse offer clear evidence that Job is an obvious candidate for membership into the category of apocalypse, over against its traditional wisdom label.

Comparing Job to the Genre Apocalypse
The biblical books most commonly considered apocalypses are Daniel in the Hebrew Bible/Old Testament and Revelation in the New Testament. However, the majority of books studied in the field of apocalypse come from the Intertestamental Period where a number of diverse cultures contributed to the growth of the genre. Like studies in Wisdom Literature, research in Apocalyptic Literature has increased in the last few decades. In fact, it can be argued that both began to flourish after the demise of the so-called Biblical Theology Movement in the early 1960s, and after the publication of Gerhard von Rad's extraordinarily influential *Weisheit im Israel*, published in 1970.[6]

Shortly thereafter, research into apocalypses exploded and took on a life of its own. Little attention was paid to methodological consistency, which resulted in the need for order within the field. Robert L. Webb, whose work has greatly influenced the initial portion of this survey, provides a concise review of the significant historical phases associated with the progress from chaos to order in apocalypse research.[7]

Robert L. Webb
Also calling 'apocalyptic' a slippery term, Webb seeks to clarify the four major grammatical referents for apocalypses. The term 'apocalyptic' is an adjective that is commonly misused as a noun, thus causing semantic

---

6. See Gerhard von Rad, *Wisdom in Israel* (trans. James D. Martin; Nashville: Abingdon Press, 1972). Collins (*Apocalyptic Imagination*, pp. 1, 12-13) suggests that interest emerged when Wellhausen's grip on Old Testament research began to decline. However, John N. Oswalt ('Recent Studies in Old Testament Apocalyptic', in D. Baker and B. Arnold [eds.], *The Face of Old Testament Studies: A Survey of Contemporary Approaches* [Grand Rapids: Baker, 1999], pp. 369-90 [369-70]) disagrees with Klaus Koch's assertion that interest began after Käsemann's 1959 lecture on apocalypse's role in Christian theology, arguing that much had occurred prior to this address.

7. Robert L. Webb, 'Apocalyptic: Observations on a Slippery Term', *Journal of Near Eastern Studies* 49 (1990), pp. 115-26.

confusion.⁸ Apocalypse itself is reserved for the designation of a literary genre. Apocalypticism describes an ideology that is distinct from social phenomena (i.e. apocalyptic movement) but is intimately related to the genre of apocalypse. Relying on Paul Hanson, Webb distinguishes apocalyptic eschatology from prophetic eschatology because the former conceives of 'deliverance out of the present order into a new transformed life'.⁹ Webb then begins to distinguish chronologically between the four major approaches to defining an apocalypse as found within contemporary scholarship.

(1) The traditional approach, as represented by Klaus Koch, compiles lists of characteristics appropriate to an apocalypse. For example, Koch lists fourteen traits, including: pseudonymity, paraenetic discourses, mythical images rich in symbolism, composite literary works, imminent overthrow of earthly conditions, and so on.¹⁰ This approach emphasizes apocalyptic eschatology while at the same time it neglects the equally prevalent features of mysticism, existential anthropology and historiography.

(2) The literary-form approach, as championed by Christopher Rowland, responds to the traditional approach by emphasizing literary features over against pure content. Because the content of apocalypses is so diverse, content itself does not adequately serve as a brand for the genre. Instead, the literary form of revelation predominates in all apocalypses as God's direct unveiling and communication of his esoteric truths.¹¹

A particular strength of this approach is the simple fidelity to the meaning of the word apocalypse, that is, as deriving from the Greek ἀποκαλύπτω ('to reveal, disclose').¹² The noun for this Greek verb, as found in the title to the book of Revelation, is commonly regarded as the source for the name of the 'apocalyptic' field of study.¹³ On the other hand, Webb notes that a fundamental weakness with the literary approach is that by minimizing the central function of content, namely, apocalyptic eschatology, it embraces a much wider body of literature under the 'apocalypse' rubric than would otherwise normally be accepted.

8. Some have called for the elimination of the term. Webb, 'Apocalyptic', p. 115, cites T.F. Glasson, 'What is Apocalyptic?', *NTS* 27 (1980), pp. 98-105 (105). See also Michael E. Stone, 'List of the Revealed Things in Apocalyptic Literature', in F.M. Cross, W.E. Lemke and P.D. Miller (eds.), *Magnalia Dei: The Mighty Acts of God* (Garden City, NY: Doubleday, 1976), pp. 414-52 (443).

9. Paul Hanson, 'Apocalypticism', in *IDBSup*, pp. 27-34 (30).

10. Klaus Koch, *The Rediscovery of Apocalyptic* (trans. M. Kohl; London: SCM Press, 1972), pp. 18-35.

11. Christopher Rowland, *The Open Heaven: A Study of Apocalyptic in Judaism and Early Christianity* (New York: Crossroad, 1982), p. 14.

12. *BAGD*.

13. On the other hand, Collins (*Apocalyptic Imagination*, p. 3) points out that the word itself may not necessarily designate a particular class of literature and instead may generally denote a revelation.

(3) In somewhat of a return to the traditional views of Koch, E.P. Sanders has coined the 'essentialist' approach as one comprised of 'the combination of revelation with the promise of restoration and reversal'.[14] For Sanders, revelation is the essential literary element while restoration and reversal are the essential contents of the genre. Again, this approach suffers from its broad appeal, namely, that it also describes biblical prophecies and political oracles of the ancient Near East. Additionally, it too does not take into account central themes such as the cosmological and mystical.[15]

(4) As noted, in order to overcome the diversity of approaches, a task force undertaken by the SBL's Genres Project sought to establish a set of criteria by showing the extent and limits of the conformity among the allegedly apocalyptic texts. The group hoped to determine whether a collection of texts 'share a significant cluster of traits that distinguish them from other works'.[16] Webb views the study group's results published in *Semeia* in 1979 as an 'eclectic' approach: one that attempts to inductively incorporate recurring features and highlight distinctive traits affiliated with a typical apocalypse.

Master Paradigm

One of the significant outcomes of the SBL Study Group is the compilation of features listed as the 'Master Paradigm'. This paradigm can serve as an excellent point of departure for determining how closely the book of Job conforms to an apocalypse. It is important to note that not all apocalypses share every feature listed in the paradigm. However, any work commonly considered an apocalypse will exhibit several of the traits listed. The paradigm consists of thirteen main features:[17]

Manner of Revelation
1. Medium by which the revelation is communicated
    1.1 Visual revelation in the form of:
        1.1.1 Visions, or
        1.1.2 Epiphanies (describing apparition of mediator)
    1.2 Auditory revelation usually clarifies the visual by:
        1.2.1 Discourse (uninterrupted speech by mediator), or
        1.2.2 Dialogue (between mediator and recipient)
    1.3 Otherworldly journey (heaven, hell, remote places)
    1.4 Writing (revelation contained in written document)

---

14. E.P. Sanders, 'The Genre of Palestinian Jewish Apocalypses', in D. Hellholm (ed.), *Apocalypticism in the Mediterranean World and the Near East* (Tübingen: J.C.B. Mohr, 1983), pp. 447-59 (458).
15. Collins, *Apocalyptic Imagination*, pp. 9-10.
16. Collins, *Apocalyptic Imagination*, p. 4.
17. Collins, 'Morphology', pp. 5-8.

2. Otherworldly mediator communicates revelation
3. The human recipient
   3.1 Pseudonymity
   3.2 Disposition of recipient (circumstances, emotions)
   3.3 Reaction of recipient (often awe and/or perplexity)

Content of Revelation: Temporal Axis

4. Protology (pre-history or beginning of history)
   4.1. Theogony and/or Cosmogony (origin of God/Pleroma, and/or cosmos)
   4.2. Primordial events having paradigmatic significance
5. History, viewed as:
   5.1 Explicit recollection of the past, or
   5.2 *Ex eventu* prophecy
6. Present salvation through knowledge (in Gnostic texts)
7. Eschatological crisis, in the form of:
   7.1 Persecution, and/or
   7.2 Other eschatological upheavals (disturbing the order of nature or history)
8. Eschatological judgment and/or destruction upon:
   8.1 The wicked, or the ignorant (in Gnostic texts)
   8.2 The natural world
   8.3 Otherworldly beings
9. Eschatological salvation, may involve:
   9.1 Cosmic transformation (renewal of entire world)
   9.2 Personal salvation
      9.2.1 Resurrection in bodily form, or
      9.2.2 Other forms of afterlife (such as exaltation to heaven with angels)

Content of Revelation: Spatial Axis

10. Otherworldly elements
    10.1. Otherworldly regions (described usually in otherworldly journeys)
    10.2 Otherworldly beings (angelic or demonic)

Paraenesis

11. Paraenesis (by mediator to the recipient)

Concluding Elements

12. Instructions to the recipient
13. Narrative conclusion

For Webb, the strengths of the earlier approaches to apocalypse are incorporated within this eclectic approach. Both form and content are central, as with the traditional and essentialist. The importance of revelation is compatible with the literary and essentialist approaches. The eschatological emphasis found in the traditional and essentialist is contained as well as the cosmic/mystical emphasis of the literary. Similarly, John J. Collins, an important architect of the paradigm, feels that the inner coherence of the paradigm revolves around the term 'transcendence', by which both the form of the revelation and the content are characterized.[18]

---

18. Collins, 'Morphology', pp. 10-12.

From this study group emerged a working definition for an apocalypse:

> Apocalypse is a genre of revelatory literature with a narrative framework, in which a revelation is mediated by an otherworldly being to a human recipient, disclosing a transcendent reality which is both temporal, insofar as it envisages eschatological salvation, and spatial insofar as it involves another, supernatural world.[19]

Webb observes that the major weakness of the eclectic approach is that it does not consider the function of apocalypse. While the form and content are adequately dealt with, an apocalypse's function required further examination. Initially responding to that concern, David Hellholm proposed that the *Semeia* 14 definition be emended by adding that an apocalypse is:

> intended for a group in crisis with the purpose of exhortation and/or consolation by means of divine authority.[20]

Collins concedes that 'the illocutionary functions of exhortation and consolation can generally be maintained for the Jewish apocalypses'.[21] He cautions, however, that exhortations can certainly vary and that the literary function must be regarded as intimately related to the form and content. That is, the distinctly apocalyptic perspective is framed spatially by the supernatural and temporally by the eschatological judgment. Thus, the function of apocalypse is to shape the reader's imaginative perception, thereby establishing the groundwork for some course of action.[22]

Collins here relies on Adela Yarbro Collins, who views apocalypse as:

> intended to interpret present, earthly circumstances in light of the supernatural world and of the future, and to influence both the understanding and the behavior of the audience by means of divine authority.[23]

Since Hellholm and Yarbro Collins ultimately entertain issues of setting, either of their efforts will naturally influence how one conceives of the literary origin of an apocalypse. Like efforts in wisdom, apocalyptic studies have failed to achieve a consensus with respect to the apocalypse's *Sitz im Leben*. More will be said on a possible setting in life for Job in Chapter 5.

Scholarly Intimations of Job as Apocalypse
My contention is that the literary form of apocalypse can, in fact, accommodate all of the seemingly disconnected facets of Job. It was noted that

19. Collins, 'Morphology', p. 9.
20. David Hellholm, 'The Problem of Apocalyptic Genre and the Apocalypse of John', *Semeia* 36 (1986), pp. 13-64 (27).
21. Collins, *Apocalyptic Imagination*, p. 41.
22. Collins, *Apocalyptic Imagination*, pp. 41-42.
23. Adela Yarbro Collins, 'Introduction: Early Christian Apocalypticism', *Semeia* 36 (1986), pp. 1-12 (7).

many of the failed attempts at identifying the overall genre suffered by their inability to distinguish between form and function. In other words, just because a form exists in the text does not mean that it is the unifying form intended by the author/redactor. This was most evident in the various form-critical proposals. Still, one would expect that various clues to the 'structural genre' would also be present. Job does contain several apocalyptic clues, the existence of which has led to previous scholarly formulations or suggestions that Job may in fact be a kind of apocalypse.

As cited earlier, John J. Collins asserts that the book of Job has the greatest affinities with apocalypses over against any of the Hebrew wisdom books.[24] Collins contends that Job, like other apocalypses, 'arises out of a failure to find order and justice in the world', and is therefore forced to rely on a 'supernatural revelation', which he receives from God out of the whirlwind.[25] It would seem, then, that Collins identifies both an apocalyptic element of content, that is, a crisis with respect to order and justice, and an element of form, namely, the supernatural revelation, as evidence of Job's intersection with apocalypse.

Others also acknowledge apocalyptic features contained in Job. For example, part of Sewall's rejection of Job as 'tragedy' is that, 'in formal tragedy there is no such *apocalypse* as Job presently experiences'.[26] With particular interest to forms, Katharine Dell suggests that the dream account of Job 4.12-21 may represent the form apocalypse.[27]

Furthermore, Ithamar Gruenwald all but asserts that Job is in fact an apocalypse. He argues that the wisdom tradition of ancient Jewish apocalypticism provided revelations of 'cosmological secrets and its relation to the problem of theodicy'.[28] To sustain this assertion, Gruenwald employs the book of Job as an example.

Finally, no one has said more about the possible relationship between Job and apocalypse than Christopher Rowland, who remarks that 'the whole structure of the book of Job offers an embryonic form of the later apocalypse'.[29] Rowland suggests that two particular features within Job lend themselves to apocalypse.

The first feature is the divine 'self-revelation' from the whirlwind.[30] This revelation 'transforms' the book of Job from a human-centered search for

---

24. See my Introduction, n. 2.
25. Collins, 'Cosmos and Salvation', p. 140 n. 3.
26. Richard B. Sewall, *The Vision of Tragedy* (New Haven: Yale University Press, enlarged edn, 1980), p. 23 (emphasis added).
27. Dell, *Job as Sceptical Literature*, p. 104.
28. Gruenwald, *Apocalyptic and Merkavah Mysticism*, pp. 14-15.
29. Rowland, *Open Heaven*, p. 207.
30. Rowland, *Open Heaven*, p. 206.

answers to the questions of unjust suffering to an appreciation of the import contained in God's dimension. Thus, the story of Job transcends its humanness and enters into the divine.

The second critical apocalyptic feature found in Job is the reader's inability to participate in the human speculation occurring in the story because the reader learns in the prologue why Job is suffering. Thus, the reader is in a privileged position as compared to the hero of the story.[31] As noted earlier, Dell notices this as well, and argues that typical wisdom books address the reader within the contents of the book, which is not the case in Job.[32]

It is clear that several significant scholars acknowledge that Job is indeed compatible with the genre apocalypse. However, as noted, hitherto no one had subjected Job to a thoroughgoing apocalyptic analysis. Given the prominence rightly attributed to the valuable apocalyptic 'Master Paradigm', a comparison between the paradigm's central tenets and the literary features of Job will assist in evaluating the proposal.

Comparing Job to the Master Paradigm

In this section only preliminary exegetical points are discussed. Further exegesis appears only in those instances where it is absolutely necessary. Chapter 4 is dedicated to the interpretive model established in Chapters 1, 2 and 3. The reader is encouraged to refer frequently to the Master Paradigm in order to ensure that the basis for the comparative analysis is clearly appreciated.

Sections one through three of the Master Paradigm treat elements associated with the revelatory process. All told, I maintain that three revelations exist in Job: Eliphaz's vision from Job 4, the revelation from Job 28 and the theophany from Job 38–41. While the theophany and to a lesser extent Eliphaz's vision are generally recognized as revelations, ch. 28's designation is perhaps less well attested in scholarship. However, as the first three sections of this comparative analysis proceed, the reader will find increased support for each of the three instances cited.

Section One: Medium by Which the Revelation is Communicated
Eliphaz's vision (4.17-21), which Dell considers an apocalyptic form,[33] appeals to many senses. Eliphaz attempted in vain to *behold* the 'spirit' that was before him (4.16), he *heard* a voice (4.16) and he was impacted physically through 'trembling' (4.14), 'bones shaking' (4.14) and the 'hair of my

---

31. Rowland, *Open Heaven*, p. 206.
32. Dell, *Job as Sceptical Literature*, p. 71.
33. Dell, *Job as Sceptical Literature*, p. 104.

flesh bristled' (4.15). The vision reveals knowledge in the form of a discourse, and while the vision does contain mystical overtones, it does not clearly transport Eliphaz to an 'otherworldly' realm. Still, the revelation contains many of the characteristics suggested in section one of the paradigm.

The importance of the apocalypse cannot be underestimated. Of all the genres and literary devices found in the lengthy Dialogue Speeches (chs. 4–27), an apocalypse is found in the very first response to Job's lament from ch. 3. Furthermore, this revelation is regarded by some as 'the only vision report by a wise person in Scripture'.[34] The fact that such a unique feature is presented so early on in the story intimates that the reader is not handling a traditional wisdom book.

The revelation of ch. 28 might be considered an auditory revelation containing a discourse that also borders on a less-developed theophany, or what I will term a minor theophany. Many might question the legitimacy of my assertion that ch. 28 contains a revelation at all, auditory or otherwise. Stephen Geller, however, considers v. 23b an absolutely astounding breakthrough in the poem, referring to it as, 'almost as much a theophany as the divine speech out of the whirlwind'.[35] Verse 23 reads:

> God understands the way to it,
> and he knows its place.

Geller continues, 'Light from this sudden revelation immediately transfigures the preceding parts of the poem'.[36] Much more will be said on Geller's interpretation in Chapter 4, but for the moment, I am comfortable recognizing the validity of my conclusion that ch. 28 does include an important revelation.

As noted earlier, scholars acknowledge that God's appearance out of the whirlwind (Job 38–41) serves as the fundamental revelation in Job.[37] It offers visual and auditory revelations mostly via discourse, but also through dialogue since Job does respond, albeit briefly and impotently. One could also argue that God's epiphany might be akin to an otherworldly journey

---

34. W.S. LaSor, D.A. Hubbard and F.W. Bush (eds.), *Old Testament Survey: The Message, Form, and Background of the Old Testament* (Grand Rapids: Eerdmans, 2nd edn, 1996), p. 476. The difficulty in their assertion is that they fail to define their terms. For example, what constitutes a 'wise person'? Certainly Daniel could be a candidate for such a person, and he clearly receives visions. Nonetheless, the main point is to draw attention to the unconventional use of a vision report in a so-called wisdom book.

35. Stephen Geller, '"Where is Wisdom?": A Literary Study of Job 28 in its Settings', in J. Neusner, B.A. Levine and E.S. Frerichs (eds.), *Judaic Perspectives on Ancient Israel* (Philadelphia: Fortress Press, 1987), pp. 155-88 (165).

36. Geller, 'Where is Wisdom?', p. 163.

37. See Rowland, *Open Heaven*, p. 207.

from Job's perspective. The mythological images conjured up with Leviathan and Behemoth themselves certainly support such an assertion.

While these three revelations might appear infrequent in comparison to the extensive length of the book, it is understood in scholarship that an apocalypse is not necessarily the exclusive or dominant genre within an apocalypse.[38] It is also important to point out that an apocalyptic revelation is not limited to 'future expectations'; it can also reveal 'heavenly secrets', which is the primary content of the revelation in the Yahweh speeches.[39] More importantly, the function that these revelations play in the story is critical to its development.

Not only do the revelations occur at pivotal points in the story, indeed, they dictate the subsequent phases of the story. For example, Eliphaz's vision in ch. 4 closes the first stage of the story and also ignites the furious dialogue speeches. The revelation in ch. 28 effectively ends the fruitless dialogue speeches while also spurring Job on to both an emboldened lamentation in chs. 29 and 30, and an impassioned assertion of his innocence in ch. 31, which includes a demand for a hearing from Yahweh. And God's revelation in chs. 38–41 cuts off Elihu's bombastic monologue while essentially completing the story, which leads to Job's total submission before God.

It is clear that the foundational element of an apocalypse, namely, revelation, plays an important role in Job's literary composition.

Section Two: Otherworldly Mediator Communicates Revelation
The vision or apocalypse of ch. 4, which begins in v. 17, contains the clearest use of a mediator. Job 4.12-21 reads:

> [12]Now a word came stealthily to me,
>   my ear received the whisper of it.
> [13]Amid thoughts from visions of the night,
>   when deep sleep falls on mortals,
> [14]dread came upon me, and trembling,
>   which made all my bones shake.
> [15]A spirit glided past my face;
>   the hair of my flesh bristled.
> [16]It stood still,
>   but I could not discern its appearance.
>   A form was before my eyes;
>   there was silence, then I heard a voice:
> [17]'Can mortals be righteous before God?
>   Can human beings be pure before their Maker?

---

38. Hanson, 'Apocalypticism', p. 29.
39. J.J. Collins, 'Apocalyptic Eschatology as the Transcendence of Death', *CBQ* 36 (1974), pp. 21-42 (22). He also states that apocalypses do not have to refer to the end of the world, as seen in Daniel (p. 25). Cf. Hanson, 'Apocalypse, Genre', in *IDBSup*, p. 28.

> ¹⁸Even in his servants he puts no trust,
>   and his angels he charges with error;
> ¹⁹how much more those who live in houses of clay,
>   whose foundation is in the dust,
>   who are crushed like a moth.
> ²⁰Between morning and evening they are destroyed;
>   they perish for ever without any regarding it.
> ²¹Their tent-cord is plucked up within them,
>   and they die devoid of wisdom.'

The identification of this mediator is unclear, but the content of his revelation (4.17-21) is unmistakable, namely, that human beings are unable to claim any standing before an omnipotent God. C.S. Rodd supports the position that some mediator exists, for he argues, 'the essential point is that what Eliphaz meets is a messenger from God with a revelation for him'.[40]

Identifying the speaker of the puzzling ch. 28 continues to stymie students of Job. Even though many have traditionally thought that Job speaks these words, Pope declares that the traditional acceptance of Job as the speaker is incongruent with Job's prior burden to force God into court in order to question him.[41] Andersen concurs, stating that most scholars cannot accept that Job is the speaker because it is so incompatible with what precedes and follows the chapter.[42] This line of argumentation has led others to suggest either Bildad or Zophar as possible speakers.[43] More are beginning to consider the author/redactor himself as the speaker.[44] None of these suggestions has gained a consensus, which leaves open the possibility that an unidentified mediator conveys the message. The text simply does not make it clear. However, the speaker offers an important revelation, namely, that only God understands the way of wisdom (28.23) and that wisdom is the fear of the Lord (28.28).

While it is true the theophanic revelation in Job 38–41 does not utilize a classic use of a mediator, the revelation is intended to persuade the reader that the human view of the situation is too narrow. Instead, the divine perspective is more complete, accounting for both the past and the future, which seems to be a common practice in apocalypses.[45] Therefore, the absence of an identifiable mediator does not detract from the apocalyptic dimension that the theophanic revelation contributes to the book of Job.

---

40. C.S. Rodd, *The Book of Job* (Narrative Commentaries; Philadelphia: Trinity Press, 1990), p. 15.

41. Pope, *The Book of Job*, p. xxvi.

42. F.I. Andersen, *Job* (TOTC; Leicester: Inter-Varsity Press, 1976), p. 223.

43. Andersen, *Job*, p. 223.

44. See Murphy, *The Book of Job*, p. 67, and Dhorme, *A Commentary on the Book of Job* (trans. Harold Knight; London: Nelson, 1967), p. li.

45. See Rowland, *Open Heaven*, p. 207.

2. Comparing Job to Apocalypse

Thus, it is clear that mediator(s) (or their equivalents) of revelations do indeed exist within Job in some manner, and their messages play particularly significant roles in the movement of the story and in the theology contained within.

Section Three: The Human Recipient
Before evaluating the recipients in each of the three revelations, it is important to say a word about pseudonymity because of the consistent role this literary device plays in apocalypses. Collins remarks, 'In all Jewish apocalypses the human recipient is a venerable figure from the distant past, whose name is used pseudonymously'.[46] In each of the three revelations, the narrative indicates that Job is ultimately the intended recipient of the content of the revelations. This may not be quite as obvious in either Eliphaz's vision or the revelation from ch. 28. However, Job is clearly the intended recipient for the whirlwind revelation.

Outside of a few biblical references (Ezek. 14.14, 20; Jas 5.11), little is known about the identity of the character Job. Some assume that the story may in fact relate to a historical person,[47] while most contend that the characters are nothing more than literary fabrications.[48] However, Pope argues that the name 'Job' was a fairly common name in the second millennium BCE and it may have been the name of 'some ancient worthy bearing that name'.[49] Given the near-unanimous agreement that the final story of Job experienced some degree of later editing, it is possible to conceive of a story that either embellishes the sufferings of an ancient legend or affixes the name of such a legend to this story. In either case, the story of Job can be better declared as pseudonymous rather than merely anonymous. In fact, it may be argued that the story of Job served as a kind of model for later pseudonymous writings, many of which have come to be recognized as apocalypses. In this way, the prevalence of the practice of pseudonymity so commonly associated with later apocalypses might be seen as a fuller, more explicit expression of pseudonymous attribution foreshadowed in the proto-apocalypse book of Job.

Perhaps recognizing this stratagem, the authors of both LXX Job and the *Testament of Job* used the name 'Jobab' for Job. Most suspect that Jobab, which is derived from Gen. 36.33, was applied to Job as a way of aligning biblical Job with the ancient patriarchs. For example, the appendix of LXX

---

46. Collins, *Apocalyptic Imagination*, p. 6. He notes that this is not the case in either *Hermes* or in the New Testament book of Revelation (n. 16).
47. See Westermann, *Structure*, pp. 6-7, and John Hartley, *The Book of Job* (NICOT; Grand Rapids: Eerdmans, 1988), pp. 65-66, esp. n. 11.
48. See Murphy, *Job*, pp. 4-6.
49. Pope, *Job*, p. 6.

Job notes that Job was formerly known as Jobab and was a direct descendant of Esau, who was fifth in the line of descent from Abraham. The *Testament of Job* extends this practice by identifying Job as Jobab in the first verse and shortly thereafter identifies Job's second wife as Dinah the daughter of Jacob.

Thus, while the theory that later translators/redactors sought to identify Job with the patriarchs is not without reason, it might also be the case that these translators/redactors linked Job with Jobab to establish credibility for the story. Not unlike the author(s) of the Enochic literature, the translators/redactors of LXX Job and the *Testament of Job* might have used a relatively obscure person from Genesis pseudonymously as a means of elevating the legitimacy of the story. Greg Carey has argued that establishing an 'apocalyptic ethos' through pseudonymity was crucial to the crafters of apocalypses.[50] The fact that Job's name is so closely related to Jobab might have made such a maneuver too tempting to avoid.

Thus, the issue of pseudonymity does apply to the character Job, the human recipient, and therefore allows for the suggestion that pseudonymity plays a role in identifying the book of Job as nascent apocalypse.

With respect to the three specific revelations occurring within the story of Job, characteristics associated with the recipients are shared with other apocalypses. Again referring to the text of Job 4, it is clear that Eliphaz's disposition is one of unease.[51] The descriptions of his psychological state preceding and during the vision include such features as 'dread', trembling and 'bristled hair'. Moreover, Eliphaz's reaction to this vision is an invigorated challenge to Job in ch. 5, which, together with ch. 4, serves as the lengthiest questioning of Job during the entire discourse cycle.

The disposition of the recipient to the revelation found in ch. 28 is less certain since the intended recipient of the revelation cannot be clearly confirmed, though it likely addresses Job. The same might be assumed with respect to the recipient's reaction to the revelation. However, on this latter point, it might be argued that Job, the likely recipient, is fueled by the revelation that wisdom cannot be found with humans because the following chapter begins a more vigorous and lengthy lament than that which is found in ch. 3. Significantly, Job does not harbor a death wish in the lament of

---

50. Greg Carey, 'Apocalyptic *Ethos*', in *Society of Biblical Literature: 1998 Seminar Papers* (2 vols.; Atlanta: Scholars Press, 1998), II, pp. 731-61. Irving Jacobs ('Literary Motifs in the Testament of Job', *JJS* 21 [1970], pp. 1-10), argues that the *Testament of Job* is martyr literature and that the changing of Job's name from Jobab to Job is actually a way of identifying a new convert to the true faith of Abraham (pp. 1, 8-10).

51. See Rowland, *Open Heaven*, p. 481 n. 39. Rowland considers Eliphaz's reaction on a par with the 'emotional upheaval' connected with prophetic visions as seen in Jer. 4.19-26 (p. 231).

chs. 29–30, as he did in ch. 3. Instead, his lament propels him into his great oath of innocence in ch. 31, which in turn contains Job's most forceful demand for a response from God.

Thus, it could be argued that Job is encouraged and revitalized by the knowledge revealed in ch. 28 that wisdom cannot be found in humans. The revelation confirms his position that the friends are simply 'worthless physicians' (13.4), unworthy of Job's attention. He thus returns to the 'pre-dialogue' state of lament over his condition, though he does so with much greater resolve perhaps as a direct result of the revelation offered in ch. 28. Habel notes that Job now takes on the air of hero[52] and Hartley describes Job as one now willing to 'take a daring step'.[53]

This resolve is, in turn, the disposition of Job prior to Yahweh's theophanic revelation. The intervening speeches of Elihu apparently do nothing to affect Job—rather, they pave the way for the theophanic revelation itself. Thus, Job, the recipient of God's direct revelation from ch. 28, is assumed to remain in his bold anticipatory state of ch. 31 after Elihu's bluster.

After each of God's speeches in chs. 38–41, Job briefly responds in resigned humility and awe. Scholarship has long questioned from what Job felt compelled to 'repent' (42.6) in his second response. I will address that question in Chapter 4, but for now it is clear that Job has received knowledge that he did not have prior to the whirlwind confrontation. He is enlightened, and this enlightenment has saved him.

Job's responses to the revelations in both ch. 28 and the whirlwind speeches reflect hope, encouragement, awe, terror, humility, reverence, and finally, submission, all of which are consonant with recipients of apocalypses. For example, in Dan. 7.15, after seeing a vision, Daniel says, 'my spirit was troubled within me, and the visions of my head terrified me'.

Sections four through nine of the Master Paradigm consider the revelation's content as it relates to matters of time.

Section Four: Protology (Pre-History or Beginning of History)
Eliphaz's vision contains one small but meaningful protological reference. In 4.17b, Eliphaz asks, 'Can mortals be righteous before God? Can human beings be pure before their Maker (מעשהו)?' The revelation recalls the images of humanity's creation. Habel suggests that 'the substance of this mysterious revelation received by Eliphaz…is simply that all humans inherit the ills of their creaturehood', and argues that the specific creation image conjured by this revelation is found in Gen. 2.7.[54] Thus, part of Eliphaz's

---

52. Habel, *The Book of Job*, p. 406.
53. Hartley, *The Book of Job*, p. 385.
54. Habel, *The Book of Job*, pp. 128-29.

revelation reflects on the primordial relationship between God and humans. This reflection establishes the paradigm that Eliphaz and the friends utilize as their basis for attacking Job. For the friends, Job's claim to be pure before God simply cannot be sustained.[55]

The revelation of ch. 28 can be treated along similar lines. Just as creation plays a profound role in establishing humanity's relationship with God as viewed in Eliphaz's vision, so too does it function with respect to the revelation of wisdom here. Job 28.23-28 reads:

> [23]God understands the way to it,
>   and he knows its place.
> [24]For he looks to the ends of the earth,
>   and sees everything under the heavens.
> [25]When he gave to the wind its weight,
>   and apportioned out the waters by measure;
> [26]when he made a decree for the rain,
>   and a way for the thunderbolt;
> [27]then he saw it and declared it;
>   he established it, and searched it out.
> [28]And he said to humankind,
>   'Truly, the fear of the Lord, that is wisdom;
>   and to depart from evil is understanding'.

God reveals wisdom during the primordial process. Commenting on v. 27, Habel posits that an eternal mystery surrounds Wisdom, one that is primordially discovered by the Creator.[56] On this reading, Hartley suggests that Wisdom 'played a pivotal role in creation'.[57] Wisdom, as also seen in other texts, has at its domain God's cosmos.

If one considers the common wisdom form found in Job 28.28 (also found in Prov. 1.7; 9.10 and Ps. 111.10) from a purely narrative analysis across the entire Hebrew Bible, it can be argued that the form in Job 28.28 represents God's initial and direct revelation of this biblical truth. In that sense, Job 28.28 could be considered the paradigmatic use of the form on which the other verses rely. If that is held, then not only is the cosmological reflection on wisdom in Job 28.23-28 considered central for the book of Job, it is central for 'narratively later' treatments of the form.[58] This would then suggest

---

55. It is not clear, however, that Job has made such a claim. More will be said on the translation of this pivotal verse in Chapter 4. For now, I merely seek to demonstrate that the revelation contains important apocalyptic elements identified within the Master Paradigm.

56. Habel, *The Book of Job*, p. 400.

57. Hartley, *The Book of Job*, p. 382.

58. I am not here referring to Job's placement in the canon, which varies in several witnesses. Instead, Job's 'antiquity' seems to suggest that it is an ancient book, which therefore preceded Psalms and Proverbs. Murphy also seems to suggest this. Referring to

that the revelation of Job 28.28 represents the initial 'creative' revelation to humanity that 'the fear of the Lord, that is wisdom'.

It goes almost without saying that the great theophanic revelation of Job 38–41 is one of the most profound creation revelations in the Hebrew Bible. The content of the revelation, however, finds closer parallels to the ancient Near Eastern mythological accounts of creation as well as to some creation psalms (Pss. 74 and 104) than it does to the Genesis accounts. This relationship is further developed with references to various aspects of the cosmos, including its origins (Job 38.33), which present the revelation as ancient. Perdue refers to these speeches as 'hymnic images having their origins in combat myths of creation and world maintenance', which 'portray both the nature and operation of creation and the character of divine rule'.[59] Perdue compares these speeches to the ancient Near East combat myths whereby God appears in order to combat chaos and establish his own sovereignty.

Further contributing to the protological features in the whirlwind speeches are the detailed discussions of the inner workings involved in both the celestial and animal realm. It is as though, again from a purely narrative perspective, God is truly revealing truths that Job simply did not know of or, at least, did not comprehend. God confirms what was revealed in Job 28.23-27, namely, that he is the bearer and giver of human wisdom.

Section Five: History, Viewed as Explicit Recollection of the Past, or Ex eventu *Prophecy*

At first this may not seem applicable to Job. However, in all three revelations, there is a looking-back to creation as the beginning, whether it be from the perspective of the human–divine relationship of Eliphaz's vision, the wisdom-divine relationship of Job 28 or the details surrounding the creative order as depicted in the theophanic speeches.

All of Job 29 is an exceptional example of Job nostalgically recalling his past. Job recounts in detail how he was respected in the village square, took care of the needy and stood up to the unrighteous. Most importantly, he reminisces about the days 'when the friendship of God was upon my tent' (29.4) and 'when the Almighty was stil with me' (29.5).

The closest the book of Job comes to *ex eventu* prophecy is Eliphaz's forecast of how a suppliant Job will benefit from accepting reproof from God. This occurs, significantly, in the graded numerical saying found in Job 5.19-26. It is significant because the passage completes the first speech of

---

Job 28, Murphy (*Tree of Life*, p. 135) notes that 'within the context of wisdom literature, one may say that a mysterious figure of personified Wisdom has made her initial appearance'.

59. Perdue, *Revolt*, p. 202.

Eliphaz, which contains the important first revelation. In the numerical saying, Eliphaz describes several ways in which Job will prosper if he will recognize that God is disciplining him for some concealed unrighteous behavior. For example, Job would be protected from war, famine and wild animals, and he will live a long life producing many offspring. All of these predictions, perhaps more ironically than prophetically, come to pass in the epilogue. It is fascinating, however, that the exhorter in Job 5, Eliphaz, is judged by God in the epilogue. The exhortee, Job, does not capitulate, and receives the very blessings forecast by Eliphaz. While not specifically related to an eschatological prophecy, as indicated by Collins's description of this section in the Master Paradigm, the pattern in Job, again, shows some similarities.[60]

Section Six: Present Salvation through Knowledge (in Gnostic Texts)
Once again, this may not seem applicable to Job. Yet after both the revelation in Job 28 and in the theophanic utterance, Job is able to extricate himself from a previous entanglement and successfully negotiate the next obstacle. And while Job is certainly not a Gnostic text, the existence of patterns in Job that are also found in Gnostic texts does not weaken the demonstration that apocalyptic features appear in Job.

By realizing that wisdom is not to be found in humans, as revealed in Job 28, Job is able to dismiss the rhetoric of the friends, and he returns to his original state prior to the friends' arrival with even greater confidence. Furthermore, he is emboldened to appeal to God (Job 31.35).

Similarly, the theophanic revelation not only assists Job in separating himself from Elihu's bombast, he rises to a new state of comprehension regarding the divine. He understands something about God that he did not know before, which results in the 'confession' that apparently yields his doubled reward.

In both cases specific knowledge, which was previously unknown to Job, provides the timely antidote required for Job to progress in his trial.

Sections seven through nine together treat eschatological elements of apocalypse, which Job explicitly lacks. Still, as demonstrated in the previous discussions, certain shared patterns do exist that are worth considering.

Section Seven: Eschatological Crisis
While there may be no clearly explicit eschatological crisis in Job, a cosmological crisis undergirds the entire story. In brief, how Job responds to his material and physical sufferings, the friends' speeches, Elihu's speeches and even God's speeches, will directly affect the reader's decision about who

---

60. Collins, 'Morphology', p. 7.

wins the 'bet' between the Satan and God. The earthly battleground for this cosmological crisis is Job's ability both to maintain his integrity and to resist the temptation to curse God to his face.

In that sense, Job is suffering nothing short of full-blown persecution. He is persecuted, unbeknown to him, by the Satan on two occasions in the Prologue. He is also persecuted by his wife (Job 2.9), who entreats him to curse God and die. His three friends and Elihu insist that Job has deserved his plight and that nothing short of complete repentance will result in God's retraction of the pain.

Thus, cosmic crisis is manifested on an earthly stage. One result of this crisis is an 'upheaval' of the view of wisdom. Job's view of wisdom contrasts severely with the friends' understanding, which leads to a complete disturbance of the prevailing order of the day. This upheaval serves as a way of 'disturbing the order of nature or history' (see the Master Paradigm 7.2) in two ways. First, his personal history is completely disrupted. He has lost his family, possessions, the trust of his wife and his health. The magnitude of this historical upheaval is captured in Job's questioning of his very birth and existence (Job 3.3). Second, Job struggles with the whole notion that the wicked do not suffer (21.7), which is an upheaval of massive proportion. The regnant 'theology of retribution' simply does not hold true with Job's situation. What was once so easily accepted as a 'natural' order has now become completely undone; Job experiences this through his own miserable condition.

Thus, it is not hard to argue that the principles of 'persecution' and 'upheaval' that mark an 'eschatological crisis' are present in Job.

Section Eight: Eschatological Judgment
At first glance, the only clear judgment appears to come in the Epilogue where God rebukes the friends and commands them to ask Job for a sacrifice on their behalf (Job 42.7-9). Eliphaz is singled out, but Job's wife and Elihu apparently escape God's wrath. More will be said later about this apparent oversight.

Perdue argues that the Yahweh speeches represent a theophanic judgment on a par with ancient Near Eastern combat myths. Yahweh has judged Behemoth, Leviathan, the wicked and is now judging Job.[61] Perdue points out that 'whirlwind' (סערה) is found most frequently as a theophanic judgment that destroys chaos and its 'various incarnations'.[62] For Perdue, 'Theophanic

---

61. Perdue, *Revolt*, p. 202.
62. Perdue, *Revolt*, p. 202. Perdue cites the following as biblical examples: Job 9.17; Pss. 50.3; 58.10 (unclear); Isa. 29.6; 40.24; Jer. 23.19; 25.32; Hos. 13.3 (unclear); Amos 1.14; Nah. 1.3; Zech. 7.14. All but two, Ps. 58.10 and Hos. 13.3, are clear examples of Perdue's assertion.

judgment, depicted in Yahweh's coming in the whirlwind, serves as the controlling image for the two speeches'.[63]

Additionally, there are other possible judgments not frequently recognized, which will be discussed in more detail in Chapter 4. (1) Job's rebuke of his wife (2.10) might be considered a judgment. This is especially interesting because she is not explicitly mentioned as the mother of Job's 'new' children in the end (42.13-15) and tradition has assigned this role of mother to Dinah, the daughter of Jacob. (2) Insofar as human wisdom is judged by the revelation in Job 28 and the first theophanic speech, the natural world order of a 'theology of retribution' may be seen as coming under judgment. (3) Some have argued that Yahweh's first words in the theophany, 'who is this that darkens counsel by words without knowledge' (38.2), may be directed at Elihu instead of Job.[64] Thus, Elihu is judged. (4) If the Satan's original challenge to God is understood as a 'self-curse', in that failure to prove his point results in some unannounced punishment, the Satan is cursed by the very fact that Job has persevered.[65] (5) Finally, the famous verse in Job 19.25, 'For I know that my Redeemer lives, and at the last he will stand upon the earth', can be considered a judgment.[66]

There are plenty of judgments administered upon the wicked, otherworldly beings and Job's accepted natural world to merit conformity to the Master Paradigm.

Section Nine: Eschatological Salvation

Two portions of Job approach a portrayal of a renewed world. The first is the revelation of Job 28 that is later confirmed by the first theophanic speech. The wisdom of the world, centered on retribution, is completely dethroned, for that is the wisdom of humans, not of God. The second instance is the renewal of Job's personal world in the epilogue. He is completely restored, receiving 'twice as much as he had before' (42.10).

With respect to the Master Paradigm's 'personal salvation', MT Job portrays Job's double blessings in the epilogue, combined with God's judgment on the friends, as his material salvation. And while Job in the LXX is resurrected, marking an overtly eschatological salvation, in the end, like Collins, one has to acknowledge that despite similar patterns of expression, though all on an earthly present-time plane, MT Job lacks future eschatology.[67]

---

63. Perdue, *Revolt*, p. 202.
64. More will be said on this in Chapter 4.
65. As suggested by Edwin M. Good, 'The Problem of Evil in the Book of Job', in Perdue and Gilpin (eds.), *The Voice from the Whirlwind*, pp. 50-69 (53). More will be said on this in Chapter 4.
66. I treat this in more detail in Chapter 4.
67. Collins, 'Cosmos', p. 140 n. 3.

However, Chapter 3 of this work is dedicated to overcoming this seemingly insurmountable obstacle for the purpose of revealing Job's clear tendencies towards the apocalyptic genre as witnessed by the evolution of the story in later translations and accounts.

Section Ten: Otherworldly Elements

This section briefly addresses the content of the revelation with reference to spatial considerations, that is, the amount of 'otherworldly' characteristics existing in the form of 'regions' or 'beings' as defined by the Master Paradigm.

Of course, the reader needs to look no further than Job 1.6 before encountering 'heavenly beings' and 'the Satan', and he/she is automatically transferred from the material world to the transcendent region of God's divine court.[68] As I will argue later, the plotline of Job's story emerges both from this otherworldly region and from the discussion between the otherworldly beings of the Satan and God. Indeed, this transcendent realm brackets the entire story.

No clear spatial element occurs in Eliphaz's vision, despite the elaborate description of Eliphaz's physiological experience. However, the 'spirit', (4.15) whose indiscernible form 'was before my eyes' (4.16), seems to qualify nicely as such an otherworldly being. Pope acknowledges that this may be the intent of the author because 'the movement of air is often taken as a token of supernatural presence'.[69] Andersen concurs, arguing that רוח is feminine and commonly takes a feminine verb. And yet, in this case, among others, it has a masculine verb. The RSV (and NRSV) obscures this construction by translating 'it', when 'he' is a more faithful translation. With that, Andersen concludes, 'this proves it is the Spirit of God, and not the wind'.[70]

Clines advances the argument further by suggesting that 'it seems more likely that Eliphaz is describing a theophany'.[71] As noted earlier, Rodd

---

68. Most suggest this region is 'heaven'; see S.R. Driver and G.B. Gray, *A Critical and Exegetical Commentary on the Book of Job* (ICC; Edinburgh: T. & T. Clark, 1921), p. 9. However, Andersen is dubious about the location, speculating that it might just as well be on the top of a mountain (*The Book of Job*, p. 82). In either case, the point is that the reader has left the earthly realm of Job and entered into some celestial arena.

69. Pope, *Job*, p. 37.

70. Andersen, *The Book of Job*, p. 114 n. 1. Habel (*The Book of Job*, p. 28) argues that it is unlikely that the referent must be masculine because the poet may have purposely left the subject unclear, which is in keeping with his style to 'heighten the uncanny and the unknown'. For a fuller discussion of the grammar, see B. Waltke and M. O'Connor, *An Introduction to Biblical Hebrew Syntax* (Winona Lake, IN: Eisenbrauns, 1990), #16.4.f.

71. Clines, *Job 1–20*, p. 130. Clines supports his assertion by noting three traditional features of a theophany: terror, violent storm-wind and thundering sound (p. 131).

argues that Eliphaz is confronted by a 'messenger from God with a revelation for him'.⁷² Furthermore, Pope points out that רוח is never used to describe an apparition in the Old Testament, save for this occasion where 'the spirit is given a semblance of form'.⁷³ Thus, it is clear that some kind of otherworldly being is presented in Eliphaz's vision, one that is supernatural in every respect.

Chapter 28 also seems to describe a paranormal state. Though the setting described in the first eleven verses details features associated with ancient mining expeditions, which is 'thisworldly', one cannot deny the surreal nature of the account that effectively transports the reader to another world. Beginning in v. 13, the reader finds that wisdom 'is not found in the land of the living'. The immediate response comes from the voice of the personified deep, which admits that wisdom 'is not in me'.

Similarly in v. 21, wisdom is 'hidden from the eyes of all living, and concealed from the birds of the air'. The author seems to insist that wisdom's origin is not 'thisworldly'. Following the pattern from v. 13, personified Abbadon and Death can only acknowledge that they have 'heard a rumor of it' (28.22).

This technique seems to parallel a possible literary function of incorporating otherwordly regions with an apocalypse in order to divert the reader's attention away from the earthly sphere and prepare him/her for an explicit revelation. As argued earlier, this revelation begins in v. 23 and climaxes in v. 28.

These personifications surely relate to 'otherworldly beings' as well. Additionally, as noted earlier, no consensus has been reached on the identification of the speaker in ch. 28. But, since the text states that wisdom cannot be found on the earth, it is not implausible, or illogical, to deduce that the messenger is some 'otherworldly' being.

One final feature contained in ch. 28 that is related to 'otherworldly elements', though much more pronounced in the Yahweh speeches, is the existence of 'lists of revealed things' as defined by Michael E. Stone.⁷⁴ For Stone, these lists, which contain 'astronomy and meteorology, uranography and cosmology and the secrets of Wisdom', are marked by 'catalogues of the subject matter of apocalyptic speculation' and are not simply coincidental intrusions into the text; evidently they represent intentional apocalyptic devices used by the author.⁷⁵ One common tendency found among these lists is that they 'all occur at the high point of a revelation', whereby the lists

---

72. Rodd, *The Book of Job*, p. 15.
73. Pope, *Job*, p. 37. Pope seems to be following Driver and Gray, *Book of Job*, p. 46.
74. Stone, 'List of Revealed Things', pp. 414-52.
75. Stone, 'List of Revealed Things', p. 414.

offer the seers some insight into 'what the writers of the apocalypses thought to lie at the heart of apocalyptic revelation itself'.[76]

Much more will be said regarding Stone's thesis in Chapter 5, but for the moment it is instructive to point out that he considers Job 28 the basis for the apocalyptic lists revealed in the later, more mature apocalypse of 2 Baruch. Importantly, these lists in *2 Bar.* 59.5 seem to be drawn from Job 28.23-26, which is the section of Job 28 that most clearly offers revelatory material.[77]

Similarly, lists from *4 Ezra* seem to be influenced by the lists found in Job 38. For example, Job 38.18 nicely parallels *4 Ezra* 5.6, and Stone considers Job 38.16 'important for tracing the origin' of a number of elements relating to 'the deep or the abyss'.[78] Even with these striking similarities, Stone cautions that, 'at most, certain isolated cosmological elements are common to the apocalyptic lists and to Job 38'.[79] Stone suggests that other passages in Job (11.7; 36.27) are also considered lists, though these are not contained in a revelation, as indicated by the Master Paradigm.[80] While Stone never explicitly posits a correlation between Job and apocalypse, his research demonstrates affinities between the two.

It also seems apparent that the Yahweh speeches contain 'otherworldly' traits as evidenced by the theophany and the ensuing references to primordial creation motifs, afterlife entities and astronomical observations. For example, 38.7 refers to the singing of 'morning stars' (כוכבי בקר) and joy of 'all the heavenly beings' (כל־בני אלהים) expressed when the earth was founded. Referring to the otherworldly realm of the afterlife, 38.17 reads, 'Have the gates of death been *revealed* (נגלה) to you, or have you seen the gates of deep darkness?' In 38.19, astronomical wonders abound: 'Where is the way to the dwelling of light, and where is the place of darkness?'

In addition to instructing Job, God seems to be declaring what Job cannot possibly know already. In this sense, Murphy is surely wrong to answer the way he does, 'What does Job learn about creation that he did not know before?'[81] God is revealing these things now in a manner that transcends Job's known material world.

Job contains abundant examples of otherworldly beings and regions, enough, I would argue, to associate Job with at least some early form of apocalypse according to the paradigm.

---

76. Stone, 'List of Revealed Things', p. 418.
77. Stone, 'List of Revealed Things', p. 430.
78. Stone, 'List of Revealed Things', p. 433.
79. Stone, 'List of Revealed Things', p. 435.
80. Stone, 'List of Revealed Things', pp. 422, 434.
81. Murphy, *The Book of Job*, p. 89.

Section Eleven: Paraenesis (by Mediator to the Recipient)
The voice from Eliphaz's vision does not truly offer an example of paraenesis, which is the presence of eclectic and ethical admonitions unrelated to any concrete situation.[82] On the other hand, an implicit exhortation that humans cannot be considered righteous before God, and therefore should not claim as much, might be construed as a legitimate exhortation. The same kind of implicit exhortation might be seen in Job 28.28, whereby the 'mediator' exhorts the reader to fear the Lord and 'depart from evil'.

The theophanic speeches contain numerous examples of eclectic admonitions to Job. Job 40.2 serves as an excellent example: 'Shall a faultfinder contend with the Almighty? Anyone who argues with God must respond.' I have argued elsewhere that the Hebrew lends itself to the following interpretation: 'The one who reproves God must answer the reproof'.[83] God is therefore serving notice to anyone who wishes to challenge him that they need to be prepared also to respond to the very challenge that they present.

Collins notes that paraenesis is quite rare in apocalypses, and only seems to emerge in a few Christian apocalypses. Even so, it is retained in the Master Paradigm because apocalypses do attempt to influence the actions of their readers, while many apocalypses imply exhortation to various appropriate actions.[84] Collins's emphasis on the implied nature of paranaesis in apocalypse is telling in Job because Job receives numerous explicit exhortations and admonitions, especially from those who mean well but still do not understand God themselves. Job's ability to discern between constructive and destructive exhortations is central to his progress in the story.

The final two sections of the Master Paradigm fall under the category of 'Concluding Elements'.

Section Twelve: Instructions to the Recipient
Collins explains that these instructions are distinct from paraenesis because they 'come after the revelation as part of the concluding framework'.[85] Defined this way, no clear instructions are given in either the Eliphaz Vision or in ch. 28. However, God's instructions to Eliphaz in the epilogue (42.8) to provide a burnt offering are probably close to fulfilling the requirements of the study group. The very fact that God instructs *Eliphaz* is intriguing, and

---

82. See Richard N. Soulen, *Handbook of Biblical Criticism* (Atlanta: John Knox Press, 2nd edn, 1981), pp. 140-41. Deut. 6.4-5 is considered such an example, as are vv. 1-21 and 32-36 of Prov. 8.

83. The RSV reads: 'He who argues with God, let him answer it'. See Timothy Johnson, 'Implied Antecedents in Job xl 2B and Proverbs iii 6A', *VT* 52 (2002), pp. 278-84 (280).

84. Collins, 'Morphology', p. 9.

85. Collins, 'Morphology', p. 8.

scholarship has long wondered why he was singled out in the end. I offer a solution here in order to demonstrate that Eliphaz should be seen as a credible recipient of the instructions, and therefore conforms to this section of the Master Paradigm, though I will say more in Chapter 4.

Eliphaz was the first person in the story to receive a revelation (4.17-21). Is it possible that Eliphaz was the intended recipient of the *content* of that revelation, instead of merely the conduit, as commonly accepted? If so, then God's displeasure with, and singling out of, Eliphaz might be due to Eliphaz's lack of recognition that the message of the revelation from the vision was actually meant for him. In other words, Eliphaz claims to possess true knowledge of God, though he does not, and the story of Job bears that out. God's instructions to Eliphaz in 42.8, then, could be seen as a follow-up to the revelation that was originally meant for him in ch. 4.

Job has learned something from God via the theophanic revelation. Based on the revelation of ch. 4, Eliphaz (and his friends) also should have learned something, but they did not. They persisted in their own self-righteous and ignorant persecution of Job (for they too were not privy to the God–Satan confrontation). In accordance with the Master Paradigm, the instructions come after God's revelation and form a critical part of the concluding framework of the story.

Section Thirteen: Narrative Conclusion
No one questions the existence of the narrative framework of Job as represented by both the prologue and the epilogue, and Collins notes that 'There is always a narrative framework in which the manner of revelation is described'.[86]

Summary
It is clear that much of Job conforms to the elements contained within the Master Paradigm. In order for Job to be considered as some form of apocalypse, it need not comply with every element of the paradigm, for Collins even recognizes 'that no one apocalypse contains all the elements noted in the paradigm'.[87] In some instances, explicit concurrence does not exist, while similar patterns indicate potential relationship, which is the basis for my claim that Job should be considered some nascent form of apocalypse.

Finally, after this relatively detailed comparison of Job to the Master Paradigm, it might be instructive to reiterate the Apocalypse Group's working definition of an apocalypse:

---

86. Collins, 'Morphology', p. 9.
87. Collins, 'Morphology', p. 8.

> Apocalypse is a genre of revelatory literature with a narrative framework, in which a revelation is mediated by an otherworldly being to a human recipient, disclosing a transcendent reality which is both temporal, insofar as it envisages eschatological salvation, and spatial insofar as it involves another, supernatural world.[88]

Once again, the reader can see that a large portion of Job compares nicely with even the distilled definition of an apocalypse.

Appraising the Master Paradigm

As valuable as the Master Paradigm is for establishing some parameters for an apocalypse, one of its weaknesses is its lack of attention to the historical development within the genre itself. E.J.C. Tigchelaar argues that the major weakness of such an ahistorical approach is that it relegates the historical perspective, which, in turn, 'disregards the existence of marginal cases'.[89] Instead, he argues that the study of apocalypse must engage the historical development of the genre, that is, the genre is subject to evolutionary processes with respect to its content and ideas. Such an historical approach takes the dates of various apocalypses into account and traces the internal development of ideas.[90] F. García Martínez concurs:

> The effort to determine the literary genre of the apocalypses is meritorious and enlightening. But the tendency to reduce the apocalyptic to the literary genre apocalypse leads to an ahistoric vision of the texts, to ignore the function and to be unaware of the place that the apocalyptic elements like Jubilee 23 or the Testament of Levi 2–5 have in the books in which they were transmitted.[91]

Martínez is concerned that the progress made in defining apocalypses, while valuable, fails to advance the importance of the genre's evolution.

This advance consists in the realization that this apocalyptic tradition should be

> interpreted in a historical perspective, which takes into account at the same time the date of the different apocalypses and the internal evolution of this tradition.[92]

---

88. Collins, 'Morphology', p. 9.
89. E.J.C. Tigchelaar, 'More on Apocalyptic and Apocalypses', *JSJ* 18 (1987), pp. 137-44 (142).
90. Tigchelaar, 'More on Apocalyptic', pp. 137, 142.
91. F. García Martínez, 'Encore l'apocalyptique', *JSJ* 17 (1986), pp. 224-32 (229): 'L'effort pour déterminer le genre litéraire des apocalypses est méritoire et éclairant. Mais la tendance à réduire l'Apocalyptique au genre littéraire Apocalypse mène à une vision a-historique des textes, à méconnaître leur fonction et à ignorer la place que des éléments apocalyptiques comme Jub. 23 ou Test. Lévi 2–5 ont dans les livres dans lesquels ils ont été transmis.'
92. Martínez, 'Encore l'apocalyptique', p. 230: 'Cette avance consiste dans la prise de conscience que cette tradition apocalyptique doit être interprétée dans une perspective

Paolo Sacchi

In his *Jewish Apocalyptic and its History*, Paolo Sacchi is most concerned with identifying the earliest thematic traces of an apocalypse.[93] Sacchi proposes that the dominant theme of an apocalypse is a search for the origin of sin as depicted in the search for the solution to the problem of evil.[94] This theme is attested in the earliest of the apocalypses, which he identifies as *The Book of the Watchers*. His selection of *The Book of the Watchers* is significant because the book can be dated well before 200 BCE. Since scholarship tends to emphasize the 300-year period between 200 BCE and 100 CE as the age when Jewish apocalypses flourished,[95] Sacchi breaks ranks and suggests that 'the soul of apocalyptic' can be found in those preceding this era.[96] For him, the central question to pose is: 'In the history of Jewish thought, are there some significant issues later found in classical apocalyptic, that is, in those works which tradition already indicates as apocalyptic?'[97]

This is an important question for my research because Sacchi has penetrated beyond the historical limits imposed by scholarship and proffers the idea that efforts closely related to apocalypses might have existed earlier. Furthermore, his question is different from the question that seeks to identify an apocalyptic *Sitz im Leben*. Sacchi is less concerned with an apocalypse's growth out of prophecy or wisdom, or whether it emerged in the uneducated class or among the scribes. Instead, foundational for him is the discovery of the first stages of apocalypse and their later developments.

Still, such a search requires some set of agreed-upon apocalyptic indicators. Sacchi accepts Klaus Koch's eight thematic characteristics as sufficient for the task: (1) *agonized waiting* for a quick and total change of all human relations; (2) the end is presented as a cosmic catastrophe; (3) the end time is closely connected to the past history of humanity and the cosmos; (4) earthly

---

historique qui tienne compte à la fois de la date des différentes apocalypses et de l'évolution à l'intérieur de cette tradition'.

93. Paolo Sacchi, *Jewish Apocalyptic and its History* (trans. William J. Short; JSPSup, 20; Sheffield: Sheffield Academic Press, 1996), p. 17.

94. See also D.S. Russell, *The Method and Message of Jewish Apocalyptic: 200 BC–AD 100* (OTL; Philadelphia: Westminster Press, 1964), p. 249.

95. See Walter Schmithals, *The Apocalyptic Movement: Introduction and Interpretation* (trans. John E. Steely; Nashville: Abingdon Press, 1975), p. 13, and Rowland, *Open Heaven*, pp. 266-67.

96. Sacchi, *Jewish Apocalyptic*, p. 36 n. 8.

97. Sacchi, *Jewish Apocalyptic*, pp. 40-41.

history, visible to all, is interdependent with an invisible history beyond the earthly, of which only preselected seers are aware; (5) after the catastrophe, there will burst forth a new *salvation*, with paradisiacal characteristics; (6) the passage from the state of perdition to that of definitive salvation is seen as a decree that comes forth from the throne of God; (7) very often an *intermediary with royal functions* is introduced as executor and guarantor of final salvation; (8) the term *glory* is used to designate the end-state cut off from the present and to presage a total fusion of celestial and terrestrial spheres.[98]

Sacchi is surprised that Koch does not include *The Book of the Watchers* as a member of the apocalyptic corpus because it contains so many of these traits. Sacchi considers the book an apocalypse and argues that because it dates to the fourth century BCE, it should be considered the oldest apocalyptic work.

Sacchi then seeks to determine the ideology of *The Book of the Watchers*, from which he then hopes to provide a first step towards understanding the origins and meaning of apocalyptic. His conclusion is that *The Book of the Watchers* reflects three ideological characteristics. The first is, 'The conviction that evil derives from a contamination of the natural and human sphere through the action of beings belonging to the "in-between world"'.[99] The 'in-between world' is where the souls of the just are already separated from the unjust and awaiting judgment. The contamination is one that is brought about by rebellious angels with God's full complicity.

The second characteristic is that every just human being contains an immortal element, and the third is that salvation must derive from an event in the 'in-between world' rather than from humans. There is therefore a cosmic element associated with both the contamination and resolution. The mixing of the human realm and the 'in-between world' results in a blurring of the distinction between the two, and this results in ambiguity with respect to whether humans are guilty of evil or simply victims of evil.[100]

After comparing these features to *Jubilees*, Daniel, and both the Rule of the Community and Hodayot from Qumran, Sacchi concludes that two fundamental guidelines can distinguish apocalypses from other genres: (1) belief in immortality (whether by resurrection or immortality of the soul) and (2) the conviction that evil has its origin in a sphere above the

---

98. Sacchi, *Jewish Apocalyptic*, pp. 43-47. See Klaus Koch, *The Rediscovery of Apocalyptic* (trans. Margaret Kohl; Naperville, IL: Alec R. Allenson, 1972), pp. 28-33. I will make use of Sacchi's translation of Koch in order to maintain consistency with his argument.
99. Sacchi, *Jewish Apocalyptic*, p. 60.
100. Sacchi, *Jewish Apocalyptic*, p. 61.

human. Furthermore, Sacchi contends that a distinction needs to be made between historical apocalyptic and cosmic apocalyptic.[101]

While Sacchi's argument represents a fresh approach to defining apocalypse, his is not without its own problems. He acknowledges that he must provide some kind of definition of an apocalypse before he can consider its evolution. Thus, he too is forced to establish criteria, which, though based purely on Koch's definition, do not take into account the whole of scholarship's struggle with defining apocalypse. Furthermore, in designating *The Book of the Watchers* as the earliest apocalypse, he declares that it therefore contains the key, though he does not substantiate why the earliest apocalypse, which he has determined on a definition that is based on later apocalypses, is the form to be preferred over against other later apocalypses.[102] Sacchi therefore establishes his own 'prototype' approach without the rigor evident in the Apocalypse Group's examination.

Despite these shortcomings, Sacchi's work is valuable simply because it breaks away from an ahistorical posture and grants a larger role for evolution in the endeavor to define apocalypse. For my purposes, comparing Job to Sacchi's work provides an even more balanced foundation for claiming that Job is more closely related to apocalypse than wisdom.

Job as Apocalyptic Compared to Koch and Sacchi

Sacchi's thesis is fascinating and instructive for the case at hand. The fact that he does not meaningfully engage with the Apocalypse Group's paradigm seems to confirm his lack of confidence in criteria that are mostly grounded in literary indicators. In relying so heavily upon Russell, Koch and to a lesser extent Schmithals, Sacchi's study[103] gives the impression that he might be wary of the tendencies defined by the Master Paradigm's results, which is most recognizable in the work of John J. Collins. However, Sacchi's lack of attention to this stream of apocalyptic studies also allows for a fresh and complementary approach to my argument. If I have demonstrated that Job exhibits striking affinities with the Master Paradigm and if I can demonstrate that Job shares equal kinship with Sacchi's research, my argument is strengthened.

Since Sacchi relies particularly on Koch to determine an apocalypse's characteristics, it is important briefly to compare Koch's eight features to Job. In doing this, I am not assuming that Koch's characteristics are any more or less definitive than those established in the Master Paradigm. In fact, since much of what Koch suggests is incorporated into the paradigm, it

---

101. Sacchi, *Jewish Apocalyptic*, p. 71.
102. A similar critique is offered by Tigchelaar, 'More on Apocalyptic', p. 143.
103. Sacchi, *Jewish Apocalyptic*.

would seem that the paradigm does supplant Koch's individual suggestions. However, Sacchi derives his two elementary apocalyptic features from *The Book of the Watchers* and he first establishes its place in the apocalyptic corpus by recourse to Koch. If Job conforms to both Koch and Sacchi, my argument is even further strengthened.

Koch's initial characteristic is that of 'Agonized waiting for a quick and total change of all human relations'. Few features characterize Job more accurately than a despondent man desperately waiting for some kind of response from God. Job says in 19.7, 'Even when I cry out, "Violence!" I am not answered; I call aloud, but there is no justice'. His final words before contending with God in 30.20 are, 'I cry to you and you do not answer me; I stand, and you merely look at me', and later in 31.35, 'Oh, that I had one to hear me!' Elihu confirms Job's posture in 35.14b, 'that the case is before him, and you are waiting for him!' Job's waiting, not unlike a waiting for the eschatological end, is influenced by a desire to move beyond his current dire circumstances. Yet his waiting is not necessarily devoid of eschatological impulse as evidenced in 14.14, 'If mortals die, will they live again? All the days of my service I would wait, until my release should come.'

Koch's second characteristic is that 'the end is presented as a cosmic catastrophe'. Sacchi views this trait as the contributing factor to a 'pessimistic spirit' associated with apocalypses. This pessimism, however, is not directly linked to the final catastrophe because the final catastrophe is really a vehicle for liberating one from the regnant evil circumstances.

For Job, his cosmic catastrophe is his own death, which will ultimately spare him from the torment he suffers. Job's first lament in 3.20-21 questions why he is even allowed to live when he seeks death more than anything: 'Why is light given to one in misery, and life to the bitter in soul, who long for death, but it does not come…' A similar sentiment is found in 10.18-22, but Job is more explicit in 14.13: 'Oh that you would hide me in Sheol, that you would conceal me until your wrath is past'. Job even considers Sheol his home (17.13).

Koch's third element is 'the end time is closely connected to the past history of humanity and the cosmos'. Job does not contain explicit references to an 'end time'. However, Sacchi feels that Koch addresses God's fixing of times, that is, apocalypses are particularly deterministic. Job is rife with determinism, especially as it relates to Job's relationship between history and the end. In 14.5, for example, Job says with respect to mortals, 'Since their days are determined, and the number of their months is known to you, and you have appointed the bounds that they cannot pass'.

The fourth feature states: 'earthly history, visible to all, is interdependent with an invisible history beyond the earthly, of which only preselected seers are aware'. Sacchi characterizes this as the recognition that our world is dominated by the action of angelic forces, whether good or evil, which are

2. Comparing Job to Apocalypse

superior to human.[104] That the story of Job is dominated by otherworldly activity is evident in the prologue. Indeed, the conversation between God and the Satan establishes the story's plot. The reader is able to discern the interdependence between Job's world and the heavenly realm, but none of the characters are able to perceive it. The only entities in the story that are in a position to bridge the gap between the two worlds are the speakers in Job 4 and 28.

Koch's fifth characteristic is 'after the catastrophe, there will burst forth a new *salvation*, with paradisiacal characteristics'. Sacchi describes this in eschatological terms whereby the resurrection is wholly expected for the just. As noted, outside of Job's possible allusion to a resurrection in 14.14, there simply is no eschaton or accompanying resurrection in MT Job. Yet the doubling of Job's possessions in the epilogue and his new state of harmony almost certainly represents a form of salvation. Pre-exilic Israelite thought does not seemingly know or at least promote the idea of resurrection. These writings express salvation in the material world. There simply is no concept of an eschaton. Thus, Job's climactic reward is salvation in that context.

The sixth characteristic suggests 'the passage from the state of perdition to that of definitive salvation is seen as a decree that comes forth from the throne of God'. Sacchi credits this concept with promoting dualistic impressions found in apocalypses.[105] Job's salvation comes after his confession (42.1-6), which, in turn leads to God's rebuke of Eliphaz. From that moment on, one senses a discontinuity from the previous world that Job has just emerged from, and the one that he is about to embrace. God serves as the arbiter between the world where Job is depicted as increasingly agitated and the new salvific world containing a double blessing.

The seventh characteristic states that, 'very often an *intermediary with royal functions* is introduced as executor of final salvation'. The closest figure in Job, which might represent a royal intermediary, is that of the unknown voice in Job 28. Sacchi points out that the intermediary may be either a human or an angel.[106] It is not clear what form the messenger of Job 28 takes, but its connection to the concept of wisdom may suggest a particularly 'royal' status. Indeed, Roland Murphy describes this messenger as a 'mysterious figure of a personified Wisdom' who 'has made her initial appearance'.[107] If Wisdom speaks in Job 28, then no better example of a royal intermediary can be found. The same assessment might characterize the speaker in Eliphaz's vision, though with less regal standing.

---

104. Sacchi, *Jewish Apocalyptic*, p. 45.
105. Sacchi, *Jewish Apocalyptic*, p. 46.
106. Sacchi, *Jewish Apocalyptic*, p. 46.
107. Murphy, *Tree of Life*, p. 135.

The eighth characteristic is that the term '*Glory* is used to designate the end-state cut off from the present and to presage a total fusion of celestial and terrestrial spheres'. God's speeches from the whirlwind essentially demarcate Job's previous world of rebellion and anxiety from the concluding state of harmony. At the same time, these speeches portray God in full glory as attested by Job's confession in 42.5, 'I had heard of you by the hearing of the ear, but now my eye sees you'. God is exalted because he is able to fuse the celestial and terrestrial spheres in ways that none of Job's antagonists could. This fusion results in a new world order for Job.

Koch remarks that all of these features are equally distributed throughout apocalypses, while 'nearly every one of them can also be found outside the late Israelite and early Christian apocalyptic'.[108] If Koch is correct, then it is possible that common ideas to apocalypse preceded the golden age of apocalypse and might be identifiable, more or less, in 'proto-apocalyptic' form. That is to say, the seeds of apocalypse might very well be seen in other works not commonly perceived as apocalyptic. This is essentially what Sacchi argues with respect to *The Book of the Watchers*. In my view, Koch's eight characteristics seem to be sufficiently present in Job with varying degrees to warrant its consideration as at least a 'proto-apocalypse'. One would therefore expect that Sacchi's two fundamental apocalyptic traits would also be present within Job.

I begin with Sacchi's second contention that all apocalypses demonstrate that evil has its origin in a sphere above the human. While it is true both that Job's friends maintain that he freely earned his current punishments, and that Job insists that he has not, it is the narrative framework that points to the origin of evil as existing beyond the human realm.

The prologue portrays God and the Satan engaging one another over the righteousness of Job. It is clear that the evil brought on to Job is not attributed to his or any other human's ultimate responsibility. Instead, it is instigated by these two celestial beings where God establishes the parameters by which the Satan is able to afflict Job. This heavenly origin is confirmed in the epilogue (42.11) when Job's family and friends 'showed him sympathy and comforted him *for all the evil that the Lord had brought upon him*'. God is explicitly and ultimately blamed for Job's afflictions.

Surprisingly few commentators take up this issue in much detail. Habel is one exception, suggesting that the verse's acknowledgment of Yahweh as the source of Job's misfortunes indicates that 'God does indeed cause the innocent to suffer evil; such things are part of his cosmic "design"'.[109] Furthermore, Job is not particularly shocked by the friends' remarks because

---

108. Koch, *Rediscovery of Apocalyptic*, p. 33.
109. Habel, *The Book of Job*, p. 585.

2. Comparing Job to Apocalypse

he was aware even in the prologue that God renders both good and bad to his followers (2.10).

Thus, the narrative framework of the story, traditionally viewed as a depiction of the pious Job, also may reveal the author's perspective on the origin of evil. One might suggest that the entire story of Job illustrates the futility of searching for the origin of evil because it dwells outside of human comprehension. Such a conception fits nicely into Sacchi's second suggestion.

However, it is Sacchi's first suggestion that is more difficult to establish in Job, namely, the presence of a belief in immortality (whether by resurrection or immortality of the soul). I have already alluded to one key passage that can be construed as manifesting a belief in immortality (14.14). This allusion, while somewhat ambiguous, nevertheless may represent the necessary seeds for a nascent apocalyptic work.[110]

Both Sacchi and Koch offer valuable and convincing arguments that writings that existed prior to the golden age of apocalypse might very well exhibit apocalyptic traits. Thus, Job might be considered an early, undeveloped form of apocalypse, one that contained many of the features associated with mature apocalypses, and only some of these in very embryonic forms.

Further evidence that MT Job might be legitimately considered 'proto-apocalypse' in the sense used here is that LXX Job contains an explicitly eschatological feature. One of LXX Job's 'additions' is an apparent embellishment of Job 42.17, which says that Job will be resurrected on the last day. Such a clear eschatological referent might be sufficient to overcome MT Job's eschatological void by suggesting that MT Job may have been considered akin to apocalypse, or at least so closely related as to allow for an easy eschatological addendum.

Job as an Apocalyptic Chronoscope

A final comparison to a recent essay by Michael Vines strengthens the possibility of viewing Job as part of the apocalyptic genus. Vines respects the work of the Apocalypse Group, but he considers it 'overly formalistic' and instead seeks to redefine apocalypse on the basis of some of Bakhtin's

---

110. Murphy seems to believe that, at best, Job is referring to resuscitation and not resurrection (*The Book of Job*, p. 43). Andersen remarks, 'Here is no doctrine of immortality as an intrinsic and inalienable property of the soul' (*The Book of Job*, p. 173). Pope (*Job*, p. 102) understands the passage to mean relief from duty that a soldier or slave would long for. Hartley (*The Book of Job*, pp. 236-37) is only slightly less convinced that it cannot refer to immortality, but he too concedes that, this side of the New Testament, such a yearning is unlikely.

insights in order to 'better discern its particular value as a medium for expressing a theological perspective on human affairs'.[111]

Reminding the reader that whales were once classified as fish and not mammals because they do not have four appendages, Vines suggests that classificatory approaches may fall prey to identifying incorrectly what appear to be obvious traits as equally essential traits.[112] Without a theoretical grid, we are beholden to the overly formalistic approaches that tend towards reductionism. Thus, Bakhtin's theoretical observations that a genre is a 'meta-linguistic form' that 'transcends its linguistic devices' can aid in establishing a less atomistic definition of apocalypse.[113]

Somewhat surprisingly, Vines presents Bakhtin in strikingly different ways than that presented by Newsom. In fact, one might call Vines's Bakhtin Hirschian because of the seemingly privileged role granted to the author. For example, Vines claims that Bakhtin considers a work's 'various linguistic devices' subservient to 'a more comprehensive authorial intention' in order persuasively to advance an 'architectonic form' or 'form-shaping ideology'.[114] Bakhtin is also concerned that a reader should not analyze a work but instead 'try to discern the author's voice' by 'looking for the overarching unity of the literary work; the unity imposed upon it by the author's creative intention'.[115] Genre is most influenced by how 'the author creates the world of the narrative' where 'patterns of "form-shaping ideology" coalesce around particular perspectives and themes'.[116] This Bakhtin is seemingly a far cry from the 'polyphonic', 'unsystematic' and 'unfinalizable' Bakhtin that honors the author 'without privilege', the Bakhtin that Newsom describes.[117] Admittedly, I am more sympathetic to Vines's Bakhtin for the reasons outlined in my Introduction, and I also do not intend to critique various authors' appropriation of Bakhtin, though it appears that such a critique is needed. Such strikingly opposite interpretations of Bakhtin exacerbate the uncertainty that unfortunately defines generic studies.

Nevertheless, it is Vines's discussion of Bakhtin's diachronic notion of genre that is most valuable for my argument that Job accords with apocalyptic overtones. According to Vines, Bakhtin would seemingly hold that a work contains both an internal and external aspect. The internal aspect is that which revolves around an author's creative use of genre conventions in

---

111. Michael E. Vines, 'The Apocalyptic Chronotype', in Boer (ed.), *Bakhtin and Genre Theory in Biblical Studies*, pp. 109-18 (109).
112. Vines, 'The Apocalyptic Chronotype', p. 109.
113. Vines, 'The Apocalyptic Chronotype', p. 110.
114. Vines, 'The Apocalyptic Chronotype', p. 110.
115. Vines, 'The Apocalyptic Chronotype', pp. 110-11.
116. Vines, 'The Apocalyptic Chronotype', p. 111.
117. Newsom, *The Book of Job*, p. 23.

2. Comparing Job to Apocalypse

order to establish an 'artificial context for the expression of a particular point of view'.[118] This context produces the 'axiological possibilities for the action of the hero...who generally embodies the values the author wishes to test'.[119] Thus, the author controls the message through the various literary conventions employed as they relate to the context, the hero and the values of other characters who participate in the narrative. Bakhtin considers this 'value-laden temporal and spatial quality of a work' its 'chronotope', which serves as the 'primary indicator of its generic relationships'.[120]

The external aspect of a genre refers to the author's 'conversation about life...that may change and evolve over time' and may allow for 'competing points of view to enter the world of the text'.[121] Those works that for various reasons do not account for competing voices are considered 'monologic', while those that allow for several voices are termed 'dialogic'. However, even monologic works, such as most apocalypses, are externally dialogical because their generic resources and language belong to the culture as well as the author of the work. Thus, a literary work cannot be fully understood until it is 'situated within an ongoing dialogue with other works that share a similar form-shaping ideology or genre', which offers a diachronic value more appealing than taxonomic approaches that concentrate on 'forms'. This theoretical framework seeks to discern 'the ideological framework that holds these forms together'.[122]

Vines concludes that a Bakhtinian approach to defining apocalypse would therefore entail three areas of concern: chronotope, author and hero, and dialogue. As its name implies, the feature chronotope largely concerns itself with time, especially as it establishes a 'God's-eye view on human history and activity' where 'the hero sees the splendor of heaven, the horrors of hell, and the persistent misdeeds of humanity'. The strange dimensions of the apocalypse disorient the hero, and 'the meaning of human history has become opaque' in part because the 'possibility of justice in the present has disappeared'. Human affairs and the welfare of the righteous are marked by pessimism, so that hope must be 'projected into the eschatological future'.[123]

Surely the book of Job conforms to this definition of an apocalyptic chronotope. From the very beginning the reader is confronted with a 'God's-eye' perspective where Job, the hero, is disoriented in the midst of his newly received chaotic condition. Job is doubtful that justice is possible, and he projects his hope not into an overtly eschatological future, but onto an

---

118. Vines, 'The Apocalyptic Chronotype', p. 111.
119. Vines, 'The Apocalyptic Chronotype', p. 111.
120. Vines, 'The Apocalyptic Chronotype', p. 111.
121. Vines, 'The Apocalyptic Chronotype', pp. 111-12.
122. Vines, 'The Apocalyptic Chronotype', p. 112.
123. Vines, 'The Apocalyptic Chronotype', p. 113.

encounter with God. It is strange that Vines seems to articulate an eschatological future that is not necessarily demanded by an ideological form that has merely lost hope in current conditions. Still, the point remains that Job's story parallels the pessimistic characteristics that demands a solution that transcends his current pool of possibilities. In other words, while Job may not be seeking an eschatological solution, the fact that he continues to demand an audience from God does depict someone who is unsatisfied with what his world has to offer.

The second feature, author and hero, is marked by a passive, virtuous hero borrowed from Israel's epic past who simultaneously carries the message of God's sovereignty and human hopelessness. However, the emphasis of the apocalypse is on the 'splendor and complexity of the heavenly message, along with its proper interpretation, rather than on the action of the hero'. Thus, the author is more concerned with 'testing the cosmos', where creation in particular is 'scrutinized'. Uncertainty over whether or not God will right the wrongs of the world or whether he is still in charge season the apocalypse, though the hero eventually learns that 'God has always been in control of the cosmos, even during times of great injustice and human unrighteousness'. God reveals a plan for how he intends to deal with unrighteous behavior, the disclosure of which is the primary content of the apocalypse that is designed to 'display the majesty of God and to vindicate God's sovereignty and justice'.[124]

One would be hard-pressed not to see Job, the 'blameless' hero who is perhaps drawn from Israel's past (Ezek. 14.14, 20), and who maintains God's sovereignty in the midst of retribution's collapse, as something other than a natural fit for Vines's analysis. Most significantly, the whirlwind speeches establish God's sovereignty over his own creation, obviously declaring that he is indeed in control of the cosmos even during Job's unjust suffering. Surely God's majesty is on display and his justice is vindicated.

The third and final element of a Bakhtinian definition of apocalypse concerns itself with dialogism where the hero 'normally has a heavenly guide with whom he converses'. Sometimes they argue, other times the hero prayerfully intercedes for those in need. Through this dialogue the author is able to 'express his finalizing vision of this world'. Thus, apocalypses are considered monologic because no substantive response or rebuttal is allowed or entertained.[125]

While Job does not have a pure heavenly guide per se, a mediator may be present in both Eliphaz's vision of Job 4 and the mystical voice of Job 28. Still, Job clearly argues with the friends and ultimately prays on their behalf.

---

124. Vines, 'The Apocalyptic Chronotype', pp. 114-15.
125. Vines, 'The Apocalyptic Chronotype', p. 115.

Most importantly, no rebuttal is offered after God's entrance as Job is left almost speechless. The author clearly uses the dialogue speeches between Job and the friends as a way to tease out the fundamental questions of God's justice and sovereignty, both of which are treated in the revelatory whirlwind speeches. In these speeches, God's revelation serves as an opportunity for Job, the hero, to 'view the cosmic situation from God's point of view and learn the mysteries of God's hidden plan', which Vines considers apocalyptic.[126]

While a more thoroughgoing treatment of Vines's conception of a Bakhtinian definition of apocalypse would be helpful, the general arguments are sufficiently clear, and, in my view, the general trajectory of the story of Job accords nicely with the three characteristics of apocalypse presented by Vines.

Conclusion

It is clear that the book of Job conforms to the majority of criteria established within the Apocalypse Group's Master Paradigm, and in those places where conformity is not complete, similar patterns seem to exist. However, Hanson cautions against reading too much into 'lists of characteristics which supposedly constitute an apocalyptic writing'.[127] Hanson argues that such lists indiscriminately combine three key apocalyptic elements—revelation, prophecy and eschatology—which are all casually distributed throughout several writings. He notes that these lists fail to account for the fact that apocalypses are a living entity prone to diachronic development.[128]

Hanson here raises an exceptional point, especially as it relates to genre development in Job. Perhaps no book in the Hebrew Bible reveals genre stratification more than Job. The theories regarding the various layering of Job's constitutive elements and genres are legion. Therefore, the book of Job seems to demonstrate clearly diachronic development, and even more so when one considers the eschatological addendum contained in LXX Job. My next chapter seeks to lay bare such an evolving apocalyptic trend in the development of the story of Job.

In addition to Job's stratification, Hanson outlines several thematic and theological characteristics of apocalypses that intersect with Job. For example, Hanson defines the apocalyptic universe as a 'protest against the bitter opposition from the dominant social system or foreign power'.[129] Job's opposition to the established theology of retribution finds full expression in

---

126. Vines, 'The Apocalyptic Chronotype', p. 116.
127. Hanson, *Dawn of Apocalyptic*, p. 429.
128. Hanson, *Dawn of Apocalyptic*, pp. 429-30.
129. Hanson, *Dawn of Apocalyptic*, p. 433.

his protestations against the friends. Furthermore, God's apparent absence combined with his governance of the universe receives some of Job's strongest protests.

One final comment with respect to genre analysis deserves special mention. John G. Gammie argues that genre analysis can be quite profitable when examining works that have much in common. He cautions that classifying a particular work along generic lines is not an end in itself, but instead provides the student opportunities to 'make fresh discoveries with respect to individual author's messages and intentions'.[130] I share this desire to offer a legitimately fresh approach to Job.

Gammie is influenced by Alonso Schökel's suggestion that interpreters need to distinguish between primary literary genre, secondary literary genre and sub-genres. Gammie thinks that Collins has erred by investigating apocalypses as though they were a primary literary genre when in fact they are really sub-genres of the secondary literary genre of 'Apocalyptic Literature'. Subsequently, Gammie argues that Collins's approach fails to appreciate other possible members of the broader Apocalyptic Literature.[131]

Gammie characterizes Apocalyptic Literature as a secondary literary genre that is apparently influenced by both Prophetic Literature and Wisdom Literature, two primary literary genres. He lists the following traits as part of Apocalyptic Literature: pseudonymity, doxologies, admonitions, exhortations, vision reports that employ animal symbolism, parables, lists, romances, riddles and historical surveys using *vaticinia ex eventu*.[132] Of course, most of these elements are also identified in either the Apocalypse Group's Master Paradigm or by Koch's (and others') studies.

Gammie's significant contribution to my study is his assertion that any genre analysis needs to produce two important fruits. The first is that it enables the interpreter to identify variations of the type under study and the second is that it should suggest other works that may be profitably studied within that same type.[133]

This chapter has accomplished both objectives by proposing that Job is a possible member of the apocalyptic corpus, and also by pointing to variations of the genre as they exist in Job. I have shown that Job shares significant features with what has traditionally been considered Apocalyptic Literature, most exemplified, taxonomically, by the Master Paradigm. Yet, I have also shown that Job conforms with a diachronic approach to apocalypse as evidenced through both Sacchi's and Vines's research. In the next

---

130. John G. Gammie, 'Paraenetic Literature: Toward the Morphology of a Secondary Genre', *Semeia* 50 (1990), pp. 41-71 (41-42).
131. Gammie, 'Paraenetic Literature', p. 45.
132. Gammie, 'Paraenetic Literature', p. 47.
133. Gammie, 'Paraenetic Literature', p. 46.

chapter, I intend to solidify further Job's place within the apocalyptic orbit by demonstrating that the evolution of the story of Job clearly evidences knowledge of, and appreciation for, eschatology. By elevating this eschatological mindset, I will overcome the chief categorical feature commonly attributed with an apocalyptic work that is often considered lacking in Job.

When the eschatological elements contained within the Job tradition are recognized, the interpreter enters into an entirely new world of legitimate possibilities. With Gammie, my hope is that this genre analysis will then 'contribute to the examination of the dynamics operative in works as a whole rather than arresting analysis at one of the parts'.[134] For too long, interpreters have been 'hedged in' by their submission to Job's categorization of wisdom and the lack of a tangible governing genre for the story. As a result, modern commentary has perhaps suffered.

It is true that any attempt to dislodge Job's moorings from its residency within the category of Wisdom Literature will meet with much resistance. However, George W.E. Nickelsburg reminds us that the terms we use to describe the various genres found in biblical literature are merely 'windows into another world...to which we do not have first hand access'.[135] He argues that it is simply wrong to suggest that sharp cleavages can be established between various genres. This is especially evident in the relationship between wisdom and apocalyptic. The following emphasis on the eschatological fabric organic to the story of Job highlights the issues raised by Nickelsburg, Gammie and others. Simply put, Job is closer to an apocalypse than scholarship has recognized.

---

134. Gammie, 'Paraenetic Literature', p. 46.
135. George W.E. Nickelsburg, 'Wisdom and Apocalypticism in Early Judaism: Some Points for Discussion', in E. Lovering (ed.), *Society of Biblical Literature Seminar Papers, 1994* (SBLSP, 33; Atlanta: Scholars Press, 1994), pp. 715-32 (729).

3

TRADITION'S ESCHATOLOGICAL INTERPRETATIONS OF JOB

Introduction

In this chapter I will briefly survey the main biblical and extra-biblical texts that reveal developments the story of Job underwent over time. I will show that the story of Job was often understood in eschatological terms and I will argue that the data furnish evidence for my claim that MT Job represents a nascent form of Apocalyptic Literature that ultimately lent itself to the kind of apocalyptic features that are so prevalent in later interpretations. In this way, I seek to overcome the major literary gap that hinders designating MT Job as an early form of apocalypse, namely, the apparent absence of eschatological features.

Because the final form of the book of Job is routinely considered a composite work of two or more stages of the story stemming from different hands, this chapter also engages various historical-critical hypotheses that disagree with my interpretive commitment to Job's final form as preserved in the MT. Such an investigation into Job's proposed historical stages naturally addresses issues of dating Job. These issues are controversial, but they must be addressed, and I will discuss them directly.

In this matter of dating, Saachi's attempt to date *The Book of the Watchers* to the fourth century is quite relevant, for he claims this date to be after the time of Chronicles and Job.[1] If this dating is correct, the interval between the probable final form of Job and the rise of apocalypses becomes even more uncertain. Hence it is possible to entertain the hypothesis that apocalyptic thoughts were circulating early. While some dates are given in this chapter,

---

1. Sacchi, *Jewish Apocalyptic*, p. 62. According to Pope, *Job*, pp. xxx-xxvii, scholars vary widely on the date of the final form of Job and have proposed dates ranging from the seventh to the second century BCE. Hartley, *The Book of Job*, pp. 18-20, notes that Fohrer, Dhorme and Gordis concur with a fourth-century dating due, in large part, to similarities with Second Isaiah. See Clines, *Job 1–20*, pp. lvi-lix, for an excellent overview. There does seem to be consensus, however, for a postexilic date, with which Sacchi agrees. More will be said on issues of dating in Chapter 5.

the dating of Job in its final form will receive greater treatment in Chapter 5, where issues of setting are fleshed out.

Lawrence L. Besserman's study on the traditions of Job yields some important insights, and his analysis greatly informs my work in this chapter. Besserman offers an 'analytic and taxonomic' tracing of Job's development from its earliest form through the story's various 'wanderings' and recreations through the Middle Ages.[2]

Earliest Job

Besserman takes the position widely held by scholars that the narrative sections of Job, chs. 1–2 and 42.7-17, reflect an earlier prose folktale, which the author of the poetic sections incorporates into his own later work.[3] This division of the book, however, into a prose source and a poetic source has been a matter of some controversy as well. Avi Hurvitz argues that the presence of 'The Satan' in the prologue suggests a very late postexilic date for the prose material,[4] while some, on the other hand, maintain that the book's unity can be just as easily defended.[5] A different possibility, however, is that the story of Job evolved over time, with additions here and subtractions there, before settling into the form found in the MT.

Many critics have accepted the majority view that the earliest story has Job as a pious man who found himself caught in the middle of a conflict between two otherworldly entities, and who, in the end, was rewarded for his perseverance. A later redactor, seeking to round out the story for some purpose, infuses the massive poetic section that readers of the story commonly recognize as the theological 'heart' of the story. Such an approach is not the most complete accounting of the earliest story of Job.

In a provocative work, Bruce Zuckerman has suggested that the earliest story of Job actually described a resurrected Job. Referring analogously to the *Akedah*, Zuckermann proposes that the story of Job, like the *Akedah*, spawned several other traditions beyond the original story itself.[6] What

---

2. Lawrence L. Besserman, *The Legend of Job in the Middle Ages* (Cambridge, MA: Harvard University Press, 1979), p. 1.

3. Besserman, *The Legend of Job*, p. 8. See Otto Kaiser, *Introduction to the Old Testament: A Presentation of its Results and Problems* (trans. John Sturdy; Minneapolis: Augsburg, 1975), pp. 383-84, for an extended discussion on this issue. See also N.M. Sarna, 'Epic Substratum in the Prose of Job', *JBL* 76 (1957), pp. 13-25.

4. Avi Hurvitz, 'The Date of the Prose-Tale of Job Linguistically Reconsidered', *HTR* 67 (1974), pp. 17-34 (19-20).

5. See, Clines, *Job 1–20*, p. lviii, and Habel, *The Book of Job*, pp. 25-27.

6. Zuckerman, *Job the Silent*, pp. 16-24. Zuckerman draws from Shalom Spiegel, *The Last Trial: On Legends and Lore of the Command to Abraham to Offer Isaac as a Sacrifice: The Akedah*, which was translated from the Hebrew edition 'Me-Aggadot

makes the *Akedah* so appealing, in my study, is the ease with which it can be applied to a Joban image. Consider the following rabbinic story in *Sepher Yashar Wa-Yera* 42b, which adds this prologue to the Genesis 22 account:

> Now there was a day when the sons of God came to present themselves before the Lord, and Satan came along among them. And the Lord said unto Satan, 'From where have you come?' and Satan answered the Lord, and said, 'From going to and fro on the earth and from walking up and down in it'... And the Lord said to Satan: 'Have you considered my servant Abraham? For there is none like him in the earth, a perfect and an upright man before Me... and that fears God and eschews evil. As I live, were I to say unto him, Bring up Isaac, your son, before Me, he would not withhold him from Me, much less if I told him to bring up a burnt offering before me from his flocks and herds.' And Satan answered the Lord, and said, 'Speak now unto Abraham as You have said, and You will see whether he will not transgress and cast aside your words this day'.[7]

The connection between the Abrahamic and Joban elements is obvious; two patriarchs undergoing severe testing from God. Zuckerman sees a further possibility. If a later version of the *Akedah* can be retooled in Joban clothing, then perhaps an earlier version of Job is more akin to the story of the proposed *Akedah*, namely, the legend where Abraham actually kills

---

ha-Akedah', in S. Lieberman (ed.), *Alexander Marx Jubilee Volume* (New York: Jewish Theological Seminary of America, 1950) and was reprinted in *The Sacrifice of Isaac: Studies in the Development of a Literary Tradition* (ed. E. Yassif; Jerusalem: Makor, 1978/79), pages unnumbered. The Hebrew term *Akedah* means 'binding', the original use of which in this sense is hard to date. Zuckerman refers to A. Segal who says that the *Akedah* is not likely to be any earlier than the second century BCE ('The Sacrifice of Isaac in Early Judaism and Christianity', in his *The Other Judaisms of Late Antiquity* [Atlanta: Scholars Press, 1987], pp. 109-30 [113-14]). Spiegel proposes that two stories of the *Akedah* actually existed. The biblical story emends an earlier tradition in which Isaac was actually killed by Abraham. Two key verses in the MT indicate that parts of this earlier tradition were intentionally preserved. The first key verse is Gen. 22.19, which reads, 'So Abraham returned to his young men, and they arose and went together to Beer-sheba; and Abraham lived in Beer-sheba'. Spiegel points out that the verb וישב is singular, and argues, therefore, that this is a vestige of the earlier tradition whereby Abraham descends alone, without the slain Isaac. On the basis of this reading, Spiegel then reinterprets Gen. 22.16, which reads: '...By myself I have sworn, says the Lord: Because you have done this, and have not withheld your son, your only son'. Here Spiegel suspects that another fragment from the ancient tale is preserved, again indicating that Abraham did in fact kill Isaac. Zuckerman sees two possible stories woven together in the Gen. 22 story. Based on the difference in names, this becomes more viable because YHWH is the one who speaks in v. 16, while Elohim speaks in v. 12 where Abraham is told not to lay his hand on Isaac.

7. Zuckerman follows Louis Ginzberg, *The Legends of the Jews* (7 vols.; Philadelphia: The Jewish Publication Society of America, 1928, repr. 1968), I, pp. 272-73. See also Spiegel, *The Last Trial*, pp. 143-52.

3. Tradition's Eschatological Interpretations of Job

Isaac, but Isaac is later resurrected. Zuckerman quotes from the twelfth-century poem by Rabbi Ephraim ben Jacob, which seems to preserve this tradition:

> He [Abraham] made haste, he pinned him [Isaac] down with his knees
> He made his two arms strong.
> With steady hands he slaughtered him according to the rite,
> Full right was the slaughter.
>
> Down upon him fell the resurrecting dew, and he revived.
> (The father) seized him (then) to slaughter him once more.
> Scripture bear witness! Well grounded is the fact:
> And the Lord called Abraham, even a second time from heaven.[8]

Although Zuckerman's intriguing claim does not demonstrate an organic connection between the two forms of the story, the prospect of 'recovering' ancient traditions, which might supplement or even undergird the 'authorized' versions of stories found in the biblical text, demands attention.

For Zuckerman, the earliest tale of Job contained the resurrection of Job's initial set of children from the dead, a crucial theme because it represents the original climax of the folktale.[9] He argues that the reference to the resurrection was omitted in the MT because the author wished to avoid such a 'false hope'.[10] However, Zuckerman's foundational thesis in his work is that the received story of Job is ultimately a parody, which he phrases 'counterpoint', of an earlier story. Therefore, he must claim that the received story is devoid of explicit resurrection elements even though they had been there.

One need not accept Zuckerman's parody theory to recognize the possibility that the original folktale might have contained such a resurrection motif. Zuckerman's comparison to the Akedah and the rabbinic tradition's testimony are sufficient and compelling arguments for acknowledging the possibility of an original resurrection motif.

Ezekiel's References

The earliest explicit reference to biblical Job is found in Ezekiel in two verses (14.14, 20), which are the only references to Job in the Hebrew Bible outside the book of Job.[11] They read:

---

8. Zuckerman cites from Spiegel, *The Last Trial*, pp. 148-50.

9. Zuckerman, *Job the Silent*, p. 28. See also Shalom Spiegel, 'Noah, Danel and Job: Touching on Canaanite Relics in the Legends of the Jews', in *Louis Ginzberg Jubilee Volume* (New York: American Academy for Jewish Research, 1945), pp. 305-55 (345-55).

10. Zuckerman, *Job the Silent*, p. 29.

11. It should be noted that *BHS* (Leningrad Codex B 19 a) contains the name יוב in Gen. 46.13, while many other manuscripts contain ישוב, as also do the Samaritan

> even if Noah, Daniel, and Job, these three, were in it, they would save only their own lives by their righteousness, says the Lord GOD (Ezek. 14.14).

> even if Noah, Daniel, and Job were in it, as I live, says the Lord God, they would save neither son nor daughter; they would save only their own lives by their righteousness (Ezek. 14.20).

The verses attest to Job's righteousness without any hint of his rebelliousness. Since modern critical scholarship has not completely determined the date of Ezekiel, though most argue for dates between the sixth and fifth century BCE,[12] it is impossible to know whether Ezekiel was referring to a legend of Job that consisted solely of the content found in the MT prologue and epilogue, that is, the portion that emphasizes the patient and reverent Job, or to a story that resembles what is found in the received text, which includes the more abrasive Job. Others regard the 'apocalyptic' portions of Ezekiel (38.1–39.16) as possible allusions to Alexander the Great and therefore date these segments to the fourth or third century BCE.[13] These apocalyptic images exhibit the very themes of apocalyptic, a phenomenon that has led some to consider Ezekiel the source of apocalyptic.[14]

The mere presence of Job in such a stratified book as Ezekiel cannot itself indicate that the sixth-century prophet viewed Job as an apocalyptic figure. Yet, it is striking that the four 'deadly acts' of judgment from Ezekiel 14 are found in Eliphaz's admonition in Job 5.19-26.[15] The immediate context surrounding Ezek. 14.12-23 led Zimmerli to label it 'The Inevitability of Divine Judgment'.[16] It may be possible to posit a correlation between the

---

Pentateuch and LXX. Thus, there is no reason to suspect that this name should be identified with biblical Job.

12. Brevard S. Childs, *Introduction to the Old Testament as Scripture* (Philadelphia: Fortress Press, 1979), p. 358; Kaiser, *Introduction*, pp. 251-55; Norman Gottwald, *The Hebrew Bible: A Socio-Literary Introduction* (Philadelphia: Fortress Press, 1985), p. 483.

13. W.H. Brownlee, *Ezekiel 1–19* (WBC, 28; Waco, TX: Word Books, 1986), p. xxxvii. However, Brownlee argues that the phraseology used in these verses is similar to that which is found in Isaiah, Jeremiah and other sections of Ezekiel. Paul D. Hanson (*Old Testament Apocalyptic* [IBT; Nashville: Abingdon Press, 1987], pp. 36-37) considers these chapters 'proto-apocalyptic' as well.

14. R.G. Hamerton-Kelly, 'The Temple and the Origins of Jewish Apocalyptic', *VT* 20 (1970), pp. 1-15. James Crenshaw also discusses this in his *Story and Faith: A Guide to the Old Testament* (New York: Macmillan, 1986), pp. 225-26.

15. This passage is a graded numerical saying that contains seven evils variously identified by scholars. See Andrew Steinmann, 'The Graded Numerical Saying in Job', in A. Beck, A. Bartelt, P. Raabe and C. Franke (eds.), *Fortunate the Eyes that See: Essays in Honor of David Noel Freedman in Celebration of his Seventieth Birthday* (Grand Rapids: Eerdmans, 1995), pp. 288-97.

16. Walther Zimmerli, *Ezekiel* (Hermeneia; Philadelphia: Fortress Press, 1979), pp. x, 310.

apocalyptic motif of judgment in Ezekiel 14 with Job, especially because he avoids these judgments on account of his righteousness both in Ezekiel and in the story of Job itself.

While the use of Job alongside of Noah and Daniel in Ezekiel 14 is fascinating in that each was recognized as considerably righteous,[17] it is even more intriguing that each survives divine trial and judgment and possibly saves their children from death. John Day comments:

> [W]hat is certain is that the stories of both Noah and Job have the common pattern of the righteous hero passing through the midst of disaster to deliverance, and the hero's children are in some way involved in the deliverance... That would, in fact, [also] be the case with the Ugaritic Daniel on the common view that the lost ending of Aqhat text went on to tell of Aqhat's resurrection... That Aqhat was resurrected, or at the very least a replacement for him was found, is strongly supported by the fact that the text clearly implies that the story has a happy ending.[18]

Zimmerli even suggests that each man and his family experienced a kind of miraculous deliverance.[19] If Zuckerman's theory that the earliest story of Job included his resurrected children, the coupling of Job and Danel is an obvious attempt to correlate righteous men who have suffered but found ultimate relief in restored or resurrected children.

A further aspect of the apocalyptic atmosphere is the feature that all three figures are universal figures, not privileged heroes associated exclusively with Israel.[20] Thus, Ezekiel contains readily identifiable apocalyptic overtones in both ch. 14 and chs. 38–39 with their inevitable judgments and intimations of a resurrection. The figure of Job in Ezekiel seems to be portrayed as a character that adheres to a nascent form of apocalypse. This use of Job suggests that Job was 'cast' for his role, in part, because the character was perceived as lending himself to the kind of cosmological vision that influenced Ezekiel and apocalyptic writings.

---

17. See Martin Noth, 'Noah, Daniel und Hiob in Ezechiel xiv', *VT* (1951), pp. 251-60, and Spiegel, 'Noah, Danel, and Job'. Most likely the figure Danel refers to the Ugaritic hero in the Tale of Aqhat from the fourteenth century BCE. For the text of the tale, see *ANET*, pp. 149-55. Harold H.P. Dressler, 'The Identification of the Ugaritic DNIL with the Daniel of Ezekiel', *VT* 29 (1979), pp. 152-61, argues that the figure in Ezek. 14.14, 20; 28.3, is the biblical Daniel. John Day, 'The Daniel of Ugarit and Ezekiel and the Hero of the Book of Daniel', *VT* 30 (1980), pp. 174-84, convincingly refutes Dressler.

18. Day, 'The Daniel of Ugarit and Ezekiel', p. 179.

19. Zimmerli, *Ezekiel*, pp. 30-32.

20. Joseph Blenkinsopp, *Ezekiel* (Interpretation; Louisville: John Knox, 1990), p. 73, Zimmerli, *Ezekiel*, p. 315, and Brownlee, *Ezekiel 1–19*, p. 206, all remark on the importance of this universal aspect of the three figures.

LXX Job

As noted previously, the most striking evidence that the story of Job had substantial affinities with eschatological notions is the resurrection 'plus' found in the LXX version. Most feel that the resurrection feature materialized as a Christian addition, or, at best, as the product of an apocalyptic fervor present during its translation from the Hebrew.[21] Based on textual evidence, it is impossible to prove either claim. The plus found in LXX Job 42.17 explicitly states that Job will be resurrected:

γέγραπται δὲ αὐτὸν πάλιν ἀναστήσεσθαι μεθ' ὧν ὁ κύριος ἀνίστησιν.[22]

And it is written that he will rise again with those the Lord raises up.[23]

Dating LXX Job is somewhat difficult, but scholarship is able to narrow the parameters with a degree of certainty. On the basis of the influence of Greek culture after Alexander the Great's conquests in 333 BCE and the Jewish community's need for a Greek translation, it is generally recognized that the Pentateuch was most likely translated in the middle of the second century BCE.[24] Since the Greek text of Sirach dates to about 132 BCE, and its prologue refers to a translation of the 'Law', 'Prophets' and 'the rest of the books', it seems likely to conclude that the Writings, which include Job, were translated at least by the first century BCE.[25]

The so-called 'addition' in LXX Job 42.17 is not the only eschatological reference offered in the LXX reading of Job. Zuckerman suggests that other verses in LXX Job (14.14 and 19.25-27) 'may also reflect an affirmative attitude toward resurrection'.[26] Additionally, Donald Gard includes LXX Job 5.11 along with 14.14 and 42.17 as examples of 'a definite belief in the

---

21. H.B. Swete, *An Introduction to the Old Testament in Greek* (Cambridge: Cambridge University Press, 1902; rev. R.R. Ottley, 1914; repr. New York: Ktav, 1968), p. 256. See also Driver and Gray, *Book of Job*, p. lxxi.

22. J. Ziegler, *Iob* (Septuaginta; Vetus Testamentum Graeca, 12.4; Göttingen: Vandenhoeck & Ruprecht, 1982), p. 412.

23. I am indebted to Dr Claude Cox for generously offering his pre-published translation of LXX Job, which is now published in *A New English Translation of the Septuagint* (New York: Oxford University Press, 2007).

24. Karen H. Jobes and Moisés Silva, *Invitation to the Septuagint* (Grand Rapids: Baker, 2000), p. 34.

25. Jobes and Silva, *Invitation to the Septuagint*, p. 34 n. 8. Jobes and Silva concur that 'scholars believe that most of the Writings, such as the wisdom books, were not translated until the first century B.C.E.'. Besserman (*Legend*, p. 162 n. 49), however, suggests that it was likely that Greek transcriptions were prepared as early as the fourth century BCE.

26. Zuckerman, *Job the Silent*, p. 279 n. 504.

3. *Tradition's Eschatological Interpretations of Job*

resurrection as the final event'.[27] According to Gard, these passages consider resurrection a fact where the original Hebrew only suggests the prospect, thereby demonstrating that the passages signal the transformation from possibility to fact in the theological tendencies of the translator.[28]

While the plus in 42.17 is often attributed to a later Christian redaction, the number of other eschatological allusions seems to add credibility to the notion that LXX Job, which emerged roughly a century before Christianity, contained apocalyptic overtones.[29] G.B. Gray argues that even if the plusses found in 42.17 were of Christian origin, the translator of LXX Job was not necessarily a Christian.[30] In other words, since several other passages within the 'Jewish' translation of LXX Job clearly recognize the belief and/or importance of the resurrection, the argument that Job lends itself to apocalyptic interpretation, which includes resurrection, is not discredited by the alleged Christian addition found in 42.17. Gray continues, 'the mere fact therefore that the added clause refers to a future resurrection of Job does not render it in any way incompatible with the translator's [Jewish] theological belief'.[31]

In fact, whether or not LXX Job contains sufficient exterior apocalyptic clues leading to an eventual apocalyptic designation may not be as relevant as recognizing that the story itself may be an apocalyptic work at its very core. In other words, is there something about the story of Job that naturally led to the later apocalyptic crafting? Not referring specifically to Job, Walter Brueggemann seems to suggest that resurrection was one such latent idea in Jewish apocalyptic thought:

> Perhaps resurrection (as a subset of apocalyptic thought) entered Israel's theological repertoire only later, as a result of non-Israelite influence. Already extant in Israel, though, were antecedent utterances and convictions that made resurrection faith an unsurprising extrapolation from what Israel characteristically believed.[32]

---

27. Donald Gard, 'The Concept of the Future Life according to the Greek Translator of the Book of Job', *JBL* 74 (1953), pp. 137-43 (139).

28. However, Gard's hypothesis that theological impulses characterize the majority of differences between the original Hebrew and the LXX has been refuted by Harry Orlinsky's series of articles on the differences between MT Job and LXX Job, 'Studies in the Septuagint of the Book of Job', in *HUCA* 28 (1957), pp. 53-74; 29 (1958), pp. 229-71; 30 (1959), pp. 153-67; 32 (1961), pp. 239-68; 33 (1962), pp. 119-51; 35 (1964), pp. 57-78; 36 (1965), pp. 37-47.

29. Swete, *Introduction to the Old Testament in Greek*, p. 256, suggests either a Pharisaic or Christian gloss.

30. G.B. Gray, 'The Additions in the Ancient Greek Version of Job', *The Expositor* 19 (1920), pp. 422-38 (429).

31. Gray, 'The Additions', p. 430.

32. Walter Brueggemann, 'Resurrection', in his *Reverberations of Faith: A Theological Handbook of Old Testament Themes* (Louisville: Westminster/John Knox Press, 2002), pp. 173-74 (173).

Referring specifically to Job, Judith Baskin also ascribes importance to the resurrection plus in 42.17, stating that it contributed to the 'growth of the figure in popular legend'. For her, the plus vitiates the central question regarding unjust suffering in the world.[33] Resurrection, then, is the solution to the enigma of innocent suffering. Baskin's solution is unsatisfying because it overlooks the other apparent resurrection verses, none of which appear to 'vitiate' the so-called 'central question' of Job. However, Baskin's point that the Joban legend grew is indisputable.

A further expansion of LXX Job is found in the *Testament of Job*, where much of what is found in LXX Job is preserved, and other themes receive re-interpretations. Before turning to that text, and keeping with this diachronic approach to the evolution of the story of Job, I will briefly address the manuscripts of Job found at Qumran, a community that is generally regarded as roughly contemporary with the translators of the LXX.[34]

Paleo-Hebrew Job

Some of the more interesting finds discovered at Qumran were scrolls written in paleo-Hebrew. This ancient script is the Hebrew script used during the Monarchy as opposed to the later square script that post-dated the Babylonian Captivity.[35] There are at least 15 texts from Qumran that are written in this script, three of which are from Job (13.18-20, 23-27; 14.13-18), which, along with a fragment of Joshua, serve as the only texts found from outside Torah.[36]

Many have questioned why these extant texts were written in paleo-Hebrew.[37] Some suggest that the community used the script to demonstrate

---

33. Judith Baskin, *Pharaoh's Counsellors: Job, Jethro, and Balaam in Rabbinic and Patristic Tradition* (Brown Judaic Studies, 47; Chico, CA: Scholars Press, 1983), p. 29.

34. Geza Vermes, *The Complete Dead Sea Scrolls in English* (New York: Penguin, 1997), p. 13, says, 'the general scholarly view today places the Qumran Scrolls roughly between 200 B.C.E. and 70 C.E.'.

35. F.M. Cross, 'The Development of the Jewish Scripts', in *The Bible and the Ancient Near East* (London: Routledge & Kegan Paul, 1961), pp. 133-202 (189-90 nn. 4-5).

36. See the official publication of these paleo-Hebrew texts in Patrick W. Skehan, Eugene Ulrich and Judith Sanderson (eds.), *Qumran Cave 4: Palaeo-Hebrew and Greek Biblical Manuscripts* (DJD, 9; Oxford: Clarendon Press, 1992). One of the fragments appears to be a passage from the book of Joshua. Of note, the published texts are transliterations from the paleo-Hebrew into the square script.

37. André Lemaire, 'L'épigraphie paléo-hébraïque et la Bible', in W. Zimmerli (ed.), *Congress Volume: Göttingen 1977* (VTSup, 29; Leiden: Brill, 1978), pp. 165-76 (165), remarks that, in total, about 2000 inscriptions exist.

3. *Tradition's Eschatological Interpretations of Job*

reverence for either the Tetragrammaton or for Torah.[38] Generally speaking, however, most consider the use of paleo-Hebrew as an attempt to 'archaize' the text for the purposes of preserving tradition or for nationalistic intentions, that is, to define the community through its sacred past.

For my purposes, discerning why Job existed in paleo-Hebrew at Qumran is of great interest, especially since the extant texts seem limited to Torah. Further amplifying this concern is the fact that only biblical texts from Job and Leviticus were found at Qumran in Aramaic (see the section on 'The Targums of Job [Qumran and Rabbinic]'). Three solutions have been proposed.

First, P.W. Skehan suggests that Job was commonly associated with the Patriarchal era and was therefore considered among the Pentateuchal patriarchs.[39] Second, W.H. Brownlee associates Job with Moses, tradition's designated author of Torah, who later penned the book of Job.[40] The third proposal contends that the books found in the paleo-Hebrew were considered the oldest of the Hebrew Scriptures and were therefore translated in the archaic script to symbolize their antiquity.[41]

To my knowledge, no full-scale comparison of these three fragments to both MT Job and the OG has been done outside of my own unpublished work.[42] My research endeavored to detect whether the underlying text from which the paleo-Hebrew texts were copied was closer to our MT or to the LXX manuscripts. I concluded that the paleo-Hebrew texts were extraordinary witnesses to the MT that deviate primarily in *plene* and defective writing, not in content. Of the scripts in paleo-Hebrew, only part of Job 14.14 could be considered eschatological. Unfortunately, the portion of the verse containing the possible eschatological reference was not found.

Since the MT in Job 14.14 poses the issue of life after death interrogatively, and since the LXX responds in the indicative, that section of Job 14.14 in the Qumran text would have been valuable. LXX Job 14.14 reads, 'For, if a person died, then would live again, when he has completed the days of his life, I would endure, until I would be born again'.[43]

---

38. Jonathan Siegel, 'The Employment of Palaeo-Hebrew Characters for Divine Names at Qumran in Light of Tannaitic Sources', *HUCA* 52 (1971), pp. 159-71.

39. P.W. Skehan, 'Exodus in the Samaritan Recension from Qumran', *JBL* 74 (1955), pp. 182-87.

40. W.H. Brownlee, *The Meaning of the Qumran Scrolls for the Bible* (New York: Oxford University Press, 1964), p. 555.

41. Michael Wise, M. Abegg Jr and E. Cook, *The Dead Sea Scrolls: A New Translation* (San Francisco: HarperSanFrancisco, 1996), p. 10.

42. Tim Johnson, 'Paleo-Hebrew and Qumran: With An Analysis of 4QpaleoJob(c)' (unpublished paper, Marquette University, 1999).

43. NETS. Sir Lancelot C.L. Brenton, by contrast, translates as an interrogative, 'For if a man should die, shall he live again, having accomplished the days of his life? I will wait

Drawing heavily from Mark David McLean, I concluded that the date of the paleo-Hebrew texts is around 200 BCE, thus a contemporary of the translation of the LXX.[44] Presumably no major discovery derives from the three fragments found at Qumran other than the fact that they were found with mostly Torah fragments and hence show the honor that the book of Job enjoyed within that community. An analysis of the targumic material containing Job will assist in answering questions related to the paleo-Hebrew witnesses.

The Targums of Job at Qumran

Two important Aramaic manuscripts of Job were found in Qumran and represent two of the earliest extant Targums of the Hebrew Bible.[45] Bruce Zuckerman concludes that the *terminus ad quem* for the two targums is 70 CE[46] though earlier research suggested a second-century BCE date, and recently a date from the first century BCE has been proposed.[47] Similar to the paleo-Hebrew fragments of Job, the other biblical book found in Aramaic at Qumran is from Torah (Leviticus). Once again, the question of why these Job fragments are found alongside a Torah fragment arises.

Zuckerman thinks that it may 'be more than simply a coincidence that two of the three clearly targumic texts found among the Dead Sea Scrolls are targums of Job'.[48] He hypothesizes that Job was included because the difficulty of the Hebrew text of Job demanded an accessible translation. Neither of the two translations of Job reveal any major divergences from the MT from which to draw any other conclusion concerning why they were present with Leviticus,[49] and Sokoloff comments, 'As far as we can tell, the translator's consonantal H text was, in general, quite close to MT'.[50]

---

till I exist again?' (*The Septuagint Version of the Old Testament and Apocrypha* [London: Samuel Bagster and Sons, 1851]).

44. M.D. McLean, 'The Use and Development of Palaeo-Hebrew in the Hellenistic and Roman Periods' (PhD dissertation, Harvard University, 1982).

45. Vermes, *Dead Sea Scrolls*, p. 431. For the *editio princeps* of 11Q18, see J.P.M. van der Ploeg *et al.* (eds.), *Le Targum de Job de la grotte XI de Qumran* (Leiden: Brill, 1971), and M. Sokoloff, *The Targum to Job from Qumran Cave XI* (Ramat-Gan: Bar-Ilan University, 1974). For the larger Targum of Job, 11Q10, see J.T. Milik, '4QtgJob', in *DJD VI* (Oxford: Clarendon Press, 1978), pp. 85-91.

46. Bruce Zuckerman, 'The Date of 11Q Targum Job: A Paleographic Consideration of its Vorlage', *JSP* 1 (1987), pp. 57-78 (58).

47. Zuckerman, 'Job, Targums of', in *ABD*, III, pp. 868-69.

48. Zuckerman, *Job the Silent*, pp. 281-82 n. 527.

49. Zuckerman (*Job the Silent*, p. 282) concurs.

50. Sokoloff, *The Targum to Job*, p. 6.

3. Tradition's Eschatological Interpretations of Job

Zuckerman's speculation is not satisfactory. However, the fact that Job exists at Qumran in both paleo-Hebrew and Aramaic seems to suggest a possibly significant association between the book of Job and the community. I offer two possibilities.

First, the Qumran community is widely recognized as an 'apocalyptic' community whose writings do not necessarily conform to a modern 'apocalyptic' expectation. Concerning the Qumran corpus, Collins states,

> the worldview that we find in these writings is typically apocalyptic: human destiny is ruled by superhuman forces of light and darkness, history is deemed to be moving inexorably to an end, and people will await reward or punishment after death. *But these beliefs are not expressed in the form of heavenly revelations to an ancient seer.*[51]

Since 11QtgJob ends at 42.11, one might be tempted to suggest that any such identification of Job as apocalyptic would contain a colophon similar to, if not identical to that found in LXX Job. However, all we can really say about the ending of Job is that it was in a state of flux. It is probable that the targumist was not aware of the Hebrew text that is the *Vorlage* of the LXX version of Job.[52] Furthermore, the column in the targum after 42.11 is left blank and both of the portions just after the column containing 42.11 and beginning at the top of the next column are lost. It is therefore impossible to determine whether or not a colophon existed in any form.[53]

Frank Moore Cross is fascinated with the fact that Job is preserved so well at Qumran:

> Job was a major force in the evolution of Israel's religion. It is intriguing that Job's importance was not forgotten in apocalyptic circles. At Qumran it alone outside of the Pentateuch survived in Palaeo-Hebrew script, and there is evidence that it was always so distinguished and received *de facto* canonization as early as the Pentateuch, in advance of the prophetic canon.[54]

While not quite identifying Job as an apocalyptic work, Cross's suggestion that Job was important to the Qumran community seems to suggest that something about Job aligned with the apocalyptic milieu that so dominated Qumran's worldview.

The second possibility, which I will explore further in Chapter 4, is partially related to the first. Many have wondered why the book of Job, a

---

51. Collins, *Apocalyptic Imagination*, p. 147 (emphasis added).
52. See Joseph Blenkinsopp, *Wisdom and Law in the Old Testament: The Ordering of Life in Israel and Early Judaism* (OBS; Oxford: Oxford University Press, 1983), p. 61, who suggests that the date of 11QtgJob was actually in the second century BCE, nearer the time of LXX Job.
53. Sokoloff, *The Targum to Job*, p. 5.
54. Cross, 'New Directions', p. 163.

non-Israelite, even appears in the canon. Might it be that he was, in fact, viewed as the great example of a Gentile convert who persevered in his new faith? Job is so carefully preserved at Qumran, then, not because he has legendary, relational connections to the patriarchs, but because he represents one of the core identifications marking the community, that is, to persevere under persecution. Thus, my thesis that the story of Job can be characterized as an early form of apocalypse is supported by the fact that the 'apocalyptic' community at Qumran, which represented a minority dissident community, identified with Job's perseverance and clung to the story of Job because of the book's admonition to endure suffering while being falsely persecuted.[55]

In summary, the place of the targum of Job in the apocalyptic Qumran community suggests that those who steadfastly preserved Job (in both Aramaic and paleo-Hebrew) valued the story for its theme of perseverance. As a minority community that claimed to be the true Israel and therefore defied the regnant Jewish authorities, they probably derived much inspiration from Job's fidelity to both his integrity and faith in God. Perhaps a further affinity is that Job also defied the 'orthodox' theology of retribution as advocated by Job's friends who are cast as that theology's quintessential practitioners.

Rabbinic Targum

The rabbinic targum of Job is worth mentioning here because this 'standard targum' does not demonstrate any direct relationship to the Qumran targums.[56] The rabbinic targum of Job is variously dated, but Céline Magnan has argued that the *terminus ad quem* is around the tenth century CE and the *terminus a quo* could be as early as the fifth century CE.[57] On the other hand, some cite the legend of Gamaliel the Elder who tried to suppress the targum as an indication that a targum existed in the first century CE.[58] More supportive of an earlier targum is the reference in LXX Job to the translation

---

55. Vermes notes that, on the basis of several manuscripts found at Qumran, the community 'regarded itself as the true Israel, the repository of the authentic traditions of the religious body' (*Dead Sea Scrolls*, p. 26).

56. Zuckerman, 'Job, Targums of', *ABD*, III, p. 868.

57. Céline Magnan, *The Targum of Job* (ArBib, 15; Collegeville, MN: Liturgical Press, 1991), pp. 5-8.

58. The account of Gamaliel's reaction is found in the *t. Shab.* 13.2. See *The Tosefta: Translated from the Hebrew with a New Introduction* (trans. J. Neusner; 6 vols.; repr. New York: Ktav, 1977–1986; Peabody, MA: Hendrickson, 2002), I, p. 404. Neusner describes the Tosefta as a 'supplement' to the Mishnah, the former being 'closed' around 300 CE as the second document of Rabbinic Judaism after the Mishnah (p. xii).

3. Tradition's Eschatological Interpretations of Job

'from the Syriac book', which some consider a reference to an Aramaic translation.[59]

The targumist interpolates four main ideas; the Law, the history of Israel, the phrase 'son of man' and eschatology. Concentrating on the eschatological influence, Magnan identifies five eschatological themes woven throughout.[60]

The first treats the more expanded sense of judgment, and the role of God as 'Judge'. In 2.1, the targum reads, 'Now on the day *of the great judgement, the day of the remission of offences, bands of angels* came to stand *in judgement* before the Lord. *Satan also came in their midst to stand in judgement* before the Lord.'[61] While it is true that the idea of judgment was already present in the Hebrew text, the targum expands this in several places (i.e. 1.6, 21; 3.5-9; 10.16).

Secondly, the targumist builds upon the already present theme of death by including the 'angel of death' (18.13) and the burial place of death (1.21). 'Gehenna' is more commonly used than the conventional 'Sheol', which is the case in other rabbinic midrashim as well as in the New Testament and Pseudepigrapha. Magnan notes that 'Whereas *Sheol* can still be a neutral word, *Gehenna* always implies punishment (e.g. 3.17; 5.4; 15.21), especially by fire'.[62]

A third eschatological intrusion into the text is the prominence of 'heaven', which is often used to suggest an expansion of God's power, (11.10; 21.22).[63] Fourth, and somewhat related, is the inclusion of 'angels' in the targum. Michael and Gabriel appear (25.2), as do Sammael (28.7), 'angels of service' (28.27), along with another reference to the angel of death (28.22), while 'paraclete' is even used to translate 'angel' (33.23).

Finally, the phrase 'future life' finds increased currency. References to 'life to come' (15.21), 'resurrection' (11.17; 14.14) or God's future 'kingdom' (36.7) attest to the targumist's knowledge of life beyond death. These five intrusions reveal a greater appreciation for eschatological tendencies in the story of Job, a phenomenon that is wholly consistent with the traditional development of the story in the other versions examined in this chapter.

The numerous eschatological features that surface in the Rabbinic tradition also suggest an appreciation for the story of Job's ability to speak to an apocalyptic context. Moreover, the fact that these eschatological elements

---

59. Magnan, *The Targum of Job*, p. 5.
60. Magnan, *The Targum of Job*, pp. 15-16.
61. Magnan concedes that no one single Aramaic text as the source of the others can be reconstructed. Her translation is based primarily on the Cambridge University MS Ee. 5.9, which is supplemented with the numerous variant targums (indicated by italicization) that are incorporated into the final text (p. 17).
62. Magnan, *The Targum of Job*, p. 16.
63. Magnan, *The Targum of Job*, p. 16

come from a strictly Jewish tradition lends credence to the assertions made earlier that the eschatological plusses in LXX Job were not necessarily limited to Christian redactors.

The service that Job paid to both the Qumran and Rabbinic traditions further demonstrates that Job was considered a nascent form of what has come to be known as apocalypse. These rabbinic inclinations also materialize in a roughly contemporary work of Jewish influence, the *Testament of Job*, to which I now return.[64]

The Testament of Job

Scholarship generally recognizes that the *Testament of Job* is reliant upon LXX Job and was produced somewhere within the first century BCE and first century CE, which was the period when the genre 'Testament' flourished.[65] Many traces of apocalyptic found in LXX Job are emphasized and expanded in the pseudepigraphal work, the *Testament of Job*. However, it also possible that the *Testament of Job* influenced LXX Job or later versions of LXX Job.[66] And yet, it is important to state again that the *Testament of Job* is one of a few works from the Testament corpus considered exclusively Jewish.[67] If the resurrection 'addition' to LXX Job is considered a Christian redaction, one would have to explain why such a so-called corruption would remain in the Jewish *Testament of Job*.[68] It is possible that the resurrection verse was not, in fact, a Christian addition. Furthermore, scholarship simply cannot eliminate the possibility that the *Testament of Job* influenced LXX Job, which undermines the argument that the resurrection was merely a later Christian manipulation.

The genre 'Testament' is closely related to apocalypse through a variety of shared characteristics such as predictions, warnings, cosmological motifs, Satan imagery, messianism and the resurrection.[69] Some of these are lacking

64. Collins, *Apocalyptic Imagination*, p. 128, notes that the *Testament of Job* is one of only three testaments (the other two being the *Testament of Moses* and *Visions of Amram*) that can be considered Jewish in their current form.

65. R.P. Spittler, 'Testament of Job', in *OTP*, I, pp. 829-68 (831).

66. Spittler, 'Testament of Job', I, pp. 831-33. Irving Jacobs, 'Literary Motifs in the Testament of Job', *JJS* 21 (1970), pp. 1-10 (1), notes that early research suggested a 75 BCE date for the *terminus ad quem*. He notes also that some (R.H. Pfeiffer, *History of New Testament Times* [London: A. & C. Black, 1949], p. 70) argued that the *Testament of Job* actually preceded LXX Job.

67. Collins, *Apocalyptic Imagination*, p. 128. Spittler, 'Testament of Job', p. 833, concurs.

68. Spittler acknowledges that 'Christian editing is possible', but declared that 'the work is essentially Jewish in character' ('Testament of Job', p. 833).

69. See Collins, *Apocalyptic Imagination*, pp. 127-44, for an excellent overview of the genre.

in the *Testament of Job*, but many others are present. For example, resurrection (4.9; 52.1-12), Satan's greater role in the story, angelic presence (chs. 2–5) and cosmic imagery (33.3; 47.3) contribute to an apocalyptic atmosphere. Important theological motifs of dualism (33.3-4, 8) and persevering during persecution also weigh heavily in showing that the *Testament of Job* bears significant apocalyptic garb. On this last point, the *Testament of Job* is even thought to resemble the literary style *martyria*, which was common to both Jewish and Christian writers.[70]

Collins also agrees with the apocalyptic nature of the *Testament of Job*, stating that it 'shows certain affinities with Jewish apocalyptic. Job's interest in heavenly realities and the manner in which they support his endurance are typical of apocalyptic.'[71] Collins cites examples such as individual eschatology, mediated revelations, a picture of heavenly Jerusalem and heavenly realities as indicative of apocalyptic. In fact, one gets the sense that Collins is unsatisfied with designating the *Testament of Job* as an example of a 'testament' and might even prefer to label it akin to apocalypse:

> Finally, a word on the question of genre. While TJ is written in the literary form of a testament, the genre 'testament' only indicates the surface structure of the work at a superficial level. Any meaningful generic classification of TJ must work rather from the deeper structures of the book such as we have analysed. TJ might be more purposefully located in a class of works which mediate an opposition between heavenly reality and earthly illusion, than in the class of 'testaments' to which it superficially belongs.[72]

That the *Testament of Job* can, and perhaps should, be considered something outside of the traditional 'testament' is significant. In the first place, the dominant storyline of Job is preserved. The plot remains, as do the characters, but most other testaments deviate substantially and create wholly original stories and plots. While many embellishments certainly exist, one cannot read through the *Testament of Job* without feeling at home in relation to the traditional story. Many consider it a kind of midrash on LXX Job and the deviations from the biblical story serve as an important attention-getting device, which serves as the point of departure for interpretation.[73]

Second, Spittler points out that the *Testament of Job* concentrates on one biblical character that is not mentioned in Torah, but instead comes from

---

70. Jacobs, 'Literary Motifs', p. 1. See also Cees Haas, 'Job's Perseverance in the Testament of Job', in M. Knibb and P. van der Horst (eds.), *Studies on the Testament of Job* (SNTSMS; Cambridge: Cambridge University Press, 1989), pp. 117-54.

71. John J. Collins, 'Structure and Meaning in the Testament of Job', in G. MacRae (ed.), *Society of Biblical Literature Seminar Papers, 1974* (SBLSP; 2 vols.; Cambridge, MA: Scholars Press, 1974), I, pp. 35-52 (49).

72. Collins, 'Structure', p. 51.

73. Collins, 'Structure', p. 35.

Wisdom Literature.⁷⁴ However, Spittler ignores the importance that the name 'Jobab' had on the translator/redactor of LXX Job, which he readily accepts as the prime influence on the *Testament of Job*. The translator/redactor of LXX Job goes to great lengths to associate Job with the patriarchal ancestors. He describes Job as one who was previously known as Jobab (LXX Job 42.17bα) whose name appears in Gen. 36.33. Job is also portrayed as one who was fifth from Abraham and directly descended from Esau (42.17cα). The *Testament of Job* continues this patriarchal association by highlighting the name Jobab (1.1) and by identifying Job's second wife as Dinah, the daughter of Jacob and Leah (Gen. 20.31; 46.15). Thus, Spittler is wrong to dismiss Job as a non-Torah figure, *per se*, but his point is well taken, namely, that Job is not traditionally viewed as a hero in the stories of the Patriarchs, the collection of characters on which most of the Testaments are based. Nevertheless, the overt effort to associate Job with Torah's heroes parallels pseudonymous practices.

Finally, Spittler prematurely suggests that *Testament of Job* is almost 'devoid of any apocalyptic element'.⁷⁵ A cursory reading of the story demonstrates otherwise, and Spittler himself points out many apocalyptic characteristics present in the text without realizing their nature.⁷⁶ I suspect that what throws Spittler off is the fact that the story has not been overtly *tailored* in an 'apocalyptic' manner as some testaments seem to suggest, even though it does contain many apocalyptic essentials.

I maintain that the confluence of unconventional features of the *Testament of Job*, described above, indicates that the crafters of the work did not need to tailor their story very much. In other words, the general storyline of Job indeed lends itself to an apocalyptic reading in and of itself. It did not require major thematic, theological or plot alterations to conform to the 'apocalyptic' interpretation prevailing in the Hellenistic environment that produced much of the testament writing. In effect, the story of Job simply conformed to the continuing development of the apocalyptic genre. John Collins concurs, saying that the choice of Job by the author 'simply indicates that Job provides the sort of example which the author wished to set before his audience, or at least, could be made to do so'.⁷⁷ Many of the apocalyptic characteristics found in the *Testament of Job* might then be considered natural progressions that were dormant, but present in the original story all along.

---

74. Spittler, 'Testament of Job', p. 832.
75. Spittler, 'Testament of Job', p. 832.
76. Spittler, 'Testament of Job', p. 835. Spittler identifies the use of an interpreting angel of 'light' as something 'characteristic of Jewish and Christian apocalyptic'.
77. Collins, 'Structure', p. 39.

3. *Tradition's Eschatological Interpretations of Job* 95

Letter of James

There is only one explicit reference to the figure of Job in the New Testament.[78] It is found in Jas 5.11: 'Indeed we call blessed those who showed endurance. You have heard of the endurance of Job, and you have seen the purpose of the Lord, how the Lord is compassionate and merciful.'

This verse closes a passage, Jas 5.1-11, which is commonly identified by scholars of James as one that contains multiple eschatological and apocalyptic elements. The passage reads:

> ¹ Come now, you rich people, weep and wail for the miseries that are coming to you. ² Your riches have rotted and your clothes are moth-eaten. ³ Your gold and silver have rusted, and their rust will be evidence against you, and it will eat your flesh like fire. You have laid up treasure *for the last days.* ⁴ Listen! The wages of the laborers who mowed your fields, which you kept back by fraud, cry out, and the cries of the harvesters have reached the ears of the Lord of hosts. ⁵ You have lived on the earth in luxury and in pleasure; you have fattened your hearts in a day of slaughter. ⁶ You have condemned and murdered the righteous one, who does not resist you.
>
> ⁷ Be patient, therefore, beloved, until *the coming* (παρουσίας) *of the Lord.* The farmer waits for the precious crop from the earth, being patient with it until it receives the early and the late rain. ⁸ You also must be patient. Strengthen your hearts, for *the coming* (παρουσία) *of the Lord is near.* ⁹ Beloved, do not grumble against one another, so that you may not be judged. See, the *Judge is standing at the doors!* ¹⁰ As an example of suffering and patience, beloved, take the prophets who spoke in the name of the Lord. ¹¹ Indeed we call blessed those who showed endurance. You have heard of the endurance of Job, and you have seen the purpose of the Lord, how the Lord is compassionate and merciful.

In the text given above, I have highlighted several instances where eschatological and/or apocalyptic phrases clearly appear.[79] Patrick Hartin suggests that 'eschatology provides the horizon for the letter's paraenetical wisdom

---

78. R.P.C. Hanson, 'St Paul's Quotations of the Book of Job', *Theology* 53 (1950), pp. 250-53, argues unconvincingly that Paul refers to Job in Rom. 11.33-35 and Col. 2.14.

79. For a thoroughgoing investigation into an eschatological interpretation of James, see Todd C. Penner, *The Epistle of James and Eschatology: Re-reading an Ancient Christian Letter* (JSNTSup, 121; Sheffield: Sheffield Academic Press, 1996). Penner draws a distinction between apocalyptic and eschatology, the definitions of which, he contests, have become too blurred in recent research. However, Penner's resolution is merely a synchronic division, which considers eschatological anything referring to end times motifs appearing in Second Temple Judaism and the New Testament. He then distinguishes between a 'vertical' and 'horizontal' eschatological feature without articulating how an apocalyptic account can be seen (pp. 106-14).

advice'. Beyond this, Hartin acknowledges that 'James does share some of the thought patterns that are found in an apocalyptic worldview'.[80] In support of this contention, he identifies James's knowledge pertaining to devils (2.19), to the future judgment that separates good and evil (5.1-11), to the future judgment as slaughter (5.5), to the final Judge (5.9) and to the 'crown of life' (1.12) for those who remain perfect.[81]

Bo Reicke also identifies an apocalyptic theme in this section of James by suggesting that the first portion of v. 11 ('we call blessed those who showed endurance') is an imperfect recollection of Dan. 12.12, 'Happy are those who persevere'.[82] Bolstering his assertion is the parallel placement of James's use of this admonition at the end of his 'apocalyptic' passage and at the end of Daniel as a final admonition following the author's eschatological description of the last days. Furthermore, in both Daniel (12.10) and James (5.10), it is clear that the message of endurance is meant to encourage the readers, and, in the context of James, those who will experience suffering.[83]

That Job would be considered a paragon for an apocalyptic message suggests that his story may have been heuristically valuable for the eschatological/apocalyptic context underlying the message of James. Peter Davids connects the eschatology of James with the 'world of intense apocalyptic expectancy' as found in Mark 13, Matthew 24–25, 2 Thessalonians 2 and the book of Revelation. He suggests that James's recipients would easily

---

80. Patrick J. Hartin, *A Spirituality of Perfection: Faith in Action in the Letter of James* (Collegeville: Liturgical Press, 1999), pp. 11, 54-55 n. 51. See also Hartin's, '"Who is Wise and Understanding among You?" (James 3:13): An Analysis of Wisdom, Eschatology, and Apocalypticism in the Epistle of James', in *Society of Biblical Literature Seminar Papers, 1996* (SBLSP, 35; Atlanta: Scholars Press, 1996), pp. 483-503 (494), where he suggests that James and his readers are 'aware of the apocalyptic imagination'. See also Douglas J. Moo, *James* (TNTC; Grand Rapids: Eerdmans, 1986), pp. 43-44, James B. Adamson, *The Epistle of James* (NICNT; Grand Rapids: Eerdmans, 1976), p. 27, and Ralph Martin, *James* (WBC, 48; Waco, TX: Word Books, 1988), p. 197, who all point out the eschatological component. Additionally, Matt A. Jackson-McCabe identifies James as apocalypse via the presence of dualism as manifested between God and the world ('A Letter to the Twelve Tribes in the Diaspora: Wisdom and "Apocalyptic" Eschatology in the Letter of James', in *Society of Biblical Literature Seminar Papers, 1996* [SBLSP, 35; Atlanta: Scholars Press, 1996], pp. 504-17.

81. Hartin, *Perfection*, pp. 54-55. Hartin does not suggest, however, that James should be considered an apocalypse. Instead, the eschatological and apocalyptic elements 'function in the service of the protreptic discourse, and not as an end in themselves'.

82. Bo Reicke, *The Epistle of James, Peter, and Jude* (AB; Garden City, NY: Doubleday, 1964), p. 54.

83. See Donald E. Gowan, 'Wisdom and Endurance in James', *HBT* 15 (1993), pp. 145-53 (145), who argues that Wisdom is the 'divine power which makes possible steadfastness under testing and thus leads to perfection'.

3. *Tradition's Eschatological Interpretations of Job*

recognize the 'apocalyptic teaching' as part of the 'basics of the faith'.[84] Thus, Job's presence in this foundational teaching seems to indicate that Job, and his story, were related to apocalypses by the community to which James had written.[85]

Since a primary message for apocalypses is to encourage communities to persevere in a hope for future reward, James and his audience considered the message of Job an example of writing that we now refer to as apocalypse. Zuckerman also suggests as much: 'Thus, for the author of the Epistle of James, Job can be a paradigm, the perfect example of how to endure persecution and suffering'.[86] Samuel Balentine concurs, noting that the early Christian community appealed to Job as a 'model for those who endure suffering heroically and with patient faith'.[87]

Viewing Job's value in this way is similar to how Arian exegetes seemed to employ Job during the late fourth century CE. Manlio Simonetti and Marco Conti conclude that two extant commentaries on Job are due to the difficult conditions Arianists endured and therefore felt that Job was the 'most suitable to be proposed as a model of firmness and resignation amid different calamities'.[88]

In an interesting divergence from traditional apocalyptic markers, Patrick Tiller has argued that the tension between the rich and the poor found in James is also indicative of apocalypse.[89] Tiller contends that James's use of Jesus' teachings on the poor from the Sermon on the Mount is a reflection of shared apocalyptic impulses. Calling on Psalm 72 and the prophetic voice of Amos 8.4, Tiller maintains that such railings toward the oppressive rich are

---

84. Peter H. Davids, *The Epistle of James: A Commentary on the Greek Text* (Grand Rapids: Eerdmans, 1982), p. 39. Davids is also careful to note that eschatology is not the 'burden' of the book, but is instead the context. This in no way detracts from the importance of Job in this eschatological context. Particularly intriguing is Davids's suggestion that early church resistance to James may have been due to its eschatology, which seemed to be why the book of Revelation received similar treatment from the Early Church.

85. Regardless of the dating one holds for James, this community is clearly one that follows Qumran and precedes much of the early Christian pseudepigraphal writing emerging after the apostolic period. See Reicke, *James*, pp. 5-6, who suggests 90 CE is the most appropriate date, while Moo contends an earlier date of 45–48 CE is closer to the mark (*James*, p. 34).

86. Zuckerman, *Job the Silent*, p. 33.

87. Balentine, *Job* (Smith and Helwys Bible Commentary Series; Macon, GA: Smith & Helwys, 2006), CD-ROM, 'Buried with Job, Raised like Christ'.

88. Manlio Simonetti and Marco Conti, 'Job', in *Ancient Christian Commentary on Scripture* (Downer's Grove, IL: InterVarsity Press, 2006), p. xix.

89. Patrick Tiller, 'The Rich and Poor in James: An Apocalyptic Proclamation', in *Society of Biblical Literature Seminar Papers, 1996* (SBLSP, 35; Atlanta: Scholars Press, 1996), pp. 909-20.

apocalyptic because James 'appeals to eschatology in order to encourage the pious and to threaten the wicked'.[90] Here the wicked refer to those wealthy individuals who economically oppress the poor, the very people God has chosen to protect.

Significantly, Tiller emphasizes Job's classic reiteration of his own innocence in Job 31 as the consummate example of such sensitivity to the poor.[91] Job echoes a 'Deuteronomic obligation to act toward the needy with justice and kindness', so common to James, which is mirrored in Job 31 where Job affirms 'the impropriety of failing to feed and clothe the poor'.[92] In my view, a strength of Tiller's argument, which he did not treat or simply overlooked, is that the clearest apocalyptic passage in James (5.1-11) begins with a rebuke of the rich and closes with a compliment of Job. If incisive critiques of an oppressively affluent elite indicate the possible presence of apocalypse, as Tiller argues, then the role that such a critique plays in the beginning of the apocalyptic passage of Jas 5.1-11 would be an exceptional example of his thesis. Job's presence, based on Tiller's own analysis, as seen above, only confirms this notion. Were Tiller to develop his argument in this way, which seems wholly consistent, James's use of Job further advances the notion that he considered the story of Job suitable for such an apocalyptic assessment of the rich.

Tiller concludes that moral exhortation has likely been present in the growth of apocalyptic, and that far too often scholars become transfixed with the cosmological and 'outlandish' elements normally associated with apocalypses. Such a preoccupation has had the unfortunate effect of neglecting the ethical system that is an important function of apocalypse.[93] The thought of James coincides with the 'dualistic definition of reality that is characteristic of apocalyptic literature', but should not be excluded from the rubric of apocalyptic simply because it does not flaunt the more sensational components that have attracted greater attention.[94] James and Job share a construction of reality in harmony with apocalyptic; furthermore, they both concentrate on understanding one's correct place within that reality.

Clearly the author of James fits Tiller's perspective. The suggestion that apocalypse includes the tension between rich and poor, the placement of Job in the eschatological passage in James and the emphasis on endurance all promote the thesis that the writer of James understood the story of Job as a nascent form of 'apocalypse'.

90. Tiller, 'Rich and Poor', p. 918.
91. Tiller, 'Rich and Poor', pp. 916-17.
92. Tiller, 'Rich and Poor', p. 917.
93. Tiller, 'Rich and Poor', p. 920.
94. Tiller, 'Rich and Poor', p. 920.

Apocalypse of Paul

One final Early Christian source that offers a brief reflection on biblical Job is the pseudepigraphal *Apocalypse of Paul*.[95] This apocalypse likely originated in Greek, but the best-preserved manuscript exists in Latin from the fourth century CE.[96] According to Besserman, the numerous Latin redactions indicate the work's popularity, and translations into Syriac, Armenian, Coptic and Slavonic reinforce his assertion.[97]

The author of this work expounds upon the Apostle Paul's vision of heaven in 2 Corinthians 12, an account in which the apostle is caught up into Paradise. Familiar with the apocalyptic tradition, the author offers the reader a glimpse of heaven's environs.[98] In the forty-ninth section of the apocalypse, several heroes from the Old Testament are paraded before Paul, including Lot, Noah, Elijah, Elisha and Moses. During this procession, Job also appears. After Job is introduced to Paul by an angel, Paul recounts the meeting:

> And he approached and greeted me and said: Brother Paul, you have great honour with God and men. For I am Job who suffered much through thirty years from the suppuration of a wound. And at the beginning of the sores that came out on (from) my body were like grains of wheat; on the third day, however, they became like an ass's foot; and the worms which fell were four fingers long. And the Devil appeared to me for the third time and said to me: *Speak a word against the Lord and die.* I said to him: If it is the will of God that I continue in affliction all the time I live until I die, I shall not cease to praise the Lord God and receive greater reward. For I know that the trials of this world are nothing in comparison to the consolation that comes afterwards. Therefore, Paul, you are blessed, and blessed is the race which has believed through your agency.[99]

Two points from this passage are of particular interest.

First, the directive to Job to 'Speak a word against the Lord and die' comes from the Devil and not from Job's wife, as in the MT (Job 2.9). This change seems to be a development from the *Testament of Job*, where, while Job's wife speaks these words, it is Satan who was 'leading her heart

---

95. Hugo Duensing, 'Apocalypse of Paul', in E. Hennecke and W. Schneemelcher (eds.), *New Testament Apocrypha* (trans. R. Wilson; 2 vols.; Philadelphia: Westminster Press, 1964), II, pp. 755-98.

96. Duensing ('Apocalypse of Paul', p. 755) notes that Origen wrote favorably of the work, which allows for an original date prior to the mid-third century CE.

97. Besserman, *Legend of Job*, p. 66. Duensing provides greater manuscript witness, but concurs with Besserman ('Apocalypse of Paul', II, p. 755).

98. Duensing, 'Apocalypse of Paul', II, p. 756.

99. Duensing, 'Apocalypse of Paul', II, p. 793 (emphasis added).

astray'.[100] Similarly, Dell points out that the Syriac translation of the *Apocalypse of Paul* depicts Job's sons as provoking their father to blaspheme God.[101] The trend apparently suggests that 'the evil one's' role became more transparent. What is initially seen in the MT as a furtive gamble with God transforms later into explicit influence and manipulation. The dualistic battle between God and 'the evil one' becomes more obvious.

The second interesting feature of the passage is Job's reference to his rewards for persevering, and the acknowledgment that the rewards of heaven substantially outweigh the trials on earth. This seems to be a more explicit development of James's admonition to endure in trials (5.11), for which he used Job as an example. In short, the *Apocalypse of Paul* acknowledges the value of perseverance, which, along with hope, typically characterizes apocalyptic themes. Their combined presence in the *Apocalypse of Paul* in the context of Job's story strengthens the proposition that the story of Job participated in apocalyptic thinking more than hitherto acknowledged.

Medieval References

Not surprisingly, the recognition of apocalypticism within Job continued in later ages. Besserman identifies the presence of Job in two eighth- or ninth-century poems; in Cynewulf's *Ascension* (lines 633-58) and in the *Phoenix* (lines 546-75a). In the former, Job is portrayed as a prophet of Christ's resurrection and ascension, while he generally testifies to resurrection in the latter.[102]

After the Middle Ages, a resurgence of interest in Job in the fourteenth and fifteenth centuries may have resulted from devastating wars and plagues.[103] An example from this period can be found in the Old French paraphrase of Job, a version in which Job is shown as having faith in the resurrection and judgment day, further solidifying the apocalyptic aura of the book and bringing the development to a logical high point.[104]

---

100. Robert A. Kraft (ed.), *The Testament of Job* (Missoula, MT: Scholars Press, 1974), p. 47.

101. Dell, *Job as Sceptical Literature*, p. 23 n. 62.

102. Besserman, *The Legend of Job*, p. 72. Besserman notes that his source for the *Ascension* is Gregory the Great's Twenty-Ninth Homily on the Gospels. For the *Phoenix*, the source is Lactantius's *De ave phoenice*. For the *Ascension* in Old English, see Albert S. Cook (ed.), *The Christ of Cynewulf: A Poem in Three Parts* (Boston: Ginn & Company, 1900), pp. 18-33. For the *Phoenix* in Old English, see N.F. Blake (ed.), *The Phoenix* (Manchester: Manchester University Press, 1964).

103. Besserman, *The Legend of Job*, p. 75.

104. See Urban Ohlander (ed.), *A Middle English Metrical Paraphrase of the Old Testament* (5 vols.; Gothenburg: Acta Universitatis Gothoburgensis, 1963), pp. 9-40 (p. 23, I.217).

Lawrence L. Besserman

This brief survey of the Joban tradition has sought to review the most important works associating apocalyptic features with Job, works which all clearly indicate that a very influential stream of tradition viewed Job as an important apocalyptic figure throughout the tradition's history. Besserman's study of this tradition begins with the question, 'Why is Job so often portrayed in the Middle Ages as a prophet of the afterlife, when according to most scholars there is no explicit mention of the afterlife in the Book of Job?'[105] Besserman concludes that the apocryphal and ecclesiastical adaptations of Job became the received tradition of Christianity, and that they, in turn, replaced the biblical material.[106] This conclusion is somewhat puzzling because Besserman also posits the strong presence of a highly influential 'folk tradition' that was 'in either oral or possibly even in written form', a tradition that may have been 'available to the Septuagint translator of Job'.[107]

In my view, Besserman simply raises the question and avoids the prior questions. For example, why did the supposed oral tradition view Job as apocalyptic in the first place? And why has the underlying story of Job been so carefully preserved in the traditions, unlike other pseudonymous apocalypses? My work in Chapter 2 and now here demonstrates that from a literary examination, eschatological features exist in the story of Job, even in its earliest stages prior to the apocalyptic fervor punctuated by the Hellenistic period. Besserman's suggestion that an oral tradition existed is probably correct. The community came to see Job's 'apocalyptic DNA' rather easily. Instead of manipulating the story to accommodate for the rise of apocalyptic thinking, Jewish and Christian tradition enhanced that which was already existent.

Still, while Besserman is wrong to underestimate the apocalyptic personality that is inherent to Job, he is correct to recognize that the role the LXX version of Job played in early and later Christian communities probably cannot be overestimated. Indeed, it is worth briefly considering just how substantial this role was, since my argument, while not reliant on the LXX, could certainly capitalize on an appreciated view of the LXX.

The LXX in the Early Christian Church

It is certainly true that the LXX was held in high esteem in the Early Christian Church—it was their 'Old Testament'. Subsequently, the LXX version of Job must have had a tremendous impact on later traditions,

---

105. Besserman, *The Legend of Job*, p. 2.
106. Besserman, *The Legend of Job*, pp. 114-15.
107. Besserman, *The Legend of Job*, p. 39.

especially in the Early Christian Church. In a recent, and much-needed study on the role of the LXX in the Early Christian Church, Martin Hengel acknowledges that the 'use of the LXX as Holy Scripture is practically as old as the church itself. For New Testament writings, beginning with Paul, it is the rule.'[108]

Naturally, when Jerome prepared the Vulgate from the Hebrew,[109] no small controversy ensued, and Hengel traces much of the early debates within Early Christian circles regarding the authority of the LXX relative to the supposed Hebrew original.[110] With specific respect to Job, Theodore of Mopsuestia, referred to an oral tradition of Job that he felt was the 'true' history of Job over against the Hebrew, which he considered a fiction.[111]

While these debates concerning the authority of the LXX versus the Hebrew seem far removed from the modern world, the debate has recently regained momentum.[112] A recent and persuasive attempt to elevate the status of the LXX comes from Møgens Müller.[113]

---

108. Martin Hengel, *The Septuagint as Christian Scripture: Its Prehistory and the Problem of Its Canon* (trans. Mark E. Biddle; Edinburgh: T. & T. Clark, 2002). The classic introductory text on the LXX is Swete's, *An Introduction to the Old Testament in Greek*. A more recent and wonderfully accessible work is Jobes and Silva's *Invitation to the Septuagint*. See my review of the latter in *JETS* 44 (2001), pp. 721-22.

109. For a concise treatment on the history of the Vulgate, see Ernst Würtheim, *The Text of the Old Testament* (trans. Erroll F. Rhodes; Grand Rapids: Eerdmans, rev. and enlarged edn, 1995), pp. 95-99.

110. Hengel, *The Septuagint as Christian Scripture*, pp. 51-54, for Augustine's attempt at a compromise, which comes from *The City of God* 18.43. See Augustine, *The City of God against the Pagans* (ed. and trans. R.W. Tyson; Cambridge: Cambridge University Press, 1998), pp. 884-86.

111. Besserman, *The Legend of Job*, p. 39. Besserman cites Giovanni Domenico Mansi, *Sacrorum conciliorum nova et amplissima collectio* (55 vols.; Florence, Venice and Paris, 1758–1798), IX, pp. 224-27. See also J.P. Migne, *PG* 66, pp. 697-98. For an introduction to Theodore of Mopsuestia, see Rowan A. Greer, *Theodore of Mopsuestia: Exegete and Theologian* (Westminster: The Faith Press, 1961), and Dimitri Z. Zaharopolous, *Theodore of Mopsuestia on the Bible: A Study of his Old Testament Exegesis* (New York: Paulist Press, 1989).

112. See the following: Pierre Benoit, OP, 'The Inspiration of the Septuagint', in *Jesus and the Gospel* (2 vols.; trans. Benet Weatherhead; London: Darton, Longman & Todd, 1973), I, pp. 1-10, and his 'L'inspiration des Septante d'après les pères', in *Exégèse et théologie* (Paris: Cerf, 1968), pp. 69-89; François G. Dreyfus, 'L'inspiration de la Septante: quelques difficultés à surmonter', in *Revue des sciences philosophiques et théologiques* 49 (1965), pp. 210-20; Roger Lapointe, 'Les traductions de la Bible sont-elles inspirées?', *Science et esprit* 23 (1971), pp. 69-83; Harry Orlinsky, 'The Septuagint as Holy Writ and the Philosophy of the Translators', *HUCA* 46 (1975), pp. 89-114. Charles Perrot, 'L'inspiration des Septante et le pouvoir scripturaire', in *ΚΑΤΑ ΤΟΥΣ Ο' Selon les Septante: trente études sur la Bible grecque des Septante, en hommage á*

For Müller, the LXX serves as more than just a witness to the development of Jewish and Christian traditions. The LXX offered new prophetic interpretations relevant for their time. This proposal is somewhat analogous to Wellhausen's contention that the prophets embarked on a new religion themselves.[114] Müller states:

> To all appearances any idea that a Hebrew Bible text should already at this time, i.e., the 4th, 3rd and 2nd centuries BC, have been so established as to allow an evaluation of the Greek translation on its basis, had better be abandoned. On the contrary it seems reasonable to see the Greek translations as part of a process of ever changing traditions which only gradually came to a standstill when one particular Hebrew text became normative.[115]

Later, Müller argues that until 70 CE, 'the Hebrew text was fluid, i.e. there was a plurality of Bible texts'.[116] Thus, the many so-called discrepancies found in the various LXX translations do not necessarily indicate a lack of accuracy on the part of the translators. In fact, Müller labels what many consider the Hebrew 'original' as merely a 'coping stone' that only later found its way into common use.[117]

In a recent and stimulating reflection on the impact of the Dead Sea Scrolls on scholarship, Eugene Ulrich declares that Qumran Studies confirm the pluriformity of the Hebrew text rather than the MT.[118] Subsequently, greater attention needs to be given to variant editions, including the LXX version of Job.[119] Since neither the MT nor a so-called proto-MT can be considered authoritative before Qumran, the LXX and Samaritan Pentateuch 'have regained their rightful status alongside the MT as serious witnesses to the Hebrew Bible in antiquity, and [so it can be argued] that the MT was not

---

Marguerite Harl (Paris: Cerf, 1995), pp. 169-83; Richard Rex, 'St John Fisher's Treatise on the Authority of the Septuagint', *JTS* 43 (1992), pp. 55-72. Most assertions upholding the superiority, or at least the value, of the LXX share several common arguments, many of which are merely upgrades of earlier statements. For example, most appeal to the wide use of the LXX by both the authors of the New Testament as well as the Early Church Fathers. Many argue that the translation of the LXX must have been inspired because it was written for a new divine dispensation in which pagans could be proselytized.

113. Møgens Müller, 'The Septuagint as the Bible of the New Testament Church: Some Reflections', *SJOT* 7 (1993), pp. 194-207. Müller further develops his case in a book-length treatment, *The First Bible of the Church: A Plea for the Septuagint* (JSOTSup, 206; Sheffield: Sheffield Academic Press, 1996).

114. Müller, 'The Septuagint', p. 196.
115. Müller, 'The Septuagint', p. 197.
116. Müller, 'The Septuagint', p. 198.
117. Müller, 'The Septuagint', p. 199.
118. Eugene Ulrich, 'Our Sharper Focus on the Bible and Theology Thanks to the Dead Sea Scrolls', *CBQ* 66 (2004), pp. 1-24.
119. Ulrich, 'Our Sharper Focus', pp. 8-9.

the standard text of the biblical books or collection in the Second Temple period, but simply one of the available text forms'.[120]

Such statements further support Müller's argument that the text traditions of the LXX should be 'included in the speculations on the shape of the Jewish Bible in centuries around the birth of Christ'.[121] Doing so ultimately allows the LXX to be treated on equal terms with the MT, an idea that would have profound implications for my argument.

For example, if LXX Job were considered authoritative today, the eschatological elements contained within it could not be as readily dismissed as they might otherwise be. Augustine's great Solomonic declaration that both the Hebrew and the LXX should be considered inspired simply demands that greater attention be given to the apocalyptic impulses so clear in LXX Job and only latent in MT. These impulses, in turn, further confirm the apocalyptic trajectory that the Joban tradition contained from its very inception.

Confirming this assertion is the fact that Origen, in his defense of the LXX, cites the specific verse in LXX Job referring to the resurrection.[122] In addition, Origen claimed that the Greek version produced by Theodotion, a convert to Judaism who revised the existing Greek *toward* the Hebrew, also contained the resurrection verse in a similar sense to that of the LXX.[123] Furthermore, many postulate that Theodotion's Greek translation was based on an earlier Greek version very similar in sense to his rendering, which both Symmachus and Aquila possibly used as a base for their translations.[124]

Conclusion

In the final analysis, it is not conclusive that the specific reference to Job's resurrection in the LXX was a Christian 'addition'. The eschatological references are found in various Jewish versions of Job too, thereby adding further credibility to the notion that the story of Job itself may have had a greater 'apocalyptic' feel than otherwise thought. I conclude that the story of Job, and its interpretive tradition, does in fact contain significant eschatological dimensions. Therefore, the evidence defeats the claim identified in Chapter 2 that Job is devoid of eschatological impulses.

---

120. Ulrich, 'Our Sharper Focus', p. 13.
121. Müller, 'The Septuagint', p. 199.
122. Origen, 'Letter to Africanus', in *Ante-Nicene Christian Library* (trans. F. Crombie; Edinburgh: T. & T. Clark, 1869), X, p. 373.
123. Origen, 'Letter to Africanus', p. 373.
124. Jobes and Silva, *Invitation to the Septuagint*, pp. 41-42. Jobes points out (p. 37) that, unfortunately, none of these works has survived.

However, even if tradition's clear indication that Job was a story receptive to apocalyptic interpretation does not convince, Collins reminds us that not all apocalypses mention the end times. He writes:

> When the most significant action is situated among the heavenly beings then the main hope of human beings is to be elevated to this higher sphere of life. If human beings are elevated to the heavenly form of life, whether this happens by a resurrection after death or already before death, the restrictions of the human condition are cast off and in particular death is transcended.[125]

Such an observation corresponds neatly with the apex of Job's story, the Yahweh speeches, because it is there that the most significant lessons are learned. It is there that Job rises above the earthly chains of ineffective reflection.

My proposal, that Job is a nascent form of apocalypse, shows its validity if it passes the test of interpreting and uniting all the seemingly disparate literary units of the book. I now turn to that effort.

---

125. Collins, 'Apocalyptic Eschatology', pp. 25, 30.

4

READING JOB THROUGH APOCALYPTIC EYES

Introduction

In this chapter I offer a reading of Job employing the apocalyptic proposal that I developed earlier. In effect, I am testing my hypothesis. I pay special attention to the three revelations outlined below since they constitute the foundation of my approach.

I first propose a unique literary structure of Job, one which provides generous parameters from which to proceed. Conventional approaches to Job typically offer the following literary structure:[1]

Job 1–2	Narrative Prologue
Job 3	Job's Lament
Job 4–27	Debate between Job and his Friends
4–14	Cycle One
15–21	Cycle Two
22–27	Cycle Three
Job 28	Wisdom Poem
Job 29–31	Job's Oath of Perseverance
Job 32–37	Elihu Speeches
Job 38–42.6	Yahweh Speeches
42.7–42.17	Narrative Epilogue

Treating Job as proto-apocalyptic, I suggest that a broad structure based on the revelations is more appropriate.[2] Interestingly, dividing Job in this way yields a structure that is similar to traditional outlines. Thus, I offer the following broad outline:

---

1. See, for example, Blenkinsopp, *Wisdom and Law in the Old Testament*, pp. 52-53. Pope collapses Job 3–31 into one 'Dialogue' or 'Symposium' (*Job*, p. xiii). Murphy (*The Book of Job: A Short Reading*) includes ch. 3 in the first cycle of debates.

2. Raymond E. Brown divides the book of Revelation broadly in somewhat similar fashion: Prologue (1.1-3); Letters to the Seven Churches (1.4–3.22), Part I of the Revelatory Experience (4.1–11.19), Part II of the Revelatory Experience (12.1–22.5), Epilogue (with Concluding Blessing) (22.6-21) (*An Introduction to the New Testament* [New York: Doubleday, 1997], pp. 780-95). He further subdivides the larger sections into more manageable units.

1.1–4.11	Job's Demise and Challenge
4.12–28.22	Revelation of Humanity's Unrighteousness: Job Persecuted
28.23–37.24	Revelation of Humanity's Lack of Wisdom: Job Encouraged
38.1–42.6	Revelation of Humanity's Powerlessness: Job Repents
42.7–42.17	Job's Victory and Rewards

Further subdivision is certainly required to account for the nuances present in each of the larger units, and I will incorporate these smaller units in the reading. However, the broad framework I propose allows the reader to recognize the timely placement of each of these revelations according to content instead of basing division on changes in genre, which may not reflect the cohering intention of the author/redactor.

Deviating from certain internal textual divisions is not uncommon or unnatural. For example, one practical way to divide Daniel is along language, that is, based on the book's use of Hebrew from 1.1 to 2.4a, Aramaic from 2.4b to 7.28, and again Hebrew from 8.1 to 12.13. Such a structure is legitimate, but it breaks up the contents of Daniel since it divides most easily into two parts, the court tales (chs. 1–6) and the visions (chs. 7–12).

Since the following interpretation presupposes that the final form of Job represents some nascent form of apocalypse, I am suggesting that the ancient writers would have understood that Job was meant to be interpreted through the paradigm of such a style of writing, though ancient interpreters would not have articulated that style as 'proto apocalypse'. Thus, the thematic expectations of perseverance and hope would have been acknowledged and assumed at the outset, which I will further demonstrate below.[3]

Up to this point, I have concentrated my efforts on identifying apocalyptic literary features, which are particularly germane to a study of genre. That said, I have purposely limited my comments on matters of themes, messages or a theology of apocalypses. At this stage of interpretation, however, the assumption of a governing genre naturally presupposes that certain theological freight is carried along as well. More will be said on these matters later, but for now, my goal is to interpret Job from the eyes of a 'first time' reader. Such an attempt, though laden with difficulties, may assist the more seasoned reader of Job in laying aside some of their own assumptions concerning Job and its governing genre.

Job 1.1–4.11: Job's Demise and Challenge

Job 1–2: Prologue

In Job 1.1-5, Job is described as a perfect (תם) one who was righteous and feared God. The numbers attest to his perfection; seven sons, three

---

3. LaSor, Hubbard, and Bush (eds.), *Old Testament Survey*, p. 569.

daughters, 7000 sheep and 3000 camels.[4] Job is such a good man that he even offered sacrifices on behalf of his children, lest they 'cursed God in their hearts' (1.5).

But then the reader is immediately removed from the material world and is confronted with cosmological imagery. Job 1.6-12 depicts the heavenly realm of God where 'the sons of god' and 'the Satan' seem to congregate routinely. God and the Satan communicate directly with each other, and the reader is inserted into the divine council, which is a feature frequently found in the classic apocalypses.[5]

At this point in the story, there is no indication that this work qualifies as 'wisdom'. With respect to God's role in the prologue, Norman Habel remarks, 'This is not the typical God of the wisdom tradition', and later, 'God acts in a way that appears to contradict the typical *modus operandi* of God in the wisdom tradition'.[6]

As the first chapter unfolds, the reader sees that the story hinges on the so-called wager between God and the Satan.[7] Significantly, it could be argued that the Satan plays the largest role in the opening chapters. Christopher Rowland notes that one of the angels that emerges is 'the representative of all that is opposed to God, namely Satan'. He later observes, 'Jewish apocalyptic literature never really loses the view of Satan which we find in passages like Job 1–2'.[8] The Satan's prominent presence may alert the reader that something akin to a modern apocalypse is before them, and an initial assessment of this likelihood is probably unconsciously considered.

Fundamentally, the Satan questions the motives behind Job's blamelessness. He argues that Job is only trying to please God for his own personal benefit, and that if all Job's wealth is removed, Job's true nature will be revealed and he will be exposed as a charlatan. The Satan is so confident that Job will fail, that he assures God that Job will 'curse (ברך)[9] you to your face' (Job 1.11), which is no small matter. Exodus 22.28a reads, 'You shall not revile (קלל) God'. God consents to the challenge but restricts the Satan's ability to harm; he may harm anything but not Job's person. Signifying subservience, the Satan silently accepts these parameters and departs.

---

4. See Andersen, *Job*, p. 79, who comments on Job's completeness as a product of divine favor.

5. Adela Yarbro Collins, 'Apocalyptic Themes in Biblical Literature', *Interpretation* 53 (1999), pp. 117-30 (119).

6. Norman Habel, 'In Defense of God the Sage', in Perdue and Gilpin (eds.), *The Voice from the Whirlwind*, pp. 21-38 (26).

7. I label it 'so-called' because, as I will show later, the exchange between God and the Satan simply may not depict a wager, *per se*.

8. Rowland, *The Open Heaven*, p. 91.

9. Most argue that ברך is a euphemistic replacement of קלל, since the latter would be considered too offensive (see Würtheim, *The Text of the Old Testament*, p. 112).

4. *Reading Job through Apocalyptic Eyes*

This exchange between God and the Satan launches the main plot of the story, but the way the Satan challenges God is absolutely critical to understanding the development of the story. In fact, if this element is missed, the reader will jeopardize a fair interpretation of the story from its very inception. In the NRSV, Job 1.11 reads:

ואולם שלח־נא ידך וגע בכל־אשר־לו אם־לא על־פניך יברכך

> But stretch out your hand now, and touch all that he has, and he will curse you to your face.

This translation is typical of most.[10] However, it misses an important nuance to the second half of the Satan's words to God. Interpreted literally, the second half of the Hebrew reads, 'If he does not curse (bless) you to your face'. Edwin M. Good argues that this phrase is 'rhetorically a formula of curse upon the speaker'.[11] The implications for his assertion turn the traditional interpretation of Job entirely on its head.

Good notes that most curses in the Hebrew Bible omit the final clause but imply some disastrous result, 'if he does not curse (bless) you to your face, [may something awful happen to me]'.[12] In other words, the Satan issues a 'self-curse' and is strongly assuming that Job will curse God. It simply cannot be overstated that in offering the self-curse, the Satan 'is laying himself drastically on the line'.[13] Good even suggests that since we do not hear from the Satan after ch. 2, the Satan 'was put out of commission' because of the self-curse.[14]

Others argue that the oath is directed to God rather than the Satan. T. Linafelt translates, 'If he does not bless you to your face—[may something horrible happen to you.]'[15] Linafelt rejects what he terms 'the standard euphemism theory' whereby ברך is interpreted negatively (curse) instead of positively (blessing).[16]

10. The NAB reads, 'surely he will blaspheme you to your face'.
11. Good, 'Problem of Evil', p. 53. See also Good's *In Turns of Tempest: A Reading of Job with a Translation* (Stanford: Stanford University Press, 1990), pp. 194-95. Good notes that Dhorme and others have recognized that a curse formula exists, but only St Thomas intuited that the end of the curse should be included in the biblical text. St Thomas proposed that *malum mihi accidat* ('let evil happen to me') be included (*Expositio in libro Sancti Iob*, p. 411 n. 15).
12. Good, 'The Problem of Evil', p. 53. F. Rachel Magdalene, 'Curse', in D.N. Freedman (ed.), *Eerdmans Dictionary of the Bible* (Grand Rapids: Eerdmans, 2000), p. 302, writes that self-curse was common in the ancient Near East and is used in 1 Kgs 8.31-32.
13. Good, 'Problem of Evil', p. 53.
14. Good, 'Problem of Evil', p. 54.
15. T. Linafelt, 'The Undecidability of ברך in the Prologue to Job and Beyond', in *Biblical Interpretation* 4 (1996), pp. 154-72 (164-65).
16. Linafelt, 'The Undecidability', p. 157. Magdalene, 'Curse', p. 301, argues that in the case of Job 2.9, ברך was likely an early scribal substitute for the more common קלל

As will be shown, interpreting ברך as a blessing attempts to redeem Job's wife in Job 2.9. However, such efforts are untenable simply because Job clearly rebukes his wife's words in order to defend God's actions, even though Job suffers. Still, Linafelt's work further demonstrates the significance that recognizing the oath formula has on interpreting Job. Good's proposal, by contrast, is a more faithful expression of the narrative.

Two important ramifications from Good's suggestion emerge. First, what Good does not suggest, but can easily be deduced from his line of thinking, is that it is possible to solve the puzzling question of why the Satan is not punished by God in the epilogue. Is it possible to conclude that there is no reason to punish the Satan in the epilogue because the Satan has earned his just desserts from his self-curse? We do not know what the punishment was because the Satan did not mention it. Good ponders whether the Satan's punishment was his downward spiral into the figure of the Devil, never to appear before God again.[17]

Second, the narrative's trajectory is firmly established by Good's proposal. Since the Satan has so much at stake, whatever that is, he has a vested interest in seeing Job curse God to his face. The Satan's self-curse seems to dispose of the idea of a wager. The Satan does not win anything if Job does curse God to his face, while the Satan's self-curse assures some negative outcome if Job does not curse God to his face. In other words, the Satan is counting on Job cursing God to his face and nothing short of that will suffice because of the self-curse.

God relents and grants the Satan authority to touch all that Job has, but he is forbidden to harm Job (1.12). Up to this point, the story is all about a cosmological tussle between God and the Satan in the heavenly court, which can be viewed as a form of the combat myth so prevalent in apocalypses.[18] The righteous Job is caught between these two otherworldly beings, and the reader, observing from a distance, is forced to wonder how this challenge is going to play itself out and whether or not Job can survive. Most importantly, the reader wants to know if Job is eventually going to curse God to his face, as the Satan so brazenly forecasted. The Satan figure is not as interested in luring Job into various acts of sin as he is in tempting him to the most egregious sin—disloyalty to God,[19] which would be realized if Job curses God to his face.

because God is the object of the cursing by Job's wife. While Magdalene does not apply this to the other uses of ברך in the prologue, her argument is persuasive and may explain the enigmatic use of the word.

17. Good, 'Problem of Evil', p. 54. This suggestion might not be as flippant as one might think because it appears that scholarship has come to a level of consensus that curses originate in the holiness of God (Magdalene, 'Curse', p. 301).

18. Collins, 'Apocalyptic Themes', p. 123.

19. LaSor, Hubbard, and Bush (eds.), *Old Testament Survey*, p. 494.

In vv. 13-22, Job loses all of his material possessions, servants and children. Even after suffering such heinous losses, Job blesses the Lord with the famous words of 1.21, 'the Lord gave, and the Lord has taken away; blessed be the name of the Lord'. Yet, despite Job's very own words of blessing, the narrator is compelled to extol Job's righteousness in v. 22, 'In all this Job did not sin or charge God with wrong'.

Why is this verse needed when Job has already spoken words of allegiance to God? In my view, it is an elaboration that specifically counters the Satan's prediction in 1.11. The narrator wants to ensure that the reader knows that Job did not, in fact, curse God to his face.

Chapter 2 begins almost identically as Job 1.6 with a repeat of the heavenly scene where the sons of God and the Satan are present again. In v. 3 the reader notices a departure from what was presented in ch. 1 when God commends Job's persistence, almost tauntingly, in the wake of the Satan's initial attacks on Job. The Satan retorts, 'Skin for skin! All that people have they will give to save their lives. But stretch out your hand now and touch his bone and his flesh, and he will curse you to your face' (2.4-5).

Distraught at his initial failure and concerned (if not insecure) that his self-curse (אם־לא) might be imposed, the Satan is forced to take his challenge to the next level. Again he speculates that under the right amount of pressure, Job will curse God to his face. God relents again, but this time he limits the Satan by ensuring that Job's life is spared. Satan inflicts Job with 'loathsome sores' from his head to his toes, and Job finds himself sitting in a 'dung' heap.[20]

At this point, the nadir of Job's life, his wife is introduced, stating in 2.9, 'Do you still persist in your integrity? Curse (ברך) God, and die.' Job rebukes her for speaking as foolish women do, stating that followers of God should accept whatever God provides, whether good or bad. With this statement, Job again demonstrates his allegiance to God. Once again, the narrator is compelled to add something to reconfirm that Job's actions did not result in the way the Satan anticipated, 'In all of this Job did not sin with his lips' (2.10).

Unlike the narrator's earlier portrait of Job's loyalty to God, this second confirmation explicitly refers to Job not sinning with words from his mouth. In other words, in both sets of upheaval, the narrator is very careful to point out that Job is not cursing God, let alone to God's face.

In my view, Job 2.9-10 further solidifies the main plot to the story of Job and, as such, reconfirms the paradigm through which the reader should

---

20. I have argued that instead of finding himself in an 'ash' heap, as traditionally accepted, Job actually is sitting in an even more repugnant 'dung' heap. See my 'Critical Note on Job 2:8', *Bulletin of the International Organization for Septuagint and Cognate Studies* 36 (2003), pp. 87-92.

ultimately interpret the story. These verses represent the climax of the prologue because when Job's wife recommends that he should curse God and die, she is, in effect, taking up the Satan's cause. If Job were to curse God, as the Satan predicted he would, then the Satan proves that God is wrong; and the reader recognizes this. The Satan is unsuccessful and essentially recruits Job's wife, who is fundamentally acting as Satan's agent by encouraging Job to curse God.[21] Augustine, Chrysostom and Calvin all viewed Job's wife as a temptress, with Chrysostom suggesting that the only reason she did not die with the rest of the family was so that she could remain as an acute plague to Job.[22]

But note carefully her words: 'Do you still *persist* in your integrity?' (2.9). Up to this point the reader is wondering the same thing: 'Will Job persist?' As noted, one of the hallmarks of apocalypse is to engender perseverance, especially in the context of a cosmic struggle with forces that are in opposition to God. Furthermore, Job's wife wonders why Job is persisting in his integrity. The Hebrew underlying 'perfect' is a form of the root תמם, as is the very word used to describe Job as 'blameless' in the introduction (1.1). She directly challenges Job to recant his fidelity to God, which is exactly what the Satan needs.

The final section of ch. 2 (2.11-13), simply serves to introduce the three friends without any particular comment about their character, except to depict them as authentically concerned about Job's miserable state. They appear as supporters of Job, willing to remain with him for a full seven days and nights. Their entrance, along with Job's wife, indicates a shift from the cosmic realm to the earthly.

It is interesting to see how large a role cursing God plays in the first two chapters of Job.[23] Recall that Job was concerned even for his children's potential cursing (ברך) of God in their hearts (1.5). The Satan picks up on this pious concern and uses it against Job, twice claiming that under the right conditions, Job will curse (ברך) God to his face. Finally, Job's wife demands that Job curse (ברך) God to his face.

---

21. Norman Habel says, 'the narrator has Job's wife serve as the earthly mouthpiece for the hidden Satan' (*The Book of Job*, p. 96).

22. Pope, *Job*, p. 22. See, however, David Penchansky, 'Job's Wife: The Satan's Handmaid', in D. Penchansky and P. Redditt (eds.), *Shall Not the Judge of the Earth Do What is Right? Studies on the Nature of God in Tribute to James Crenshaw* (Winona Lake, IN: Eisenbrauns, 2000), pp. 223-38, and Claire Mathews McGinnis, 'Playing the Devil's Advocate in Job: On Job's Wife', in S. Cook, C. Patton and J. Watts (eds.), *The Whirlwind: Essays on Job, Hermeneutics and Theology in Memory of Jane Morse* (JSOTSup, 336; Sheffield: Sheffield Academic Press, 2001), pp. 121-41, who both seek to 'rehabilitate' Job's wife's image and reputation.

23. Linafelt, 'The Undecidability', pp. 154-72.

4. *Reading Job through Apocalyptic Eyes* 113

Thus, in the first two chapters, the primary thematic question is whether Job will curse God to his face or persevere in his faithfulness. The repetition of this theme is countered only by the narrator's twofold response that Job did not capitulate. The reader observes the obvious theme of perseverance under persecution, as well as the overt cosmic and dualistic imagery. These markers are absorbed and categorized during the reader's initial genre impression. In my view, from the very outset, the reader is prepared for a story that is more along the lines of apocalypse than some didactic exhortation.

Job 3

Chapter 3 shifts to Job's reaction to his plight. It is true that the story makes a dramatic break from narrative into poetry, but this does not warrant separating ch. 3 from the prologue because the storyline has not been disrupted. Again, the entrance of the friends at the end of ch. 2, who arrive in order to 'console' and 'comfort' Job (2.11), functions as a transition suggesting continuity in the plot.

Job's lengthy curse and lament is the kind of reaction any reader would expect from someone who suffered as egregiously as Job. However, as the reader observes Job's disposition altering from patience to anguish, they remember the interpretive paradigm formed by the cosmological discussion between God and the Satan. In that context, the reader simply wonders if Job, in his depressed state, will actually curse God to his face.

The first verse responds to this question, 'After this Job opened his mouth and cursed (קלל) the day of his birth'.[24] Given the predominance of ברך in the prologue, it is interesting that the narrator chooses another word to describe cursing the first time it is associated directly with Job. Perhaps the narrator's zeal to disassociate Job from even the possible hint of cursing God led him to choose קלל over ברך. Job does not curse God, but his cursing the day of his birth and the following incantations are latent with apocalyptic overtones. These only enhance the level of his despair and also remind the reader of the gravity the cosmic struggle plays in the story.

The initial apocalyptic sense emerges in the first ten verses, which depict Job requesting a complete reversal of creation. In contrast to Gen. 1.3, 'Let there be light', Job complains, 'Let that day [of his birth] be darkness' (Job 3.4).[25] Job's penchant with darkness is further elaborated in the following verses, which include an appeal to those who curse the sea and can rouse Leviathan. The sea represents both the apocalyptic forces of evil and chaos, while Leviathan is the apocalyptic ally of death who battled Baal in the

---

24. BDB states that קלל is interpreted as curse in the Piel and Pual forms only.
25. On this point, see Murphy, *A Short Reading of the Book of Job*, p. 19.

Ugaritic creation accounts.²⁶ Many of these images will re-appear in the Yahweh speeches, but then as expressions of God's handiwork.

The incantations in vv. 3-10 are not so much challenging God's role in creation as they are referring to Job's personal misery. In other words, Job should not be viewed as cursing God in any of these so-called curses, as some intimate.²⁷ It is better to identify the first ten verses as one curse, which is not the curse that the Satan was trying to provoke in Job.²⁸

The remainder of the chapter, vv. 11-26, represents a lament that also employs creation language to exacerbate Job's despair in the context of God's creative order. The joyous Sabbath rest from Gen. 2.1-3 is transformed into the silent rest of Sheol. In Sheol, 'the weary are at rest' (3.17).²⁹ Light is contrasted with darkness, with preference given to the latter—'Why is light given to one in misery?' (3.20)—over against light breaking through the primeval darkness of the pre-creative world (Gen. 1.2-3).

Habel identifies an 'intricate pattern of reversals: from birth to prebirth death, from order to primordial chaos, from light to darkness, from gloom in life to pleasure in the underworld...'³⁰ These dramatic reversals, 'ranging from the cosmogonic and universal to the existential and individual' were used by the narrator to 'shock the audience and thereby prepare it for a traditional rebuke by the friends'.³¹

I question whether the narrator intended to prepare the reader for the ensuing discussion with the friends. The first-time reader does not yet know that the friends intend to speak to Job. Furthermore, it is not altogether clear that Job is directly addressing any part of his lament to God, as many conclude.³² Instead, Job's first words in ch. 3 seem to tantalize the reader, who is anxiously waiting to read whether or not Job is going to curse God. Anticipating this anxious disposition on the part of the reader, the narrator begins ch. 3, 'After this Job opened his mouth *and cursed*...' The reader quickly identifies the narrator's shift from ברך to קלל, which reveals that something new is happening, and eventually discovers that Job does not curse God. Nevertheless, the reader continues to filter out the ongoing story through the prism that was so intricately established in the prologue.

---

26. Collins, 'Apocalyptic Themes', pp. 122, 124.
27. See Hartley, *The Book of Job*, p. 101, and Habel, *Job*, pp. 102-103, who concurs with my assessment.
28. Murphy, *A Short Reading of the Book of Job*, p. 19, concurs.
29. See C.S. Rodd, *The Book of Job* (Philadelphia: Trinity Press International, 1990), p. 10.
30. Habel, *Job*, p. 105.
31. Habel, *Job*, pp. 105-106.
32. Claus Westermann, *The Structure of the Book of Job*, p. 37, argues that it is not directed specifically to God.

Job 4.1-11

The first five verses of ch. 4 paint a picture of Eliphaz cautiously approaching Job and pointing out that at an earlier time Job was the strong person helping others. Now Job finds himself in the opposite position, and Job does not like it. Gradually the reader discerns that this 'friend' is not as transparent and sympathetic as one might have presumed from the final verses in ch. 2.

Verses 6-11 confirm the reader's suspicion. Eliphaz asserts in v. 6, 'Is not your fear of God your confidence, and the integrity (תֻּמַּת) of your ways your hope?' Two dramatic points are worth noting in this verse. First, Job has not claimed that his fear of God was his confidence or his strength, nor has he claimed that his integrity was his hope. The fact that Job is considered תָּם and one who fears God (1.1) is not based on Job's self-assessment; up to this point in the story, they are based both on the narrator (1.1) and God's assessment (1.8). As Murphy intimates, Eliphaz is attempting to trap Job by using these very characteristics in convincing Job that he has done something wrong.[33] By contrast, Andersen, and most others, deny that Eliphaz is accusing Job of sinning because they tend to presuppose that Eliphaz's theological starting point is the same as Job's.[34] However, such an assertion by commentators is simply without warrant at this point in the narrative because Job has yet to make a theological rationalization for his situation. The reader is better off holding to the existing knowledge, namely, that Job has not actually done anything to merit his current demise. The reader, unlike Eliphaz, knows that already and implicitly Job knows it as well.

The second dramatic point in v. 6 is that what Eliphaz is ascribing to Job is essentially what the Satan alleged, namely, that Job served God only because he was confident that God would bless him and that his righteousness would be his means of gaining favor with God. It was God, and only God, who identified Job as righteous. The Satan has challenged the motivation behind that righteousness, and now Eliphaz has taken up the Satan's mantle and is beginning to establish an argument against Job that is a misrepresentation from the beginning of his very first words to Job. The reader recognizes this and realizes that Job is left to his own devices.

In vv. 7-11 Eliphaz utilizes traditional, reliable wisdom to emphasize his foundational deception. In Job's world, Eliphaz's theology, that those who fear God will be blessed, is hard to combat. Who can argue with his words in v. 8, 'As I have seen, those who plow iniquity and sow trouble reap the same'. Eliphaz begins a line of attack against Job that all three friends take up. Traditional wisdom will be invoked to support their deceptive contention that Job is wrong to claim that he is righteous and therefore innocent.

---

33. Murphy, *A Short Reading of the Book of Job*, p. 21.
34. Andersen, *Job*, p. 112.

Alonso Schökel concurs with this finding and depicts the wife and friends in collusion with the Satan. He writes, 'Job's wife and the friends, in an indirect way, support the thesis of the Satan'.[35] And again, 'the friends take up and amplify the position of the Satan'.[36] Still later he reveals why the friends seek so desperately to elicit a confession of guilt from Job, 'to confess his guilt would be to disprove what God said in the prologue, it would be to declare that his friends, and through them the Satan, had been right'.[37]

Is it any wonder that God singles out Eliphaz for a special rebuke near the end of the story (Job 42.7)?[38] It is Eliphaz's deceptive portrayal of Job's condition that serves as the foundation for the following dialogue, which essentially persecutes Job because he claims to be innocent. All of the friends' arguments (and Elihu's) in one way or another can be traced back to Eliphaz's misrepresentation. Recalling the primary plot, that God and the Satan have a cosmological discussion and that the Satan needs Job to capitulate and curse God to his face, Eliphaz is unknowingly serving as one of the Satan's advocates in the same way that Job's wife had. Mindful of this foundational plot, the reader wonders if Job will be able to persevere.

Job 4.12–28.22: Revelation of Humanity's Unrighteousness— Job Persecuted

Job 4.12-21; 5.1-8: Beginning the First Cycle
Eliphaz begins this section by transitioning from his misrepresentation of Job and dependence on a theology of retribution to a description of the setting from which he received his vision. Verses 12-16 set the stage for the ensuing vision:

> ¹²Now a word came stealing to me,
>   my ear received the whisper of it.
> ¹³Amid thoughts from visions of the night,
>   when deep sleep falls on mortals,
> ¹⁴dread came upon me, and trembling,
>   which made all my bones shake.
> ¹⁵A spirit glided past my face;
>   the hair of my flesh bristled.
> ¹⁶It stood still,
>   but I could not discern its appearance.
>   A form was before my eyes;
>   there was silence, then I heard a voice...

---

35. Alonso Schökel, 'Dramatic Reading of Job', p. 52.
36. Alonso Schökel, 'Dramatic Reading of Job', p. 53.
37. Alonso Schökel, 'Dramatic Reading of Job', p. 55.
38. Murphy (*A Short Reading of the Book of Job*, p. 21) notes that Eliphaz was a bit pompous to assert that he had seen a vision, perhaps portraying a 'superior attitude'.

The circumstances of Eliphaz's vision are not given. Why did Eliphaz receive this vision in the first place? When did he receive it? Presumably, Eliphaz feels that the vision was given so that he could apply it to Job at this very moment in the story. The actual vision is found in vv. 17-21:[39]

> [17]'Can mortals be righteous before God?
>   Can human beings be pure before their Maker?
> [18]Even in his servants he puts no trust,
>   and his angels he charges with error;
> [19]how much more those who live in houses of clay,
>   whose foundation is in the dust,
>   who are crushed like the moth.
> [20]Between morning and evening they are destroyed;
>   they perish for ever without any regarding it.
> [21]Their tent-cord is plucked up within them,
>   and they die devoid of wisdom.'

Traditionally, commentators argue that Eliphaz is using this vision to 'reject Job's defense of his innocence'.[40] The problem with this approach is that Job has yet to defend either his innocence or his righteousness! Some even suggest that these words are 'plainly inappropriate to Job's case'.[41] Andersen concurs, writing, 'Eliphaz is reading a lot into this to find implied criticism of God'.[42]

Such a conundrum has led scholarship to debate whether the vision is actually given to Eliphaz. Some suggest that Job is the more likely recipient of the vision. Gary Smith commendably covers this thorny problem, assessing others who have had equal difficulty determining the vision's intended recipient.[43]

Smith treats the vision as a vehicle intended to 'give some sort of supernatural insight into the problem of Job'.[44] He contends that Eliphaz is quoting an earlier vision that *Job* actually had by pointing to similar wording shared between the vision and Job's own speeches in Job 7.14 and 9.11. Additionally, Smith claims that Eliphaz's questions to Job in 15.8—'Have you listened in the council of God? And do you limit wisdom to yourself?'—are indicative of an earlier revelation claimed by Job. Finally, in Job 15.11, Smith sees an admission that the words of the vision were actually

---

39. Not all agree that the vision is constituted by all five verses. Clines, for example, considers only v. 17 revelatory, while the remaining verses are 'wisdom's extensions of it' (*Job 1–20*, pp. 133-34).
40. Hartley, *The Book of Job*, p. 113.
41. Clines, *Job 1–20*, p. 132.
42. Andersen, *Job*, p. 114.
43. Gary Smith, 'Job iv 12-21: Is it Eliphaz's Vision?', *VT* 40 (1990), pp. 453-63. Clines (*Job 1–20*, p. 132) also intimates the need to investigate this, but does not.
44. Smith, 'Eliphaz's Vision', p. 453.

Job's, 'Are the consolations of God too small for you, or the word that deals gently with (to) you?'[45]

Smith's strongest argument is that Eliphaz's first words after the revelation in 5.1 seem to rebut the vision, if one assumes that Job claimed the vision, 'Call now; is there anyone who will answer you? To which of the holy ones will you turn?' Eliphaz seems in 5.8 to be denigrating Job for seeking this vision from lesser beings, and prefers that Job would seek God.

Many question whether the vision even addresses human depravity, as is widely accepted. Instead, the vision, especially in vv. 19-21, seems to align more with Job's thought. The despair and helplessness of life and of humans is much more in line with Job's lament in ch. 3. Eliphaz is more concerned with the fool and the simple (5.2) than he is with humanity as a whole.

Smith admirably challenges conventional approaches, but there is absolutely no indication in the text that this is Job's vision. Given the precision with which the editor identifies speakers during the dialogue, it seems a stretch to assign this vision to Job. Furthermore, Smith's interpretation still presupposes that Job is claiming to be righteous, even if that presupposition is based on one's knowledge of how the story will develop. While Smith helpfully forces interpreters to question how the vision functions in the story, I maintain that the most natural reading associates the vision with Eliphaz.

Since the reader is unsure when and why Eliphaz received this vision, I suggest that the vision at some point was intended for Eliphaz, not Job. The meaning of the vision is not in doubt. In fact, its message is so banal that one wonders why it required a divine revelation (theophany) at all. Since v. 17 seems to accuse Job of claiming to be righteous, which further amplifies Eliphaz's misrepresentation of Job earlier, the reader now knows that Eliphaz is distorting the situation. Eliphaz is trying to redirect a vision that was intended for him (indicating that Eliphaz is the one in need of understanding) by applying it to Job. And the reader, who does not have any preconceived 'wisdom' notions or understanding of the rest of the story, is able to see that. The 'wisdom' of v. 21, which apparently was lacking in Job according to Eliphaz, is lacking in Eliphaz; and the story's epilogue confirms that. In the end, if Eliphaz is actually taking up the Satan's mantle, as I argue, then such a deceptive tactic of inappropriately applying his vision to Job would not be unexpected.

The vision from Job 4 is absolutely pivotal to understanding the apocalyptic features of the story. The reader is now completely prepared for the ensuing dialogue with the friends, which represents nothing short of an earthly manifestation of the inaugural cosmic war begun by God and the

---

45. Smith, 'Eliphaz's Vision', p. 457. Smith translates 'to' instead of the more common 'with'.

Satan over Job's faith. In the cosmic battle, the question is whether Job will persevere and not curse God to God's face, as the Satan stated he would. Now the earthly battlefront has intensified, for Job was able successfully to deflect his wife's attempt to force him to capitulate. Now, however, he has to contend with three 'wise' men, the leader of whom misappropriates a divine revelation for the Satan's own purposes.

In Job 5.8, the reader sees that the new earthly tactic is to convince Job that repentance will alleviate his suffering. Eliphaz says, 'As for me, I would seek God, and to God I would commit my cause'.[46] By contrast, traditional readings of Job assume that Eliphaz is not demanding confession or guilt.[47] But these interpretations have to wrestle with Eliphaz's words directed to Job in 5.17, 'How happy is the one whom God reproves; therefore do not despise the discipline of the Almighty'.

Such divergences in interpretation aptly demonstrate how the starting point that I propose ultimately deviates from traditional approaches that assume a 'wisdom' reading instead of an apocalyptic reading. Eliphaz is being used by the Satan—he is not merely some innocent sage willfully trying to persuade Job of Job's own self-righteousness. The reader knows that Job is righteous and innocent, and the reader also knows that the Satan needs Job to curse God to his face. Job's wife implored Job to curse God, but her direct and lackluster impact likely forces another strategy.

For the Satan, the first step to success is getting Job to admit that he has done something deserving of his punishment. Eliphaz therefore is used to elicit this confession from Job, which will result in Job admitting that he deserves his punishment. That such a strategy is in place is borne out by Eliphaz's appeal to it in the beginning section of each of his three speeches (4.17; 15.15-16; 22.2). However, such an admission by Job will demonstrate that Job has served God for his own personal benefit and consequently will refute God's claim that Job is indifferently righteous. More importantly, such a concession on the part of Job may ultimately lead him to curse God to his face.

Much is at stake in this battle between God and the Satan, a battle whose implications are nothing short of apocalyptic.

Job 5.9–14.35: Completing the First Cycle
The remainder of ch. 5 is a continuation of Eliphaz's attempt to promote his view in such a way as to force Job to repent, encouraging Job not to 'despise the discipline of the Almighty' (5.17). Again, Job has not despised God. He has only despised himself in ch. 3. Still, Eliphaz has aligned himself with

---

46. See Pope, *Job*, p. 43: 'Eliphaz, having admitted that trouble and suffering are inescapable, still advises Job to resort to God who can deliver him'.
47. Habel, *The Book of Job*, p. 133.

God and goads Job to repent in order to avoid seven 'troubles' identified in 5.19-26.[48]

Of interest, four of the seven troubles from which Job could be protected through his own repentance (famine, sword, wild animals, destruction) are almost identically mirrored in Ezek. 14.21 where God declares that Jerusalem will receive 'four deadly acts of judgment, sword, famine, wild animals, and pestilence'. The similar language of judgment found here in Job only reinforces the reader's perception that this story is no mere work of Wisdom Literature.

Not unimportantly, Eliphaz's last words in this first speech use the first person plural: 'See, *we* have searched this out; it is true. Hear, and know it for yourself' (5.27). Eliphaz is now speaking for the two friends, and not just himself. Andersen wrongly suggests that Eliphaz speaks for all wisdom scholars and that the reason Eliphaz is rebuked later in 42.7 is because of his 'ineptness as a counselor'.[49] This interpretation is a common example of scholars forcibly applying a wisdom interpretation on a plot that is simply not wisdom. Eliphaz misrepresents Job's words in 4.6, he misuses his own vision in 4.17-21, and he aligns himself with God in ch. 5 without any justification. Furthermore, he corrals his two duped friends into accepting all that he has said to this point without them having said one word. Eliphaz is much more than an inept counselor; he is the tool of the Satan.

Job's response to Eliphaz in Job 6.8-9 reiterates his despair from ch. 3, 'Oh that I might have my request, and that God would grant my desire; that it would please God to crush me, that he would let loose his hand and cut me off'. Job even denies his own ability to persevere—'In truth I have no help in me, and any resource is driven from me' (6.13)—which is the exact opposite sentiment that Eliphaz falsely accuses Job of maintaining.

Job then recognizes that Eliphaz's words are in error: 'Teach me, and I will be silent; make me understand how I have gone wrong. How forceful are honest words! But your reproof, what does it reprove?' (6.24-25). Conventional interpretations suggest that Job is asking why he has suffered, even if only slightly, but that is not the case within my apocalyptic reading.[50] Instead, Job is wondering why the friends are falsely accusing him of claiming to be righteous before God. He is confused and defensive.

Job continues his response to Eliphaz in ch. 7 by shifting the object of his attention from Eliphaz to God. In the sense that Job addresses God, his theme is an extension of the lament in ch. 3. He questions why God has

---

48. This passage represents a graded numerical saying where identifying the seven 'troubles' has been variously debated. See Steinmann, 'Graded Numerical Saying in Job', pp. 288-97.
49. Andersen, *The Book of Job*, p. 123.
50. Hartley, *The Book of Job*, p. 140, and Pope, *Job*, p. 52.

4. Reading Job through Apocalyptic Eyes 121

plagued him with such difficulties and he wonders why God does not pardon him (7.21). It is true that Job appears to be challenging God, which is not unexpected. However, it is important to frame this challenge in the overall cosmic plot. Job has suffered greatly and been abandoned by his wife and three friends. He is completely alone. Still, he does not curse God. His struggle, which is universal to those suffering, is only a sub-theme, important as it is, to the greater question of whether or not Job will persevere.

Bildad enters the scene in ch. 8 and picks up where Eliphaz left off. He appeals to the universal theology of retribution and asks Job, 'Does God pervert justice? Or does the Almighty pervert the right? If your children sinned against him, he delivered them into the power of their transgression' (8.3-4). Bildad's solution is to 'seek God and make supplication' (8.5). The argument is this: 'since you are suffering you must have done something wrong, just as your children must also have. Therefore, ask for forgiveness and God will restore you'. Bildad expands on what Eliphaz has begun and points out several natural examples of how life works, especially for those who have parted from God. And this is Bildad's primary issue, 'Such are the paths of all who forget God; the hope of the godless shall perish' (8.13).

Bildad broadens Eliphaz's argument by suggesting that beyond simply claiming to be righteous, Job has abandoned God. This is no minor point because there is absolutely no indication that Job has left God. Job laments his predicament and questions God, but he never rejects God. However, Bildad is careful not to avoid Eliphaz's argument, stating, 'if you are pure and upright, surely then he (God) will rouse himself for you and restore to you your rightful place' (8.6), and 'See, God will not reject a blameless (תם) person, nor take the hand of evildoers' (8.20).

Yet the reader knows that God has already declared Job תם (1.8). The reader also knows that Job has done nothing to deserve his suffering and that Bildad is also misrepresenting the situation.

Job's response in chs. 9 and 10 continues to reaffirm that he loathes his life. He adumbrates God's magnificence and his own smallness and God's purity and his own filth, but he does not curse God. Two large issues emerge in this response that remind the reader of the cosmic plot.

First, Job explicitly states that he knows he is innocent. In 9.15 he says, 'Though I am innocent, I cannot answer him', and in 10.7, 'although you know that I am not guilty'. For the first time in the story, Job does explicitly assert his innocence. While the reader knows that Job is right, the reader also knows that Job does not know why he is, in fact, right. What is most interesting is that both of Job's claims are followed by allusions to a desired third party.

In 9.15b, Job says, 'I must appeal for mercy to my accuser'. The underlying word translated 'accuser', מְשֹׁפְטִי, could just as easily be translated 'judge', as in the NASB. The idea of a judge fits better with Job's later words in 9.33, 'There is no umpire (מוֹכִיחַ)[51] between us, who might lay his hand on us both', and in 10.7, 'there is no one to deliver out of your hand'.

The reader who has thus far witnessed Job persevere begins to see a weakening in Job's rhetoric. The flagging is not that Job is starting to 'shake his fist at God', as so many interpreters tied to the wisdom assumption assert. The sign of deterioration is that Job begins to demonstrate, on at least two separate occasions, the need for a third party. Such a request suggests that he might be losing faith in God after all, which the reader may interpret as a first step toward Job becoming increasingly capable of cursing God.

Such a modified disposition in Job progresses, and the remainder of ch. 10 seems to initiate the process whereby Job is going to curse God, and in so doing, give the Satan the victory. In Job 10.8-17, Job reminds God that he created Job, so why now does God choose to destroy him? Then, in vv. 10.18-22, Job returns to the lament motif of ch. 3, questioning his very existence and instead longing for the gloom of Sheol. Still, Job does not curse God, nor does he admit that he has done anything wrong to deserve his current dismal state of affairs.

Chapter 11 introduces Zophar for the first time. Like Eliphaz and Bildad, Zophar argues that Job has claimed to be righteous, saying in v. 4, 'For you say, "My conduct is pure, and I am clean in God's sight"'. Zophar seems to be twisting Job's words from 6.10, 'This would be my consolation; I would even exult in unrelenting pain; for I have not denied the words of the Holy One', and in 10.7, 'although you (God) know that I am not guilty, and there is no one to deliver out of your hand'. Yet Zophar is simply misrepresenting Job, as Murphy notes, 'Job has never made such a statement'.[52] The reader is not surprised to see this strategy here, even though it is a new speaker. By now the reader fully understands that the friends, especially because of Eliphaz's initial misrepresentation, are only earthly reflections of the Satan's scheme.

Again, in accordance with the first two friends, Zophar also directs Job to God, in whom Job might find renewed hope. He too suggests that Job's twofold sin is that he claims to be righteous and has departed from God. The apocalyptic battle continues in that sense, though Zophar's words commence a sub-theme that will become much more important as the story progresses. Can a human truly understand the Almighty? In v. 7 Zophar asks, 'Can you find out the deep things of God? Can you find out the limit of the Almighty?'

---

51. This word is derived from יכח, meaning 'decide, adjudge, prove' (BDB, p. 406b).
52. Murphy, *A Short Reading of the Book of Job*, p. 34.

4. *Reading Job through Apocalyptic Eyes* 123

These questions will arise with greater frequency, reaching their crescendo in the final and most powerful revelation of the story; God's words from the whirlwind.

In chs. 12–14, Job begins to disdain his friends, accusing them of assuming a superior position over him. He draws their attention to the majesty of God and to God's absolutely inscrutable ways. Job re-establishes the high ground by pointing out to the friends that, 'He uncovers the deeps out of darkness, and brings deep darkness to light' (12.22); 'He makes nations great, then destroys them' (12.23). Job knows this too, so he reiterates his equality with the friends (13.3).

Then Job explicitly announces that he would speak with God and argue his case after only alluding to such a maneuver in 9.16. Now, after hearing all three of his friends, Job knows that their arguments are impotent, and instead of wasting his time with them, he is ready actually to speak with God. The reader who has kept the cosmic context in mind recognizes that there may be a chance that Job and God will meet. Rejecting his friends, Job is ready to take his chances with God, even though he knows that he is unlikely to survive. This is a common biblical theme: few survive who have seen God's face (cf. Hagar, Gen. 16.13 and Jacob, Gen. 32.30). Job 13.15b piques the apocalyptic-minded reader, 'but I will defend my ways *to his face*' (אל־פניו אוכיח אך־דרכי). There is no chance that the reader will miss this point. God and Job will possibly have a showdown face to face, but the reader wonders if Job will curse God to his face if given the opportunity.

Job continues to cling to his belief that he has not done anything to deserve his punishment (13.23b), and he eerily identifies, also explicitly for the first time, the friends' deceptive role in this battle. In 13.7 Job says, 'Will you speak falsely for God, and speak deceitfully for him'? Justifying his own position to speak for God, Job asks in 13.8, 'Will you show partiality toward him, will you plead the case for God?' For Job, this dramatic disclosure is pivotal because he, like the reader, recognizes that the friends' claim to speak for God is based on deception. Once again, the cosmic battle manifests its way to the earthly scene. For all intents and purposes, the dialogues could end here because Job knows, and the reader confirms, that the friends do not speak for God—they speak for the Satan.

Job concludes the first cycle of speeches in ch. 14 by appealing to his stock lament, as first seen in ch. 3. A mortal born of a woman is described as fleeting. There is little hope: mortals die and are laid low and Job wishes to be hidden in Sheol. Job now knows the friends' ultimate role, and once again it is clear that he is on his own. All but dismissing the friends, the larger object of Job's struggle is now redirected to his relationship with God.

Job 15–21: Second Cycle

As in the first cycle, Eliphaz again begins the second cycle and admonishes Job for his 'windy' words. He initiates a theme that will emerge in each of the friends' opening lines, namely, to accuse Job of acting in a condescending manner. In 15.9 Eliphaz asks, 'What do you know that we do not know?' The attacks on Job will become more personal. Instead of challenging Job's apparent self-righteous position, Eliphaz accuses Job of 'doing away with the fear of God, and hindering meditation before God' (15.4). And later in 15.13, Eliphaz claims that Job has turned his own spirit against God. In 15.25 Eliphaz compares Job to those who are wicked, 'Because they have stretched out their hands against God, and bid defiance to the Almighty'. Finally in 15.35, Eliphaz identifies these wicked ones as those that 'bring forth evil and their heart prepares deceit'.

This first attack on Job in the second cycle is far less interested in Job's claim of self-righteousness, and instead concentrates on portraying Job's behavior as his own departure from God. Of course, the reader knows that Job has now claimed to be righteous; yet, the reader also knows that Job is innocent. The reader also knows that Job has questioned God, sometimes quite strongly, though he has yet to abandon or curse God.

Job's response in ch. 16 includes words of innocence in v. 17, 'there is no violence in my hands and my prayer is pure'. Job also relies on God in 16.19, 'my witness is in heaven, and he that vouches for me is on high'. Both verses suggest that Job knows what the reader knows, namely, that Job is truly innocent and that God is the one who has vouched for him in the very beginning. Indeed, were it not for God, the Satan may have already killed Job. Job's continued response in ch. 17 contains more language that is similar to ch. 3's lament.

One important part of Job's response, which is easy to overlook if one is following the RSV, is his plea to speak with God. This is important because Job's final response in the first cycle begins to emphasize this desire. That the request also surfaces in this first response in the second cycle is extremely important to the reader, who continues to wonder if Job and God are ever going to have the chance to meet. Again, for the reader, this meeting is vital because the reader wants to know if Job will curse God to his face and vindicate the Satan.

The RSV translates 16.21, 'that he would maintain the right of a man with God, like that of a man with his neighbor'. By contrast, the NASB translates, 'O that a man might plead with God as a man with his neighbor', and the NEB reads, 'If only there were one to arbitrate between man and God, as between a man and his neighbor'. The Hebrew for 16.21 reads:

ויוכח לגבר עם־אלוה ובן־אדם לרעהו

Here again, a form of יכח is used, but this time Job is the one seeking to judge or argue. BDB gives this word as 'decide' or 'judge', and suggests 'adjudge', 'convince', 'prove', and 'argue' for other uses of the Hiphil.[53] The main point is that Job is actively seeking to speak with God, and this will not be missed by the reader.

Bildad continues the trend of personal attacks, asking Job in 18.3, 'Why are we counted as cattle? Why are we stupid in your sight?' He then begins a tirade against Job that is dominated by descriptions of the wicked. Like Eliphaz, he too has minimized the charge that Job is self-righteous and leapt to associating Job with the evil ones. The culmination of his invective is to claim, not unsurprisingly, that Job does not know God. Job 18.21 reads, 'Surely such are the dwellings of the ungodly, such is the place of those who do not know God'. The friends are turning the screws on Job and attacking his fidelity to the one God.

Recognizing the intensity of this latest allegation, Job points to God's sovereign role during his predicament in 19.6, 'know then that God has put me in the wrong, and closed his net around me'. And again in v. 21, 'Have pity on me, have pity on me, O you my friends, for the hand of God has touched me'. Job is redirecting his friends' insistence that he is leaving God by inextricably tying himself to the very God who has caused his despairing plight. His friends will not pin down Job.

Job concludes ch. 19 with one of Christianity's most revered verses in Scripture, 19.25. Combined with the verses following it, the end of ch. 19 once again accords with the storyline presented thus far, and points to rudimentary apocalyptic. Job 19.25-29 reads:

> [25]For I know that my Redeemer lives,
>   and that at the last he will stand upon the earth;
> [26]and after my skin has been thus destroyed,
>   then in my flesh I shall see God,
> [27]whom I shall see on my side,
>   and my eyes shall behold, and not another.
>   My heart faints within me!
> [28]If you say, 'How we will persecute him!'
>   and, 'The root of the matter is found in him';
> [29]be afraid of the sword,
>   for wrath brings the punishment of the sword,
>   so that you may know there is a judgment.

With particular attention to the identification of the redeemer (גאל) figure, scholars have variously interpreted this powerful passage. Some suggest that Job is actually the figure.[54] The traditional view is that the redeemer figure is

---

53. BDB, pp. 406-407.
54. For a discussion on some of the views, see Clines, *Job 1–20*, pp. 459-60.

not God, and is more likely to be a third-party mediator.[55] But all of these interpretations presuppose that Job views God as the 'adversary', 'enemy', 'hunter' or 'spy', to name a few. The storyline never argues that Job will not question God or even view him as an enemy. As already discussed, the chapter opens up with Job assuming that it is God who has caused him his anguish. The question of whether or not Job loses patience with God is never at stake—the issue is whether or not Job will succumb to his condition and curse God to his face, as the Satan insisted would happen.

Others suggest that the redeemer is none other than God.[56] The fact that Job refers to 'seeing' God three times (vv. 26b, 27a, b) in such a compact context seems to support the conclusion that he is referring to God.[57] Murphy points out that these verses prepare the reader for the climactic theophany (final revelation according to my scheme), which, combined with other elements, confirms that 'the author-poet never allows Job to give up or to give in, to give up on God or to give in to any accusation of infidelity'.[58]

However, on my reading, Job is appealing to a third party, which is consistent with similar appeals in both chs. 9 and 16. The use of גאל simply amplifies the author's message that Job is looking outside of God for assistance. In my view, this is an eschatological passage whereby Job is putting his hope in the hands of some third-party figure. Job is not abandoning God, he projects a day when God will be on his side, and Job will not see another, 'and not another' (19.27). Job may be upset with God along the way, and he seems to increasingly doubt God's faithfulness, but he has yet to curse God. Job's tendency towards doubting God simply heightens the reader's anticipation of Job and God's first meeting. Murphy is right to point out that this appeal for a גאל points to the theophany, yet the importance of the theophany is the fact that it is there that Job meets God face to face. Will Job, if given a chance, curse God to his face?

Two additional and substantive components further confirm an apocalyptic interpretation. First, in 19.25b, scholars have struggled to translate אחרון, which is typically viewed as an adverbial descriptor instead of its given adjectival form. Habel observes that 'unless there are cogent reasons to the

---

55. See Pope, *Job*, p. 135; Habel, *The Book of Job*, p. 306; Clines, *Job 1–20*, p. 459, as examples of this view.

56. Andersen, *The Book of Job*, p. 194. The REB translates vv. 25-27: 'But in my heart I know that my vindicator lives and that he will rise last to speak in court; and I shall discern my witness standing at my side and see my defending counsel, even God himself, whom I shall see with my own eyes, I myself and no other'.

57. This is also the position adopted by Murphy (*A Short Reading of the Book of Job*, p. 56).

58. Murphy, *A Short Reading of the Book of Job*, p. 56.

contrary the term should be retained as an adverb'.⁵⁹ If Job is taken as proto-apocalyptic, 'last' is a better translation than Habel's 'afterward'. The word can then be understood in its most natural substantival sense without emendation or theological contortion.⁶⁰ Job can be construed as making a statement that is eschatological, that is, he is talking about the end of the age.⁶¹ God will rise up in a judgment posture and Job will behold him, and 'not another'. This judgment allusion represents an eschatological element contained within this passage.

The second observation on this passage is the fact that the LXX reads so differently from the Hebrew. The text reads:

οἶδα γὰρ ὅτι ἀέναός ἐστιν ὁ ἐκλύειν με μέλλων ἐπὶ γῆς

To be sure, I know that he who is about to undo me on earth is everlasting.⁶²

Many Christian interpreters past and present assume that Job 19.25 validates the resurrection. Calvin, and others, consider such an assertion far too much of a stretch, even though we now know that ideas of the resurrection prevailed in ancient times as well.⁶³ I concur. I do not treat that debate here, but it is interesting to note that the LXX rendering seems less inclined toward an eschatological interpretation than the Hebrew. If early Christian editors interpreted the Hebrew of Job to conform to a Christian perspective, it seems odd that such an important verse as 19.25 was not evidently included, while the Hebrew easily suggests a personal resurrection. In fact, the LXX is almost enigmatic compared to the Hebrew. So different is the LXX from the MT that one wonders what the *Vorlage* before the LXX translator actually contained. Ziegler lists no significant manuscripts even suggesting that later Christian editing might have occurred, and, significantly, the verse does not contain Origen's asterisks.⁶⁴ At the very least, then, one can conclude that, based on the lack of LXX editing on 19.25, the hypothesis that early Christians 'tailored' Job to a more Christian worldview is quite suspect.

In vv. 28 and 29, Job warns the friends that they who have persecuted him and claimed that the problem lies within Job himself should be afraid of the

---

59. Habel, *The Book of Job*, p. 305. Habel translates 19.25 as '*I myself know* my redeemer lives. And coming *afterward*, he will...' Pope (*Job*, p. 135) suggests translating it as 'at last'.

60. BDB, pp. 30b-31a, cites the following options: 'a. of place, behind, hindermost', and, 'More commonly b. of time, latter or last'.

61. Andersen (*The Book of Job*, p. 194) concurs.

62. NETS translation.

63. Andersen (*The Book of Job*, p. 194) also cautions against assuming a resurrection is intimated in this passage.

64. Ziegler, *Iob*, p. 296.

sword. The idea of sword is connected with a punishing wrath that can only be attributed to judgment. Job is confident because he knows that he is innocent and that God will vindicate him, despite his angst with God over his state of affairs.

Zophar's second speech begins similarly to the two previous friends' speeches. Offended by Job's condescending attitude, he too says in 20.3, 'I hear censure that insults me'. And in v. 5 he immediately implies that Job is one of the godless. The remainder of his speech describes the miserable conditions that such wicked persons will experience. He concludes in the same way, stating that the terrible portion of the wicked is from God. Thus, his speech accords with his two compatriots that Job has left God and should be counted as one of the wicked.

Job's entire response in ch. 21 contradicts Zophar's dire description of the wicked. Job declares that the wicked do prosper, even though they oppose God. While some go to Sheol in peace, others die in their bitterness. The fact of the matter is, Zophar is wrong. Yet Job makes clear that he knows what the friends are up to in 21.27, 'Oh, I know your thoughts, and your schemes to wrong me'. Job is completely aware that the friends are no comforters and are attempting to deceive him into believing that he himself is wicked and separated from God. The reader knows that Job has gradually come to acknowledge this, and his words at the end of ch. 21 leave no doubt. In 21.34 he says, 'How then will you comfort me with empty things? There is nothing left of your answers but falsehood.'

In cycle one the friends sought to convince Job that his self-righteousness was in fact his downfall. Job, however, responded effectively enough to each of them that their second cycle of speeches intensified. Each friend began by defending their honor from Job's apparent condescending answers, and then each friend attempted to convince Job that he was a partner of the wicked and had deserted God.

In two cycles, the friends have failed to incite Job into cursing God, even though Job expresses his dissatisfaction with God. In the midst of the second cycle, Job begins to cry out loudly for an audience, which encourages the reader to continue, for the reader is constantly wondering if Job will persevere, as it seems he will, or will actually curse God to his face. Job's world hinges on this apocalyptic moment.

Job 22–27: Cycle Three
Since his first two approaches were unable to persuade Job, Eliphaz begins the third round of speeches with a new tactic. He wonders if human beings could ever be useful to God at all, no matter how wise or righteous they are. Of course, Job has been useful to God because of his perseverance. Eliphaz persists and begins to enumerate specific sins that Job must have committed.

He accuses Job of stripping the naked of their clothes (22.6), denying water to the weary (22.7), dismissing widows empty-handed (22.9) and crushing the strength of orphans (22.9). These are despicable sins, particularly the last two, which cut to the heart of scriptural morality.

The reader knows that these charges are false for two reasons. First, God himself declared that Job was blameless in chs. 1 and 2. Secondly, Eliphaz himself, in his first speech from Job 4.3-4, said: 'See, you have instructed many, and you have strengthened the weak hands. Your words have supported those who were stumbling, and you have made firm the feeble knees.' While not explicitly identifying widows and orphans, one suspects that Eliphaz at 4.4 is referring to these and other less fortunate ones. Thus, Eliphaz is contradicting himself, which occurs frequently when one lies. Job will assert his 'blamelessness' in ch. 31 by refuting these blasphemies.

Eliphaz continues his speech by revering God in another attempt to associate himself with the deity. By contrast, and not surprisingly, he associates Job with the wicked. In 22.15 he asks Job, 'Will you keep to the old way that the wicked have trod?' He completes his speech by again asking Job to make peace with God. If there was any doubt that Eliphaz thought Job had forsaken God, it becomes clearer in 22.23 where he advises, 'If you *return* (שוב) to the Almighty, you will be restored...' This verse assumes that Job has departed from God, and that this departure is the root of his abysmal condition. In an ironic and fitting end to Eliphaz's role in the story, he tells Job in 22.30 that God 'will deliver even those who are guilty; they will escape because of the cleanness of your hands'. Neither Eliphaz nor the reader knows yet that in order to save the friends from God's wrath, Job will intercede, especially on behalf of Eliphaz.

Job's response simply ignores Eliphaz. The friends have completely lost Job's attention and instead he moves immediately to his increasing obsession—meeting God. He says in 23.3, 'O that I knew where I might find him, that I might come even to his dwelling'. He continues to long for such a meeting, stating that he would bring his case before God.

Job continues by specifying the evil ways of wicked men, rehashing many items that Eliphaz had just affixed to Job, but Job includes the murderer (24.14) and the adulterer (24.15) as further examples of the wicked. Further, in a cosmological reference, Job points out that the wicked 'rebel against the light' (24.13). Habel considers this reference a rejection of God's righteous and ordered world.[65] Job feels that the wicked have all too often gone unpunished, despite their disastrous impact on the world. And while it is not incorrect to accept that Job is questioning why the wicked prosper, his main concern is why they prosper when 'those who know him never see his days'

---

65. Habel, *The Book of Job*, pp. 360-61.

(24.1). Job's passion is to meet God, and the fact that this request is going unheeded causes Job to ponder why the wicked flourish. However, in the end, Job argues, 'they wither and fade like the mallow' (24.24). Seemingly implying that he is not wicked, Job taunts the friends into explaining why he then still lives.

Bildad briefly re-enters for his third speech with only six verses, also primarily intended to denigrate the status of human beings before God. In a final attempt to wound Job, Bildad wonders again how a human can be righteous before God (25.4). Bildad's words are the last of any of the friends', thereby serving as a kind of *inclusio* with Eliphaz's words from his vision in ch. 4.

Job retorts that Bildad's attempts to support 'one who has no power' (26.2) have been vain. It can only be assumed that he is referring to Eliphaz, but it may also refer to the Satan. Since the Satan has not been mentioned since the beginning, and since Job, unlike the reader, does not know of the cosmic dialogue, it is probably best to identify the recipient as Eliphaz.[66] Of course, by this time, the reader is clear that Eliphaz is carrying the Satan's water. Yet Job seems to press this very point in 26.4, asking, 'With whose help have you uttered words, and whose spirit has come forth from you?' The reader knows, and Job seems to be discerning the source behind the conspiracy as well. The remainder of ch. 26 is another praise of God's creative splendor as manifested in various natural wonders, which also prepares the reader for the coming theophany.[67]

Job reaffirms his commitment to God, despite God's role in making Job's life bitter and taking away Job's right, apparently to speak before God. Job says in 27.3-4, 'as long as my breath is in me and the spirit of God is in my nostrils, *my lips will not* speak falsehood, and *my tongue will not* utter deceit'.

Job confidently holds fast to his integrity and righteousness before the friends (27.11). One can picture them speechless, which, in addition to Job's very forceful completion to his response to Zophar's second speech, may be why Zophar never speaks a third time. Importantly to the reader, however, is

---

66. Murphy (*A Short Reading of the Book of Job*, p. 64) wonders whether Bildad is referring to God. Andersen (*The Book of Job*, p. 217) thinks that Job is referring to Bildad's uninspired words.

67. To account for the combination that Bildad's final speech is seemingly abbreviated and Zophar does not have a third speech at all, scholars have generally assumed the following reconstruction: Job speaks in 26.1-4; 27.1-12, Bildad in 25.1-6; 26.5-14, and Zophar in 27.13-23 (Hartley, *The Book of Job*, pp. 24-25). To legitimate such reconstructions, scholars are forced to presuppose two important matters. First, that symmetry must exist in poetry, and second, that Job is a piece of Wisdom Literature that concentrates on solving the book's 'problem'. Again, my approach to the text assumes what is found in MT.

Job's statement that he will not speak ill of God with his lips (27.4). The reader immediately recalls the Satan's confident conclusion that Job will curse God to his face. While Job's own confidence is a fitting end to this major assault offered by the friends, the reader still wonders if Job will, in fact, curse God to his face if given the opportunity.

The reader reaches the conclusion of the dialogue speeches in 27.11-12, where Job shifts gears, 'I will teach you concerning the hand of God; that which is with the Almighty I will not conceal. All of you have seen it yourselves; why then have you become altogether vain?' Job has secured the high ground again with the friends, and he provides an excellent segue into the enigmatic wisdom poem found in ch. 28. Job closes ch. 27 with an unsettling account of the portion of the wicked evidently to distance himself even further from the friends and also from the profile of the wicked as ascribed to him by the friends.

Summary of the Dialogue Speeches
The friends first enter the story at the end of ch. 2 in a rather benign way. They mourn with Job and patiently wait alongside for seven full days before approaching him. By all accounts, they appear to be authentic friends. Yet once the dialogues begin, things change. The dialogue between Job and the friends represents the earthly playing field for the Satan, who seeks to defeat Job in order to avoid his own curse. The deceptive tactics employed by the friends functions as an important component of Apocalyptic Literature. Adela Yarbro Collins comments:

> The harsh portrayal of opponents as archetypal monsters, demons, or sinners is hardly conducive to the resolution of conflict through mutual understanding and acceptance. Such language merely intensifies the polarization already present. But it is an effective tool at times for unmasking the *forces that pretend to be benign*, but actually exploit. Or perhaps more accurately, apocalyptic rhetoric can be a revelatory corrective to propaganda. Propaganda stresses what is supposedly benign and constructive, whereas apocalyptic rhetoric has the potential to unmask what is exploitative and corrupt.[68]

The propaganda that the friends promote is the universal certainty and application of retribution theology. This is the comfortable theology that the friends appealed to in order to extract a confession from Job. Thus, a conventional wisdom theme is exploited for the Satan's purposes, but it is ultimately rendered ineffective and errant. The escalating polarization between the friends and Job only convinces the reader of the propaganda's failure.

---

68. Yarbro Collins, 'Apocalyptic Themes', p. 128 (emphasis added).

As noted, the Satan's argument is fundamentally stored within the strategy employed by the friends. The Satan seems to have failed in this attempt, but Job seems aware of his influence on the friends.

Job has correctly accused the friends of persecuting him (21.27) and in so doing, reveals that this dialogue, in part, functions as a form of apocalyptic war. Job has survived the earthly, material challenge from his wife and now the three friends. He has maintained his integrity and passed the first major test. The larger question, however, is whether or not he will contribute to a cosmological victory for God. Only if Job finds a way to meet with God will the reader know whether or not Job will succeed.

Job 28.1-22

Job 28 has long puzzled scholars. First, most scholars consider this chapter a later interpolation,[69] though not all agree that it came later or indeed what its purpose is in the story.[70] A second more profound difficulty in view of the narrative is the identification of the speaker. Most interpreters are uncomfortable assigning Job as speaker because the beginning of ch. 29 starts, 'Job again took up his discourse and said' (v. 1), indicating that Job may not be speaking in ch. 28. Murphy agrees and argues that there is no sign of continuation from Job's speech in ch. 27 to ch. 28.[71] A possible rebuttal to Murphy and his proposal is the fact that both Job 27 and 29 begin with the same phrase, 'Job again took up his discourse and said'. Since Job is clearly speaking in ch. 26, one could argue that the author's use of the phrase in ch. 29 is no different than his use of it in ch. 27. On the other hand, Job is 'answering' his friends in ch. 26, while ch. 27 signifies the opening of a lengthy summary, which is not the same pattern one finds between Job 28 and 29.[72]

Andersen suggests that there could be some continuity in the narrative, though he is content to consider ch. 28 an interlude that is capable of standing independently of chs. 27 and 29.[73] Pope accepts that the poem was 'put into the mouth of Job', though he too views it as an extraneous addition.[74]

In my view there are two significant reasons to support Job as the speaker. The first argues that since God is clearly the speaker in Job 28.28—'And he said to humankind'—the narrator is forced to identify Job as the speaker in ch. 29. That the speaker is quoting God at the end of ch. 28 does not discount the possibility that Job could be speaking in earlier parts of the

---

69. Pope, *Job*, p. xviii.
70. See Habel, *The Book of Job*, pp. 391-92, for a discussion of these issues.
71. Murphy, *A Short Reading of the Book of Job*, p. 67.
72. Andersen, *The Book of Job*, p. 219.
73. Andersen, *The Book of Job*, pp. 222-24.
74. Pope, *Job*, p. xviii.

chapter. Thus, the argument that the opening words of ch. 29 indicate that Job could not have spoken in the preceding chapter at all is without warrant.

The second reason that Job could be the speaker in ch. 28 is the thematic transition from ch. 27 to 28. In my reading of the book to this point, Job already realizes the ineptness of his friends, and he even seems to recognize their involvement in a larger plan to sabotage his own faith. The combination of Bildad's brief third discourse and Zophar's absence suggests that the editor is showing that the friends' efforts have been exhaustive, but ultimately ineffective. Similarly, Hartley argues that ch. 28 'authenticates Job's turning away from his comforters to petition God directly'.[75] In that context, Job's words in 27.11 seem to point to what will follow in ch. 28, 'I will teach you concerning the hand of God; that which is with the Almighty I will not conceal'.

This statement forecasts Job's role in divulging material apparently not available to the friends. Since ch. 28 essentially addresses the inaccessibility of wisdom, and since the friends unsuccessfully attempted to teach Job about their perceptions of wisdom, Job proclaims that he will teach them, and he will expose that which has otherwise been unavailable to them. Thus, the narrative itself supports the conclusion that Job is speaking in ch. 28.

Miners' language is used to compare the friends' futile efforts to discover wisdom with similar efforts by the miners. In 28.1 Job says, 'Surely there is a mine for silver, and a place for gold to be refined'. The major distinction between miners and the friends is that a miner is able to discover various minerals as in 28.11b, 'hidden things they bring to light'.

Importantly, Job then immediately asks in v. 12, 'But where shall wisdom be found?' One would think that some would be able to locate wisdom with the appropriate tools and sufficient persistence, as the miners do. The more optimistic view of wisdom's accessibility is promoted in Proverbs 1–9, a far more traditional 'wisdom' work. Yet the friends have not found wisdom.

Verses 12 and 13 initiate the transition from the accessible minerals of human mining to the inaccessible wisdom of God, and the text heightens the reader's anticipation for some kind of answer to the location of elusive wisdom:

> [12]But where shall wisdom be found?
> And where is the place of understanding?
> [13]Mortals does not know the way to it,
> and it is not found in the land of the living.

Not only are humans unable to discover it, the chaotic deep and sea (both representing ancient creation antagonists) do not know where it is (28.14).

---

75. Hartley, *The Book of Job*, p. 384.

No valuable stones can be exchanged for it (28.15). The wealth of the wicked, as Job indicates in 27.16, 19, 20-21, is incapable of establishing a home for wisdom. So again, Job asks in v. 20, 'Where then does wisdom come from?' It is not to be found by humans or by the birds. Extending the sea and deep metaphors, Job reports that both Abaddon and Death declare, 'We have heard a rumor of it with our ears' (28.22). This personification of the underworld enhances the apocalyptic images already present.[76]

Of all the precious stones mentioned, Job especially emphasizes gold's inferiority when compared to wisdom. Gold is mentioned six times (28.1, 6, 15, 17 [twice], 19). While gold was a highly prized possession, the numerous references are striking in that Eliphaz's name means, 'God is fine gold'.[77] Might it be that Job's frequent references to gold seek to rebuke the friend who initially misrepresented Job's position and who apparently exalted himself above the others? Job might very well be saying that God is not found in gold, nor is he found in the man whose very name suggests that God can be equated to gold. Perhaps Job is exposing Eliphaz's superficial understanding of God by means of Eliphaz's own name.

Similarly, in response to the second rhetorical refrain asking where wisdom is found (v. 20), Job responds that it is hidden from all humans and from the birds of the air. It is likely that birds were chosen to represent the animals of creation because they have an aerial advantage and can view all things, except where wisdom is found.[78] On the other hand, perhaps the futility that birds have in discovering wisdom symbolically alludes to Zophar, whose name means, 'young bird'.[79] In this way, these initial verses (28.1-21) utilize a common apocalyptic convention of using symbols to mask the identity of the entity in mind.

The mining metaphor, though used to distinguish between that which is accessible and that which is not, also bears significant apocalyptic characteristics. Furthermore, terms such as 'darkness', 'gloom' and 'dust' anticipate 'underworld themes'.[80]

Additionally, the reader of the Bible might associate the mining minerals of Job 28 with Nebuchadnezzar's troubling dream in the apocalyptic book of Daniel, which included gold, silver, bronze, iron and clay (Dan. 2.31-45). All but the obscure mixture of clay and iron from the dream are found in

---

76. Magnan's quotation of the targumic translation of 28.22 seems to corroborate this: '*The house of* Abaddon and *the angel of* death say: "We have heard a rumor with our hearing *of its being given to Israel*"' (*The Targum of Job*, p. 66). I understand the underlined portions to be '*Variant Targum[s]* incorporated in the text' (p. 17).
77. Hartley, *The Book of Job*, p. 85.
78. Pope, *Job*, p. 182.
79. Hartley, *The Book of Job*, p. 86.
80. Geller, 'Where is Wisdom?', p. 159.

Job 28. Even more uncanny are the striking similarities between Daniel's words of gratitude after having received his revelation of Nebuchadnezzar's dream and Job's words in 12.13, 16-22; 26.6; and in ch. 28. Daniel 2.19-23 reads:

> ¹⁹Then the mystery was revealed to Daniel in a vision of the night,
>   and Daniel blessed the God of heaven.
> ²⁰Daniel said: 'Blessed be the name of God from age to age,
>   for wisdom and power are his.
> ²¹He changes times and season, deposes kings and sets up kings;
>   he gives wisdom to the wise and knowledge to those who have understanding.
> ²²He *reveals deep and hidden things*;
>   he knows what is *in the darkness*, and light dwells with him.
> ²³To you, O God of my ancestors, I give thanks and praise,
>   for you have given me wisdom and power...'

An obvious relationship between the wise person and revealed knowledge is shared between Daniel's first vision and Job's description in ch. 28. This relationship between wisdom and apocalyptic was most demonstrably championed by Gerhard von Rad who argued that apocalyptic grew out of wisdom traditions.[81] While the most mature expression of apocalypse surfaces in the last half of Daniel, one cannot easily dismiss the fact that Daniel's words precede his interpretation of a vision that is nothing short of apocalyptic. Meaningful points of intersection exist between Daniel's interpretation and Job's lecture on wisdom, which suggests that proposing latent apocalyptic traits in both Daniel and in Job is well founded.

Furthermore, and in contrast to the 'darker' images of the early verses in ch. 28, v. 6 associates wealth derived from the mountains with the wealth of paradise, a motif that 'luxuriates even into apocalyptic literature'.[82] The reader senses that something is about to be 'mined', something is about to surface in the story as they continue to wonder if Job will curse God to his face.

Thus, Job's speech is consistent from 27.11 to 28.22. He is completely discarding the friends' 'wisdom' and chastising them both for their inability to recognize the nature of wisdom and for their vanity. After associating their ways with the wicked, he then establishes the necessary context for them to understand that wisdom is not something that can be 'mined' or simply obtained through human endeavor. Its source is something far more transcendent than any place on earth.

---

81. I will take up this specific argument in Chapter 5.
82. Geller, 'Where is Wisdom?', p. 163. Geller references *1 En.* 24 as an example of this motif (n. 54).

Job 28.23–37.24: God's Revelation of Wisdom— Job Encouraged

Job 28.23-28

In a compelling and iconoclastic study on Job 28, Stephen Geller argues that Job receives a divine revelation. Geller sees v. 23 as an absolutely astounding breakthrough in the poem, referring to it as 'almost as much a theophany as the divine speech out of the whirlwind', where, 'light from this sudden revelation immediately transfigures the preceding parts of the poem'.[83] A superficial reading of vv. 23-28 may fail to justify Geller's enthusiasm:

> ²³God understands the way to it,
>   and he knows its place.
> ²⁴For he looks to the ends of the earth,
>   and sees everything under the heavens
> ²⁵When he gave to the wind its weight,
>   and apportioned out the waters by measure;
> ²⁶when he made a decree for the rain,
>   and a way for the thunderbolt;
> ²⁷then he saw it and declared it;
>   he established it, and searched it out.
> ²⁸And he said to humankind,
>   'Truly, the fear of the Lord, that is wisdom;
>   and to depart from evil is understanding'.

Geller marvels at the combination of the 'unexpected' אלהים of v. 23a and the emphatic הו of v. 23b. As readers progress to the creation verses of 25 and 26, they will 'reinterpret the meaning of 23a retroactively' to understand that God has control over the workings of nature and wisdom.[84] Further, appreciating v. 23a as a revelation will cast new interpretive light on the earlier sections of ch. 28.

For example, wisdom does have a 'place', as intimated earlier in vv. 12 and 20. For Geller, this place is a *when*, that is, during creation. The reader receives this revelation (v. 23a) 'with lightning speed', and the revelation places the preceding creation language in clearer terms. Nothing in creation could possibly know wisdom because 'God used it to create the world'.[85]

With respect to the plot of Job, the wisdom to which Job refers is a cosmic wisdom, one that precedes the earth and indeed was used in fashioning the earth. Thus, a critical point in ch. 28 is that the friends *cannot* know where God's wisdom is found.[86] They speak of an earthly wisdom that is

---

83. Geller, 'Where is Wisdom?', p. 165.
84. Geller, 'Where is Wisdom?', p. 167.
85. Geller, 'Where is Wisdom?', p. 166.
86. Murphy (*A Short Reading of the Book of Job*, p. 71) argues similarly, 'It is certain that the writer of chapter 28 is underscoring the limits of human wisdom concerning retribution'.

incapable of accounting for Job's situation. The reader knows that the storyline is fundamentally cosmic, and Job is aware of this too.

After extolling God's role in establishing wisdom in vv. 23-27, Job ends with God's pietistic words to humankind: 'Truly, the fear of the Lord, that is wisdom; and to depart from evil is understanding' (28.28). Most commentators consider this last verse a later addition, designed to moderate the almost hopelessness offered in ch. 28.[87] However, the verse's claim to be original should not be too easily rejected.[88] The quietism proffered in this final verse, that humans should simply fear God and avoid evil, might seem too trite, or at least too obvious. However, this is the main point of Job's admonition to his friends regarding the ways of God in 27.12, 'All of you have seen it yourselves; why then have you become altogether vain?' Job knows that true wisdom is not as complicated as the friends have made it out to be. He knows that at its root it is to fear God. Job has come full circle because he is described in the very beginning of the story as a man who feared God and turned away from evil.

In this way, v. 28 functions in the narrative as an *inclusio* between the beginning of the story of Job and now the end of the fruitless cycle of debates between Job and his friends. But while it also ends the cycle, it also serves as the launching point, or 'next beginning', to Job's forthcoming struggle with God. Zuckerman considers v. 28 a necessary element that offers 'a significant mediating effect...especially in reference to the Theophany'.[89] Job has moved past his friends, but his desired meeting with God has not yet occurred, and the reader still anticipates some kind of showdown.

However, v. 28 also serves as the climax of God's revelation in ch. 28. Geller overlooks this function, charging that the verse is literarily 'misplaced', and as such labels it 'too bold, 'bland', and ultimately 'superfluous'.[90] His dismissal of the verse seems too hasty, however.

In my view, vv. 23-28 collectively represent the revelation that benefits Job by revealing the place where God's cosmic wisdom is found. The friends have tried to argue via earthly wisdom that Job has done something wrong to deserve his punishment. They have failed and Job knows it. Still, Job wonders why he has suffered so much, and only by an appeal to the cosmic wisdom that is beyond the material world can he obtain an answer. This is truly an apocalyptic setting.

While Geller's proposal offers a significant break from traditional exegesis, it suffers because he does not stray too far from standard assumptions. He hopes to situate Job 28 'in the larger contexts of Job and the traditions of

---

87. See Blenkinsopp, *Wisdom and Law*, p. 134.
88. Murphy, *A Short Reading of the Book of Job*, p. 68.
89. Zuckerman, *Job the Silent*, p. 143.
90. Geller, 'Where is Wisdom?', p. 174.

wisdom literature'.⁹¹ Like many others, he is blinded by the concentration of wisdom features in ch. 28 and fails to interpret this particular chapter in the larger cosmic context of the storyline. His assumption is even more troubling because he acknowledges that 'wisdom had no traffic with revelations aside from dreams'.⁹² For example, he concludes his study by suggesting that the author of Job has 'presented an "answer" to suffering'.⁹³ Such a result recalls Westermann's initial reason for breaking with a wisdom assumption for Job because such assumptions presume that the book of Job deals with a 'problem'.⁹⁴ For most, this problem is the issue of suffering, and Geller, too, falls prey to his own self-hedging assumptions, which limit the text's possibilities.

However, Geller is correct to point to a 'new pietism' in Job and that this resurgent piety (as seen in the subsequent chs. 29–31) 'results from revelation, not deduction'.⁹⁵ He is also correct to treat ch. 28 as needed preparation for the climax of the book.⁹⁶ Most importantly, his work is extraordinarily helpful in that it suggests that ch. 28 contains a major revelation, one that is pivotal both to understanding the story, and to framing the more useful genre of apocalypse.

Job is revitalized because of the revelation in ch. 28. From ch. 28 Job will immediately launch into another self-justification, and this time with much greater force than what has hitherto proceeded from his mouth. As Carol Fontaine suggests, Job is encouraged to move forward because the wisdom revealed in ch. 28 'encourages him to take the oath of innocence in ch. 31'.⁹⁷ So powerful are his ensuing words, that the friends simply yield their position, thus completely ending the cycle of debates between Job and the friends.

Finally, for interpreters who consider Job strictly wisdom, ch. 28 is commonly used as justification for that designation. However, such assumptions cannot, as pointed out, weave this chapter into a larger 'wisdom' scenario for Job. Only when one accepts that 'wisdom' is being used as a vehicle for the larger cosmic storyline, and should not be considered the centerpiece, can the interpreter lift their eyes from the page and see the story for itself.

91. Geller, 'Where is Wisdom?', p. 155.
92. Geller, 'Where is Wisdom?', p. 169.
93. Geller, 'Where is Wisdom?', p. 175.
94. Westermann, *Structure*, p. 1.
95. Geller, 'Where is Wisdom?', p. 173.
96. Geller, 'Where is Wisdom?', p. 174.
97. Fontaine, 'Wounded Hero', p. 79. Fontaine argues that Job is a form of 'poeticized folktale', where ch. 28 serves to mark the entrance of a 'magical agent' (pp. 71, 79). Naturally, what is a magical agent to Fontaine is a mediator in an apocalyptic scheme. Regardless of labels, I agree that ch. 28 functions to hearten Job's commitment to his integrity.

Chapter 28 reveals the apocalyptic moment for Job in that he is rejecting the earthly realm's ability to assist in his struggle. In ch. 28, Job makes a clean break from the friends and creation and sets his eyes more firmly on that which is beyond. He is encouraged to continue his fight because all earthly explanations are rendered impotent since they *cannot* understand or find God's wisdom.

Job 29–31
Chapters 29–31 essentially function as a unit that point to the anticipated confrontation between God and Job. Thus, the reader begins to see the symmetry between the beginning of the story and now. The second cycle of the story has begun. Job's reminders of fear of the Lord and turning from evil in Job 28.28 call the reader back to the prologue, and now, with the cosmic context still in mind, Job laments in chs. 29 and 30 again, as he did in ch. 3, though this lament is different.

The narrator reminds the reader in 29.1 that Job again has begun to speak. As noted earlier, some have seen this as evidence for denying Job's voice in ch. 28. On my reading, this is both true and false. It is false because, as I have argued, Job's continuation into ch. 28 can be defended on thematic consistency with his words in ch. 27. Additionally, since God is quoted at the end of ch. 28, the narrator seeks to clarify that Job is now resuming. Thus, even if one rejects Geller's proposal regarding the theophanic characteristics of 28.23b, the fact that God clearly speaks in Job 28.28 necessitates an editorial identification of Job as the speaker in ch. 29.

A resurgent Job appears in the beginning of ch. 29 who is no longer concerned with the friends. His attention is completely fixed on God, and his words reflect a profoundly increased piety that is the product of the revelation in ch. 28.[98] Job 29.2 reads, 'Oh that I were as in the months of old, as in the days when God watched over me', and Job's piety is especially and nostalgically seen in 29.14, 'I put on righteousness, and it clothed me; my justice was like a robe and a turban'.

Chapter 30 is an expression of contrast. Now life has changed dramatically and everything that was good has been reversed. His reputation, status with God and wealth are all gone. Job laments in 30.15, 'Terrors are turned upon me; my honor is pursued as by the wind, and my prosperity has passed away like a cloud'.

Job's lament slowly develops in 30.20 where he returns to his vain cry for an answer from God, though silence is all he receives. Increasingly, Job becomes more accusatory toward God. In v. 21, Job says, 'You have turned cruel to me'. Now that the friends are rhetorically dismissed, there can be no doubt that Job is directly addressing God. Job is hard-pressed to understand

---

98. Geller, 'Where is Wisdom?', p. 173.

how God could be so silent, especially to someone who has been as good a man as Job. In v. 25, Job begins to move slowly into one of the greatest accounts of moral correctness in the Hebrew Bible. He asks, 'Did I not weep for those whose day was hard? Was not my soul grieved for the poor?' This imprecation will reach its pinnacle in form and content in ch. 31, an incomparable selection of righteous actions in the Hebrew Bible.

Having worked through both chs. 29 and 30, the reader may not notice that an invigorated Job does not express a desire for death, as he did in ch. 3. Instead, Job seems driven, and he develops a case to gain a hearing with God, which will culminate with Job's plea in ch. 31. This new Job is no longer a defeated man longing for the grave, he is a man who has parried the friends, been emboldened by a revelation of cosmic wisdom and is now ready to speak directly with God. Despite his anxiety over God's reluctance to meet with him, he does not curse God.

In ch. 31, Job denies that he has conducted himself in an unrighteous manner by addressing various sinful acts, many of which the friends have accused him of committing. For example, Job denies being deceptive (vv. 5-6), withholding from the poor (v. 16), any reliance on wealth (v. 24) and, importantly, idolatry (v. 26). His emphatic declarations of righteousness project a sort of 'bravado' before God, which is the complete manifestation of the 'new' Job that emerged from ch. 28.[99]

However, the purpose of this speech, as prepared by the previous two chapters, may be to clarify his hope and intention to speak with God. In vv. 35 to 37, Job makes one final plea for God to hear his case. Job used to walk with God in such a blissful way, but where is God? Now that his fortunes have been reversed and Job has demonstrated that he is indeed righteous, it is time for some answers, so he says:

> [35]Oh, that I had one to hear me! (Here is my signature! Let the Almighty answer me!)
> Oh, that I had the indictment written by my adversary!
> [36]Surely I would carry it on my shoulder;
> I would bind it on me like a crown;
> [37]I would give him an account of all my steps;
> like a prince I would approach him.

The reader's expectation of a possible confrontation is once again heightened, which is stimulated by the editor's note that Job's words, and thus both his lament and appeal, are ended.[100] This anticipation is deflated again as a new figure enters the scene.

---

99. Murphy (*A Short Reading of the Book of Job*, p. 75) suggests the 'bravado' posture.

100. Hartley, *The Book of Job*, p. 425.

As the friends retreat into silence (32.1), Job is confronted with Elihu who up until now was only a silent observer. Still, despite the reader's disappointment that Job is not yet meeting God, they too recognize the repetition of the pattern that began in Job 28.28. Wisdom is fearing the Lord and turning from evil, Job is suffering and laments it and now Elihu's role repeats the literary function of the friends—to attack Job's position.

On the other hand, Elihu's role might not be merely as a literary device intended to provide symmetry. Indeed, his appearance has baffled many scholars and led many to conclude that it is a later interpolation. As I will argue shortly, Elihu is also a potential agent of the Satan, akin to the friends. Thus, his sudden arrival may have been prompted by something as equally dramatic as his entrance and long-winded bombast that follows.

Perhaps Elihu's main purpose in the narrative is to combat Job's perceived willingness to die in his righteousness, without ever admitting to some kind of non-existent sin. Such a scenario would undermine the Satan's machinations and result in his suffering the very curse he imposed on himself. The form of Job's final plea in Job 31 might indicate that Job was in fact ready to die in his own righteousness.

Job 31 seems to mirror negative confessions frequently recited in ancient Egypt, many of which are contained in the *Book of the Dead*, which was the name given to a collection of ancient Egyptian papyri. For example, Job says in 31.13-14, 'If I have rejected the cause of my male and female slaves, when they brought a complaint against me; what then shall I do when God rises up?' In the *Book of the Dead*, the writer offers, 'I have not done evil. I have not repeatedly made slaves work overtime…I have not given false witness against slaves to their masters.'[101] In Job 31.16-17, Job says, 'If I have withheld anything that the poor desired…or have eaten my morsel alone, and the orphan has not eaten from it…' And in the *Book of the Dead*, 'I have not starved the hungry'. Several other parallels exist, suggesting at least that Job 31 might indicate knowledge of the Egyptian practice.

The Egyptian texts were placed with the dead 'in order to help them pass through the dangers of the Underworld and attain an afterlife of bliss in the Field of Reeds, the Egyptian heaven'.[102] Pritchard refers to it as 'The Protestation of Guiltlessness'.[103] So close are the parallels that J. Murtagh concludes that 'it is impossible to deny the influence of the Book of the Dead on the Book of Job'.[104] Pope is more cautious, noting that while the

---

101. Matthews and Benjamin (eds.), *Old Testament Parallels*, pp. 204-205.

102. Carol Andrews (ed.), *The Ancient Egyptian Book of the Dead* (Austin, TX: University of Texas Press, 1985), p. 11.

103. *ANET*, p. 34.

104. J. Murtagh, 'The Book of Job and the Book of the Dead', *Irish Theological Quarterly* 35 (1968), pp. 166-73 (167).

'similarities are striking', they are 'not sufficient to indicate direct interdependence'.[105] Pope distinguishes the Egyptian catalogues as primarily ethical and ritual whereas Job is almost exclusively ethical.[106]

Similarly, while Georg Fohrer agreed that 'many things in Job 31 are similar to these confessions', he observed that Job's conditional formulation contrasted with the Egyptian form enough to declare that the Egyptian confessions could not 'be regarded as the immediate prototype'.[107] Hartley, however, contends that even if the sins in the lists are somewhat different from each other, the situations had the similar purpose for the swearer who sought to 'clear himself of any guilt from the slightest wrongdoing'.[108]

It seems that the Egyptian practice of proclaiming declarations of innocence or negative confessions were 'designed to bring about the resurrection of the dead and assure a blessed afterlife'.[109] If the author of Job knew that such a negative confession would depict Job as preparing for his own resurrection or blessed afterlife, two important points need to be made.

First, while indirect, once again the concept of an afterlife and even a resurrection is alluded to by the author. Job has fought his friends, dismissed them, and is emboldened through the revelation in ch. 28. Based on his own seemingly futile plea in 31.35, 'Oh that I had one to hear me!', Job does not seem to expect a hearing from God. Therefore, he prepares to die in his integrity, and now seeks to prepare the way for a more pleasing afterlife.

Second, as regards the main plot of the story, the last thing the Satan wants to see is Job dying in his righteousness, because that would signal the Satan's defeat; Job held on. In contrast to Job's damning lament in Job 3, where he was ready to die in despair, a hope-filled Job is now ready to die in his own intransigent insistence that he is righteous. In neither case does Job 'curse God'. That can only spell cosmic despair for the Satan. Thus, seizing one last chance to force Job to capitulate, Elihu emerges. Elihu represents the Satan's last opportunity to avoid his own self-curse before Job dies in his righteousness. Elihu is, therefore, anything but an expendable character in the story.

Job 32–37
In the opening five verses of narrative, the author clearly aligns Elihu with the three friends by disclosing that Elihu was angry with Job for justifying himself rather than God (32.2), which is a charge the friends directed at Job.

---

105. Pope, *Job*, p. 200.
106. Pope, *Job*, p. 200.
107. Georg Fohrer, 'The Righteous Man in Job 31', in J. Crenshaw and J. Willis (eds.), *Essays in Old Testament Ethics* (New York: Ktav, 1974), pp. 3-22 (10).
108. Hartley, *The Book of Job*, p. 407.
109. Matthews and Benjamin (eds.), *Old Testament Parallels*, p. 204.

But then Elihu directs his anger toward the friends because they had not sufficiently answered Job (32.3). Verse 3's scribal history warrants further analysis since it may be possible to shed light on its interpretation. Job 32.3 reads, 'he was angry also at Job's three friends because they had found no answer, though they declared Job to be in the wrong'.

At first glance, it seems that Elihu is upset simply because the friends were unable to prove Job's error, despite the fact that they insisted he was wrong. However, the English translations seem to tailor the Hebrew to fit a wisdom context rather than accepting what is presented. The second stich of 32.3 reads: וירשיעו את־איוב.

The Hiphil form of רשע, 'condemn as guilty, act wickedly',[110] suggests that the friends *caused* Job's guilt or wickedness. If one were to stress the causative usage of the Hiphil, translation of the clause might read, 'they caused (brought on) Job's guilt (or wickedness)'. Such a rendering would make no sense because the friends' alleged incompetence could not logically lead to Job's guilt. After all, the friends had already declared Job guilty by his own actions, as Elihu had just done in the preceding verse.

There is another possibility. According to Jewish tradition, Job 32.3 is one of the 18 'emendations of the scribes'. The earliest versions evidently contained האלהים as the object instead of איוב.[111] If the earliest versions were the most accurate, then the friends would actually have caused *God* to be 'condemned as guilty (or wicked)'! Supporting this idea, Pope translates, 'And against his three companions his anger also flared because they had not found an answer and so made God guilty'.[112] If this was the case, Elihu was angered at the friends not only because of their incompetence, but because their incompetence jeopardized God's honor. The friends consistently claimed to be speaking for God, and yet their arguments completely failed to convince Job to repent. Logically then, God's reputation would be impugned by their failure.

Elihu therefore usurps the role of God's spokesperson from the friends and is now going to speak on God's behalf. Barely into his monologue, Elihu aligns himself with God even more powerfully than the friends had. Contrasting the traditional understanding that wisdom resides with the elderly, the youthful Elihu concludes in 32.8, 'But truly it is the spirit in a mortal, the breath of the Almighty, that makes for understanding'. After

---

110. BDB, p. 957b.
111. Pope, *Job*, p. 212. See also the footnote in *BHS*.
112. Pope, *Job*, p. 210. NEB translates, 'they had found no answer to Job and let God appear wrong'. Of interest, Cox translates the LXX, 'and they made him out to be righteous', where the 'him' refers to Job, not God. Ziegler (*Iob*, p. 354) does not offer any variants that assign guilt to God.

further justifying his place in the conversation, Elihu addresses Job directly in ch. 33.

Elihu will make similar arguments to those made by the friends, and in so doing assume the role as another unsuspecting tool of the Satan. Readers who have stayed the course will pick up this nuance immediately, especially if האלהים were before them in 32.3. The reader will see that Elihu is nothing more than an extension of the Satan. Since Job has just demanded an audience with God (31.35-37) and the friends have sunk into silence, Elihu functions as the Satan's last chance to coerce Job into some form of forced repentance.

Elihu argues that Job's claims to be 'clean, without transgression' (33.9) are simply wrong. The reader recognizes, once again, that Job has not claimed that he is without transgression, of which he confesses himself in 7.20-21, but it is God who has labeled Job completely upright. Here is where Elihu maintains the same line of argument pursued by the friends; yet, in contrast to the friends, Elihu concentrates his assault on Job's insistence to be granted God's audience. Job 33.13 is critical because it serves as both the transition from Job 31 and as the underlying argument throughout the Elihu speeches. It reads: 'Why do you contend against him, saying, "He will answer none of my words"?'

This request for God's audience was Job's last and strongest demand and Elihu feels that such a request is wholly improper. Elihu even refers to Eliphaz's vision (33.15-16) and, using the same tactics that Eliphaz did, turns the message of the dream against Job. Not surprisingly, also like Eliphaz, Elihu takes up the remainder of ch. 33 to illustrate the plight of the wicked who are saved from 'going down into the Pit' if they repent. The reader recognizes the parallel of the two passages and is again reminded of the cosmic plot.

In ch. 34, Elihu apparently addresses the entire gathering and accuses Job of both claiming to be innocent and of having his 'right' unduly removed in v. 4. In vv. 7 and 8, Elihu accuses Job of associating with evil people. The reader knows that all of these are not true, at least in the way that Elihu is suggesting. This is simply the same tactic the friends had used. Elihu offers another blow at the end of the chapter, declaring, 'Job speaks without knowledge, his words are without insight' (34.35).

Elihu continues his attack in ch. 35, defending God's silence in the face of Job's request. Here again, Elihu seems incredulous at Job's request for a response from God. He says in 35.13-14:

> [13]Surely God does not hear an empty cry,
>   nor does the Almighty regard it.
> [14]How much less when you say that you do not see him,
>   that the case is before him, and you are waiting for him!

Elihu considers Job's request as pure insolence before his God. He ends this chapter in a way similar to the preceding, with a declaration that Job opens his mouth in 'empty talk'.

However, the greatest expression of arrogance arises from Elihu himself at the beginning of ch. 36:

> ¹Elihu continued and said:
> ²'Bear with me a little, and I will show you,
>   for I have yet something to say on God's behalf.
> ³I will bring my knowledge from far away,
>   and ascribe righteousness to my Maker.
> ⁴For truly my words are not false;
>   one who is perfect (תמים) in knowledge is with you.'

Elihu not only claims to speak on God's behalf, he claims to be perfect in knowledge. The use of תם is not lost on the reader. God described Job as תם and now Elihu's self-assertion contrasts that use. No greater sign of pomposity has yet existed, and no greater distance between the claims of humble service made by Job in ch. 31 and these can be fathomed. Elihu closes the chapter by repeatedly chastising the wicked, and he asserts that God brings down great men, and that God is beyond understanding.

In ch. 37, Elihu continues this appeal to God's greatness, especially through natural wonders. He then levels his final charge that it is inappropriate to demand to have a case brought before God in 37.19-20:

> ¹⁹Teach us what we shall say to him;
>   we cannot draw up our case because of darkness.
> ²⁰Should he be told that I want to speak?
>   Did anyone ever wish to be swallowed up?

Elihu persistently berates Job for seeking an audience with God, which is peculiar to Elihu over against the friends' allegations. Elihu has tried a new tactic. In fitting irony, his final words declare that God 'does not regard any who are wise in their own conceit'.

If the ancient reader understood Elihu's role in the way I suggest, it may demonstrate why the author(s) of the *Testament of Job* portrayed Elihu in such a demonic way. For example, in *T. Job* 41.5, Elihu is said to be 'inspired by Satan'. Chapter 42 reports that God 'censured Elihu' and that God revealed to Job that it was a 'beast' speaking through Elihu, not a man. Furthermore, after the three friends have been pardoned because of Job's sacrifice, they all take up a hymn against Elihu, which comprises the entirety of ch. 43—the longest chapter in the book! The friends consider Elihu 'the evil one'.

For such a seemingly innocuous character, one that most modern scholars view as a late and disconnected addition, it is rather remarkable that the ancients took such interest in condemning Elihu.[113] However, no character in the story of Job has taken such pains as Elihu to proclaim his right standing with God. Furthermore, Job has adequately dispelled the errant remarks of the friends, and Elihu generally rehashes much of what they say, thereby demonstrating that he is actually more foolish than they.

Job 38.1–42.7: God's Revelation of Divine Prerogative— Job Submits

Most commentators accept this section as the decisive stage of the story. God's sudden theophany bursts onto the scene as the story's centerpiece and apex. This revelation is what the reader, and especially Job, has been waiting for.[114] The theophany contains a heavenly revelation and in the power of the storyline, this theophany must influence one's interpretation of the entire story.[115] It is therefore imperative that the reader clearly understand the story's interpretive sequence, which, by this time, is all too often forgotten. It may be useful to remind the reader of Donald Gowan's correct assertion that the book of Job, 'provides one of the best examples...of how one's presuppositions affect an interpretation of Scripture'.[116]

These presuppositions are put to the test immediately with God's very first words. In 38.2 God questions Job, 'Who is this that darkens counsel by words without knowledge?' Traditionally, interpreters argue that God is berating Job for his presumptuousness. As an example, Robert Alter argues that God's speeches are poetry designed specifically to counter Job's maledictory words of poetry employed in Job's mournful lament from ch. 3. For Alter, God is correcting Job and thereby demonstrating that it is inappropriate to question God's regnant world order.[117]

Yet, the reader might legitimately question who is actually addressed by God's words. Given Elihu's baseless and arrogant alignment with God, one could argue that the words might have been directed at Elihu! Since God used the very words that Elihu used against Job, namely, 'words without knowledge' (34.15; 35.16), it is possible that God is parodying Elihu.

---

113. See Westermann, *Structure*, p. 139, who places the source of modern scholarship's obsession with identifying the 'problem of Job' in the Elihu speeches.
114. Robert Alter, 'The Voice from the Whirlwind', *Commentary* 77 (1984), pp. 33-41 (34).
115. Thomas F. Dailey, 'Theophanic Bluster: Job and the Wind of Change', *Studies in Religion* 22 (1993), pp. 187-95 (188, 192).
116. Donald E. Gowan, 'God's Answer to Job: How is it an Answer?', *HBT* 8 (1986), pp. 85-102 (86).
117. Alter, 'Voice', pp. 33-41.

4. Reading Job through Apocalyptic Eyes

Although silent regarding the recipient of God's question, Andersen does suggest that God's conversation with Job is not the rebuke that so many assume. For Andersen, 'there is no hint of that irritating cant that silences the honest seeker with the reminder that it is not for us to question the ways of the Almighty'. Instead, Andersen views the conversation between God and Job as 'kindly playfulness...which is quite relaxing'.[118] While Andersen does not mention it, 11QtgJob also conveys this more unperturbed tenor in both Job 38.3 and 40.7, where God says, 'Like a man, *please* gird your loins'.[119]

Is it possible that our modern interpretations have read too much into these words? Is it possible that a world that is defined by individualism and independence *desires* to view Job as 'shaking his fist' at God? While Job certainly questions God, is it possible that his questioning was not considered 'challenging', but rather mere querying?

Perhaps God was, in fact, simply addressing his question directly to Elihu. Karl Wilcox argues for such an interpretation. For him, the grammar provides the hint. Job 38.2 is asked in the third person but then shifts immediately to the second person. Wilcox argues that this switch signifies that God is initially addressing Elihu, and then turns his attention to Job.[120] H.H. Rowley also supports such a reading, stating, 'If the Elihu speeches were integral to the book, the reference here should be to him'.[121] Perhaps the premodern insights of Gregory of Rome could also be instructive because he too felt that God's question was directed at Elihu. Gregory comments, 'For Elihu had spoken arrogantly... Having then glanced with contempt on this man [Elihu!], His words are directed to the instruction of Job.'[122]

Tradition also castigates Elihu. As noted earlier, in *T. Job* 42.1-2, Job claims that God censured Elihu: 'After Elihu ended his arrogant speech, the Lord—having appeared plainly to me through a hurricane and clouds—spoke and censured Elihu'.[123] The *Testament of Job* also depicts the three friends stating in 43.5, 'Elihu, Elihu—the only evil one—will have no

---

118. Andersen, *The Book of Job*, pp. 270-71.
119. Vermes, *Dead Sea Scrolls*, pp. 433, 436 (emphasis added).
120. Karl Wilcox, '"Who is this...?" A Reading of Job 38.2', *JSOT* 78 (1998), pp. 85-95. In a rebuttal of Wilcox, John J. Bimson ('Who is "this" in "Who is this...?" (Job 38.2)? A Response to Karl G. Wilcox', *JSOT* 87 [2000], pp. 125-28 [125]) argues that Wilcox's commitment to the grammatical solution rests on the assumption that God addresses Job directly.
121. H.H. Rowley, *The Book of Job* (NCBC; Grand Rapids: Eerdmans, 1970), p. 241.
122. *Moralia on Job*, III, pp. 268-69, as cited and translated in Besserman, *Legend*, pp. 54-55.
123. Spittler, in *OTP*, I, p. 861.

memorial among the living'.[124] Rabbi Akiba also tramples Elihu by comparing him to Balaam, the enemy of Israel.[125]

Further supporting this line of thinking is that the opening formula in God's second speech (40.1-7) does not include a similar question. God's opening formula in ch. 38 mirrors the beginning of the second speech and includes similar wording, such as, 'gird up your loins like a man'. If the author intended to repeat the formula, we might expect that the question about 'who darkens counsel' would be repeated. If, in fact, Elihu is the object of the question in 38.2, then that explains why the question does not appear in the beginning of God's second speech. The absence of the specific question in the second speech opens the possibility that the question was considered a one-time comment on Elihu's words. In such a scenario, the reader would recognize God's antipathy for Elihu, which agrees with the reading I propose.

Who the reader decides is the recipient of God's revelation greatly influences how one interprets God's following words. The traditional approach argues that God is challenging Job as a 'defense against the accusation and claims of Job, a defense which sends Job reeling'.[126]

The speeches to Job simply do not have to be read as sarcastic or overly critical. It seems that they are typically accepted as such because of the presumption that Job has indeed erred. Murphy acknowledges that the majority of God's words to Job represent a 'gentle mood of instruction, an air of, "Don't you agree?"'[127] Donald Gowan argues that the theophany itself would have signaled a 'positive experience' by the reader in antiquity.[128] Thomas Dailey goes further, proposing that 'God's presence in the theophany serves as a demonstration of divine favour'.[129]

God is therefore not challenging Job; rather, he is dismissing the so-called friends' arguments against Job once and for all. In effect, God's intervention has spared Job from any further attacks by the Satan's lieutenants. This is the kind of impact that revelations have in later apocalyptic works. Apocalyptic revelations assure the recipient that God is sovereign even over the apocalyptic battle. They impart hope and offer both comfort for the future and strength to persevere under duress. For the recipient, salvation is offered through the power of the revelation. Dailey puts it well: 'like theophanies of old, it [the whirlwind] intimates a salvific presence; like images of the

---

124. Spittler, in *OTP*, I, p. 862.
125. Jacob Neusner (trans.), *The Talmud of the Land of Israel* (35 vols.; Chicago: The University of Chicago Press, 1984), XXVII, p. 160.
126. Habel, *The Book of Job*, p. 528.
127. Murphy, *A Short Reading of the Book of Job*, p. 89.
128. Gowan, 'God's Answer', p. 95.
129. Dailey, 'Bluster', p. 190.

future, it implies a definitive judgment'.¹³⁰ Further amplifying Dailey's point, Joe Lunceford observes that 'in most biblical citations', whirlwinds are 'symbolic of God's swift and thorough judgment'.¹³¹

This interpretation might also solve the problem of why Elihu is not rebuked at the end of the story. A possible solution is that he is rebuked in 38.2 already! Nothing more needs to be said, and the *Testament of Job* seems to bear this tradition out.

After this opening, Yahweh makes an unprecedented revelation of creation from 38.4 to 39.30. Many commentators have recognized the creation language of Job as more archaic and showing greater affinity to the mythological language of the ancient Near East than to the tidy and systematic Genesis accounts. Could it be that Job, a non-Israelite like Abraham and Noah, is cast by the author as the first (only?) non-Israelite to receive a direct revelation of God's creation? After all, God is revealing his massive creation more extensively than anywhere else in the Bible by addressing cosmogony, meteorology and zoology.¹³² Interestingly, God's revelation in Job does not center on, or even address, the creation of human beings. Tom Are suggests that even though humans are not discussed, the fact that a human (Job) receives God's revelation is important. For Are, 'the effect is to demonstrate that Job is not mere creature, but God's creature', because, while creation demonstrates a complex order, it remains God's order.¹³³ In other words, Job is not claiming to be God or even asserting that he understands God. He is humbled by God's revelation, but not because of his presumptuousness.

If this interpretation is correct, the magnitude and importance of the revelation is even more stunning, and the tenor of Yahweh's words clearly seeks to instruct rather than intimidate. In this way, Job is not the villain, but as recipient of this revelation, he is crowned the victor by being granted this astonishing word from God. The whirlwind speeches serve as a 'revelatory symbol'¹³⁴ that gives form to 'the proto-language of transcendent experience, and thus also of religious experience'.¹³⁵ If Job is intended to depict the earliest demonstration of such a transcendent communication, the story rises well above wisdom and enters into the milieu of the otherworldly realm more commonly associated with apocalypse.

---

130. Dailey, 'Bluster', p. 191.
131. Joe E. Lunceford, 'Whirlwind', in Freedman (ed.), *Eerdmans Dictionary of the Bible*, p. 1377. Lunceford considers the uses of whirlwind in Job 37.9 and 38.1 as 'literal' uses, which is somewhat perplexing given the book of Job's poetic tendencies.
132. See Westermann, *Structure*, p. 114, and Alter, 'Voice', p. 34.
133. Tom Are, 'Job 38:1-7', *Interpretation* 53 (1999), pp. 294-98 (297).
134. Dailey, 'Bluster', p. 193.
135. L. Alonso Schökel, *A Manual of Hebrew Poetics* (Subsidia biblica, 11; Rome: Pontifical Biblical Institute, 1988), p. 111.

In God's second speech, he becomes much less playful. There is no doubt that God is now addressing Job, asking in 40.2, 'Shall a fault-finder contend with the Almighty? Anyone who argues with God must respond.' While Job may not be guilty of 'darkening counsel', he is guilty of contending and challenging God. I have argued for a reading of the Hebrew as, 'the one who reproves God must answer the reproof'.[136] Thus, in Job 40.2, God is not accusing Job of any specific wrongdoing per se.[137] Instead, he is challenging Job to measure up to Job's own questions concerning God, which, of course, Job cannot possibly accomplish. Thus, the primary goal in God's second speech is to demonstrate Job's impotence and smallness, which would thereby render Job completely reliant upon and submissive to God.

The great mythological beasts of Behemoth and Leviathan dominate this second speech. Leo Perdue has argued cogently that both of these beasts are to be regarded as symbols of chaos.[138] The author uses them both to promote a mythical battle metaphor, which Perdue argues is a contest between God and Job. Perdue contends that Job seeks to 'dethrone Yahweh and rule over the divine council', which requires that Job defeat these beasts.[139]

In my view, Perdue is unconvincing because he reads too much into Job 40.8-14, which is the basis for his argument. However, he leads in a direction more amenable to my apocalyptic hypothesis. Perdue acknowledges that 'God is both the one who does battle with this creature of chaos, and the one who is creator. It may be that this implies divine culpability for the origins of evil.'[140] At the same time, Perdue notes that Behemoth functions not to blame God for chaos, but to demonstrate 'that the powers of darkness are mighty and fierce and must be intimidated and confronted to keep the world from entering the realm of oblivion'.[141]

Leviathan is described even more extensively than Behemoth, though Perdue advances similar thoughts emphasizing that Leviathan represents pre-existent chaos and that Job must defeat him if he is to dethrone Yahweh.[142] However, the questions that God asks in this section highlight

---

136. Johnson, 'Implied Antecedents', pp. 278-84.

137. See too, Perdue, *Wisdom in Revolt*, p. 219, who concurs, but for different reasons. Perdue is also predisposed to Job as wisdom and feels that God cannot equate Job's innocence with his guilt. Also of note, Perdue's study seeks to avoid ch. 28 and the Elihu speeches altogether (p. 85). Thus, while his study is illuminating and helpful in many areas, it is unable to accomplish narrative and literary unity, which is my essential concern in my project.

138. Perdue, *Wisdom in Revolt*, pp. 221-32.

139. Perdue, *Wisdom in Revolt*, p. 225.

140. Perdue, *Wisdom in Revolt*, p. 226. See also A.Y. Collins who identifies the combat myth with apocalypses ('Apocalyptic Themes', pp. 123-26).

141. Perdue, *Wisdom in Revolt*, p. 226.

142. Perdue, *Wisdom in Revolt*, p. 228.

4. *Reading Job through Apocalyptic Eyes*   151

the mortal Job's inability to defeat Leviathan even more powerfully than those asked in the preceding section covering Behemoth. In fact, it is even clearer that 'only Yahweh as Divine Warrior has the power to defeat Leviathan'.[143]

But Yahweh declares this sentiment as well with reference to Behemoth in 40.19, 'It is the first of the great acts of God—only its Maker can approach it with a sword'. Perdue argues that with some minor pointing alteration in the MT, a very similar reading could be found in 41.26, this time regarding Leviathan, 'the one who made him', which would provide for a reading that treats Yahweh as the subject of v. 26 instead of Leviathan. Thus, 'only Yahweh would stand before Leviathan without fear'.[144]

Like Perdue's, my reading of Job regards these two creatures as symbols of evil. Job is shown to be utterly unable to defeat evil, which is what is at stake, and only God is able to complete what Job cannot. Job has learned that his friends are part of a larger plot, but he cannot identify the plot. He can only suspect that some negative force is behind it, 'With whose help have you uttered words, and whose spirit (נשמה) has come forth from you?' (26.4). Thus, after each speech from God, Job is humbled because more is revealed to him than he knew beforehand.

Commentators who assume Job is rebellious are at pains to describe his first response in 40.3-5. Habel describes the mood as one of complaint,[145] and Andersen says that Job is 'sticking to his guns'.[146] Most see that Job is neither confessing nor submitting, which causes God to speak again, but God still has more to reveal. Murphy seems closer to the mark by recognizing that Job is simply awed: faced with God's willingness to respond (40.2), Job wisely chooses silence.[147]

However, few identify that Job's response is packaged in another graded numerical saying:[148]

> ³Then Job answered the Lord:
> ⁴'See, I am of small account; what shall I answer you?
>   I lay my hand on my mouth.
> ⁵I have spoken once, and I will not answer;
>   twice, but will proceed no further.'

This numerical saying does not enumerate the two items that Job alludes to, namely, the two specific times he spoke to God. Job clearly directs his

---

    143.   Perdue, *Wisdom in Revolt*, pp. 228-29.
    144.   Perdue, *Wisdom in Revolt*, p. 231.
    145.   Habel, *The Book of Job*, p. 549.
    146.   Andersen, *The Book of Job*, p. 285.
    147.   Murphy, *A Short Reading of the Book of Job*, p. 95.
    148.   Steinmann ('Graded Numerical Saying', pp. 288-97) cites four instances where graded numerical sayings are found in Job 5.17-27; 33.13-22; 13.29-30 and 40.3-5.

words to God in several places. Andrew Steinmann convincingly argues that the two incidences referred to are Job's first lament in ch. 3 and his second lament in chs. 29–31, which Steinmann considers 'challenges to God'.[149]

The graded numerical sayings emerge in three pivotal areas in the story. Earlier in this chapter I discussed the first occasion, which was Eliphaz's first response to Job in ch. 5.[150] The second occasion includes the two numerical sayings in Elihu's first speech (33.13-22, 29-30), which was also in response to Job's larger lament contained in chs. 29–31. Thus, Steinmann suggests that the location of each numerical saying is designed to indicate an important juncture in the story. This also seems to be the case in 40.3-5.

Neither of the two previous uses of the numerical saying successfully drew a confession from Job. Both Eliphaz and Elihu failed to achieve that goal. However, Job's use of the numerical saying in 40.3-5 seems to yield some kind of admission from Job that he was wrong.[151] Therefore, this final numerical saying is used to 'highlight God's wisdom as superior to human wisdom' since both Eliphaz and Elihu failed to elicit such an admission.[152] Once again, like the revelation in ch. 28, God reveals that human wisdom is inferior to his own.

Job's second response in 42.1-6 proves that God's message has been received. Job's question in 42.3, however, has been appropriately associated with God's initial question in 38.2. In 42.3, Job asks, 'Who is this that hides counsel without knowledge?' Most commentators argue that Job is rhetorically referring to himself by repeating the question that God directed to him in 38.2. Habel even prefaces 42.3 with 'You said' in order to influence the reader's understanding.[153]

Is such an intrusion necessary? The verb used for 'darken' in 38.2 is a Hiphil of חשך, translated in BDB as 'to obscure, confuse'.[154] However, the verb used in 42.3 is a form of עלם, translated as 'conceal'.[155] The difference between 'confuse' and 'conceal' is significant. The pejorative nature of 'confuse' lends credibility to the notion that Elihu was, in fact, misleading Job via his alleged alliance with God's will and his bold claim to understand God.

In 42.3, by contrast, Job is likely offering a self-reflection admitting that he should have known better all along. He himself should have known that God was incomprehensible, yet he persisted in asking and demanding God's

149. Steinmann, 'Graded Numerical Saying', p. 295.
150. See my discussion earlier in this chapter on the latter part of Job 5.
151. Steinmann, 'Graded Numerical Saying', p. 297.
152. Steinmann, 'Graded Numerical Saying', p. 296.
153. Habel, *The Book of Job*, p. 575.
154. BDB, p. 365a.
155. BDB, p. 761a.

4. Reading Job through Apocalyptic Eyes

response. Job uses these words to announce to God that now he has something to reveal to God. Job's revelation to God is that he now knows God in a new way, which was God's immensely privileged revelation to Job all along. Job says in 42.5, 'I had heard of you by the hearing of the ear, but now my eye sees you'. Job signals that he has received this revelation from God. He concludes by repenting not of sinning in any way, but in not truly 'seeing' what he had always 'heard'. Job had knowledge of the facts, which should have led him to the inward knowledge.

The reader is not surprised that Job does not repent of any particular sin, because God had already declared him righteous at the very beginning and Job had not earned his punishment. Murphy remarks similarly, 'Whatever be the translation of v 6, it cannot mean that Job goes back on the views expressed'.[156] However, since many consider Job 42.6 the climactic verse in the book, scholarship continues to debate its interpretation. Thomas Dailey summarizes scholarship's approaches to interpreting Job 42.6:

> Job's concluding position could be described as: 1) *juridical*, in that he is stating the retraction of his lawsuit against God; 2) *confessional*, in that he is expressing his conversion back to God; 3) *lyrical*, in as much as he is experiencing consolation in having encountered his God; or 4) *ironical*, in as much as he is deftly continuing his rejection of the defense of God.[157]

Of those cited by Dailey, Dale Patrick's approach initiated a renewed interest in Job 42.6. Patrick challenges the traditional translation:

> Therefore I despise myself, and repent in dust and ashes.

Instead he proposes translating the verse:

> על־כן אמאס ונחמתי על־עפר ואפר
>
> Therefore I repudiate and repent of dust and ashes.[158]

The key for Patrick is interpreting ונחמתי על as repenting *of* instead of *in*, arguing that the traditional rendering 'does not correspond to the pattern of usage found elsewhere'.[159] Therefore, Job repents of 'wallowing in dust and ashes', which ultimately signals a shift from lamenting his state into a praising of God.[160] William Morrow acknowledges that Patrick's interpretation is

---

156. Murphy, *A Short Reading of the Book of Job*, p. 100.
157. Thomas Dailey, 'And Yet He Repents—On Job 42,6', *ZAW* 105 (1993), pp. 205-209 (206-207). Dailey identifies advocates for each of the positions held.
158. Dale Patrick, 'The Translation of Job xlii 6', *VT* 26 (1976), pp. 369-71 (369).
159. Patrick, 'The Translation of Job xlii 6', p. 370.
160. Patrick, 'The Translation of Job xlii 6', pp. 370-71. L.J. Kaplan, 'Maimonides, Dale Patrick, and Job xlii 6', *VT* 28 (1978), pp. 356-58, noted that Patrick's view corresponded exactly to that of Maimonides (p. 356).

legitimate, but only because the author of Job 'created a situation that can be interpreted in several ways according to the theological inclinations of the reader'.[161]

Dailey argues that Job's response is neither the simple lyricism associated with Patrick's proposal, nor the ironic rebellion more common with scholars like John Briggs Curtis.[162] Instead, Dailey suggests,

> the concluding verse maintains the denunciation of cosmic mismanagement which would be consistent with Job's sapiential integrity, yet attests to the epistemological transformation effected in him as a result of his encounter with the God of the storm.[163]

Still, Job does seem to confess some kind of wrongdoing. Steinmann may be correct that Job repents of his two lamentations (chs. 3 and 29–31), yet the claim that Job 3 is directed to God is not persuasive, as argued earlier in this chapter. The book of Job has been presented as focusing on perseverance, and Job has successfully preserved his integrity. In the worldly plane of his struggle, there must be some earthly sin of which Job is aware.

On two specific occasions, Job asserts that he has a helper in heaven, who is seemingly someone other than God. In 16.19, Job says, 'Even now, in fact, my witness is in heaven, and he that vouches for me is on high'. And in 19.25, the גאל figure serves as this possible intermediary. In contrast, Job 9.33 indicates that Job is simply acknowledging the lack of an 'umpire'. Job asserts that none exists.

Thus, there are two specific places where Job seems to loosen his reliance on God and long for another heavenly figure to save the day. If there are only two such incidences, these two places will serve as a better solution to the problem of the graded numerical saying in 40.3-5 described earlier. These two 'sins' also disclose that Job was not seeking God to solve his problem and therefore indicated that his monotheism might be waning. Apocalypses teach that those persecuted need to rely on God, for God is the

---

161. William Morrow, 'Consolation, Rejection, and Repentance in Job 42:6', *JBL* (1986), pp. 211-25 (225). I find his conclusion unsatisfactory because he seems to allow for any kind of interpretation without taking the whole of Job into account. For example, Morrow's approach would treat John Briggs Curtis's position that 'the poet intended not to support the current, accepted theology but rather to undermine it by showing the poverty of a transcendent and remote God, who has lost all touch with humanity', on a similar plane to that of Patrick's praise of God. Accepting all possibilities does not seem to help solve the interpretive challenges. See John Briggs Curtis, 'On Job's Response to Yahweh', *JBL* 98 (1979), pp. 497-511 (511).

162. Dailey, 'And Yet He Repents', p. 209. See n. 160 for the citation on John Briggs Curtis.

163. Dailey, 'And Yet He Repents', p. 209.

4. *Reading Job through Apocalyptic Eyes*   155

one who will rescue the sufferer through unseen means. In 42.6, Job confesses that he was on the way toward such a possible iniquity because he had only heard of God, but now he sees God with his very own eyes (42.5). The reader senses that Job might have rejected God had it not been for God's intervention. Job confesses that his faith was foundering, and because God chose to reveal himself, Job persevered.

Robert Gordis also recognizes the value of Job's faithfulness, stating, 'It is characteristic of Jewish thought that in spite of all the calamities that came upon him, Job does not yield to atheism'.[164] That Job would even entertain the idea of another heavenly assistant challenges the author's commitment to the Hebrew Bible's mainstay that 'God is one and indivisible'.[165]

Later tradition confirms such a conviction. In the Slavonic translation of the *Testament of Job*, the author overtly identifies Job as a former idol-worshipper and Irving Jacobs opines that 'it seems clear that the author himself regarded his hero as a former pagan'.[166] Job receives even harsher treatment in the *Book of Jashar*, which portrays Job as a counselor to the Pharaoh during the period just prior to the Hebrews Egyptian enslavement. This Job, who was 'from Mesopotamia, in the land of Uz', seems to refer to biblical Job and is even saddled with the dubious distinction of suggesting that all of the male children born to the Israelites be put to death, which the Pharaoh orders.[167] If such stories actually existed during the time of the *Testament of Job*, it is no wonder that Irving Jacobs refers to this work as 'the earliest source for the motif of the convert suffering for his newly adopted faith'.[168]

And yet the most remarkable element emerging from God's confrontation with Job is what was not said. Job had demanded an audience with God, and the reader who patiently traversed this lengthy story has wondered whether Job would capitulate and actually curse God to his face as the Satan so impetuously predicted. Here, in the midst of the whirlwind, is the climactic apocalyptic moment. Would God win or would the Satan? Will Job curse God or bless him? All at once the double meaning behind Job's wife's frenzied appeal that Job ברך God and die bears immense poetic significance,

---

164. Gordis, *Poets, Prophets, and Sages*, p. 297.
165. Gordis, *Poets, Prophets, and Sages*, p. 298.
166. Jacobs, 'Literary Motifs', p. 6; see n. 29.
167. *The Book of Jashar, Referred to in Joshua and Second Samuel* (trans. M.M. Noah; New York: Noah & Gould, 1840). Job is covered in 66.15-22 and later in 67.42-43. Curiously, Job is not heard from again in this book. This book claims to be the lost book that is mentioned in Joshua and 2 Samuel. It is, however, a likely translation of a sixteenth-century work. See the introduction entitled, 'Mordecai M. Noah and the Book of Yashar'.
168. Jacobs, 'Literary Motifs', p. 7.

perhaps an intended *double entendre*. All hinged on Job, and instead of cursing God, he both blessed God and repented.

Job persevered in the midst of immense pressure that was exerted from his wife and then from his so-called friends, and finally from a crafty youth. Job weathered all of these attacks, and in so doing, defeated the unseen machinations of the Satan. As pointed out, tradition strongly recognizes that the Satan is using all of these people to influence Job. In fact, the Syriac version of the *Apocalypse of Paul* even reports that Job's sons were used by Satan to encourage Job to blaspheme God.[169] The work also portrays Job telling Paul, 'the Devil appeared to me for the third time and said to me: Speak a word against the Lord and die'.[170] Job has won this cosmological battle, and tradition has clearly recognized the magnitude of the victory and the theological significance.

Job 42.7-17: Job's Reward for Persevering

As I have pointed out earlier, Eliphaz is singled out for rebuke from God because of his leadership role in attacking Job unjustly. He and his friends did not speak genuinely about God, but Job did. Eliphaz and the friends essentially tried to 'use' God to prove Job wrong, not knowing *they* were being 'used' by the Satan. And so the author comes full circle by essentially rebuking the Satan via Eliphaz and the friends' inability to persuade Job. There is no reason to expect a specific rebuke for the Satan because his self-curse takes full effect with Job's successful perseverance.

Job's wife received her rebuke from Job, who prior to his lament in ch. 3, was still considered תם by the narrator, which signaled that God recognized Job as his own ambassador. Job himself attests to his former dispensing of justice in 29.7-10, 17, 21-22, and so does Eliphaz in 4.3. Thus, as God's ambassador, Job's reprimand, 'You speak as any foolish women would speak' (2.10), is sufficient for God. There is no need for God to rebuke her again in the epilogue.

In the interpretation of the story offered here, the reader is not surprised that God levels his anger at Eliphaz. Andersen poignantly observes that during the course of the dialogue, none of the friends even intimated that *they* might be the object of God's wrath.[171] As noted earlier, Eliphaz initiates the debates by inappropriately applying his vision to Job without considering that he might have been the target for the message contained in the vision. God's address to Eliphaz in 42.7 strengthens the idea that Eliphaz abused

---

169. See Dell, *The Book of Job as Sceptical Literature*, p. 23 n. 62.
170. Duensing, *Apocalypse of Paul*, §49, p. 793.
171. Andersen, *The Book of Job*, p. 293.

his privilege. Now the roles are reversed. The persecutors receive God's wrath, while the righteous one functions as the conduit for the persecutor's forgiveness.

God rewards Job handsomely, doubling the possessions he had earlier. Nearly every commentator resists calling these 'rewards', because doing so would signal that God is confirming the theology of retribution. These same commentators assume that the story of Job is 'wisdom' and usually regard the rejection of retribution as central to the story. This is not the case. The story of Job is all about persevering under persecution. Job has defeated all who persecuted him, and most importantly, he has caused the Satan to swallow a self-curse, which vindicated God. Thus, Job is rewarded. Such is also the case in Dan. 12.12-13:

> [12]Happy are those who persevere
> and attain the thousand three hundred thirty-five days.
> [13]But you, go your way, and rest;
> you shall rise for your reward at the end of the days.

Many have pointed out that the doubling of Job's possessions recalls Exod. 22.4, which states that when a thief, who steals various livestock, is found, he should pay double. Commentators naturally claim that God is implicating himself for stealing from Job. But this goes too far. God never stole from Job, though he authorized the taking. However, the Satan did steal the livestock and essentially received his punishment. Thus, by restoring the livestock twofold, God is simply honoring his own regulations for restitution. After all, who else could exact payment from the Satan? And if Exod. 22.4 is the guide for restitution, then none should be surprised that Job's children were not doubled in like manner. The verse in Exodus refers exclusively to livestock.

At its very core, the story of Job is not about God or Satan; it is about the man Job persevering under cosmological and earthly persecution. Job, the non-Israelite, is every man. God revealed himself to Job in a way that helped Job to persevere without which Job might not have held up. In Apocalyptic Literature, God's revelations are intended to support those who have been chosen to suffer. In my view, the story of Job is less about unjust suffering and more about persevering under persecution. The Satan felt that Job worshipped God because of Job's multiple blessings. If the Satan were able to demonstrate that suspicion, Job's faith in God would be revealed as a sham. If Job honored his possessions more than he honored God, it would have been easy to admit that he had done something wrong. Doing so would also make it easier to curse God to his face. Job came close to doing this, but in the end, he did not curse God to his face—even though he had the chance.

Conclusion

My hope is that this reading both stimulates a reappraisal of Job's conventional interpretations, and demonstrates that Job can be legitimately construed as a nascent form of apocalypse. Job has survived a battery of opponents, all of whom, in this interpretation, functionally serve the interests of the Satan. Yet even wisdom's traditional view of retribution is twisted in the Satan's plan to break Job. All of the collaborators receive their just desserts.

As noted earlier, these severe pronouncements in apocalyptic serve as a necessary means of 'unmasking the forces that pretend to be benign, but actually exploit'. Apocalyptic rhetoric serves as a revelatory corrective to propaganda, which has the tendency to exploit and corrupt.[172]

In each case—whether Job's wife, the friends, or Elihu—the propaganda of retribution, especially as falsely paired to God's intended order, is corrupted and conformed to the needs of the Satan. Since the reader knows that Job is blameless and innocent, they should be able to recognize the tactic. What holds the reader's attention is not how Job suffers, but whether he will curse God to his face.

This new interpretive paradigm challenges some traditionally enigmatic features found in Job and generates some new insights. More are expected. However, other matters pertaining to the study of Job are necessarily questioned as a result. For example, treating Job as proto-apocalypse will influence how conventional Joban themes, such as 'the problem of evil', are understood. Similarly, issues of Job's literary setting may benefit from a unique approach. I now turn to those matters.

---

172. Collins, 'Apocalyptic Themes', p. 128.

5

IMPLICATIONS FOR APOCALYPTIC JOB
ON THEMES AND SETTINGS

Introduction

Interpreting Job from the perspective that I have proposed naturally yields significant implications, ones which may happily challenge certain assumed results as well as offer fresh approaches to older, stale explanations for otherwise challenging verses and passages. This chapter briefly discusses two areas of Joban studies that relate to my proposal: (1) the theme(s) of Job and (2) the setting of Job's canonical form.

I have argued in the preceding pages that the governing genre for Job is closer to apocalypse than an unsuccessful association with the conventionally accepted genre of wisdom. In the process of presenting an apocalyptic reading of Job, it seems clear that the likely and appropriate theme for Job is perseverance. One might even proffer that Job's theology argues that in the midst of persecution, one is encouraged to endure because of a hope that is otherworldly.

This is not to say that Job contains only one theme. There are, in fact, multiple themes in Job. However, if an embryonic form of apocalypse functions as the overarching model for interpretation, then perseverance under trial founded on divine hope logically follows since such a theme is central to apocalyptic thinking. David Noel Freedman remarks:

> In times of crisis, as we know, apocalyptic becomes more relevant: it offers to the faithful hope for despair, courage for weakness, certainty for doubt, commitment for vacillation, and assurance about the nature and destiny of man in the cosmos.[1]

---

1. David Noel Freedman, 'The Flowering of Apocalyptic', *JTC* 6 (1969), pp. 166-74 (174). Earlier (p. 166), he offers the view that the Apocalyptic Literature mirrored 'sharply the vicissitudes of the Jewish community during that period of unusual instability and upheaval in the Near East (in marked contrast with the preceding Achaemenid and Ptolemaic periods of comparative tranquility); similarly, they brought a message of hope and comfort, of courage and strength, and above all of zeal in the Lord'.

As shown, the structural arrangement for Job does not require manipulation in order to be read in this way. Therefore, a search for Job's setting could be beneficially re-directed from so-called 'wisdom' settings by factoring in this appeal to an apocalyptic-informed appeal for endurance.

Paul Hanson argues that the biblical 'apocalyptic consciousness' witnessed two seasons.[2] The first began in 587 BCE with the fall of Jerusalem. Isaiah 24–27 reflects this early form of apocalypse, which 'is marked by courage and moral discernment in the face of social collapse'.[3] Furthermore, given the option, hope instead of despair reigned in the minds of the apocalyptic authors.

The second era of apocalyptic thinking flourished in the second century BCE because of Hellenism's intimidating threat to Judaism.[4] Hanson asks, 'How was it that they could endure persecution, ridicule by their own leaders, and martyrdom and still not submit to the mighty kingdoms of this world?'[5] Here again, hope overcomes despair, and even though distanced by a few centuries, the apocalyptic consciousness consistently invokes perhaps the defining apocalyptic imperative from heaven in Rev. 2.10, 'Be faithful until death, and I will give you the crown of life'. Hanson summarizes, 'All things could be endured by those who believed that their final destiny rested not in ruthless oppressors of this earth, but in the gracious God of truth and justice'.[6] Later, Hanson says that the apocalypticists' thirst for God's righteous order 'gives them courage to endure disappointment, oppression, and martyrdom'.[7]

It is therefore not hard to include Job's story in this apocalyptic consciousness. As Job grasps for an umpire, mediator or גאל, he is signaling his desire to endure, and while he may not be referring to God in any of these pleadings, he is at least looking beyond the limited realm of himself and his earthly abode.

---

2. Paul Hanson, 'Apocalyptic Consciousness', *Quarterly Review* 4 (1984), pp. 28-39. Most now identify apocalypticism as the religious phenomenon that generated apocalypses, which are the actual literary genre. For example, see Lester L. Grabbe, 'The Social Setting of Early Jewish Apocalypticism', *JSP* 4 (1989), pp. 27-47 (29).

3. Grabbe, 'Social Setting', p. 30.

4. See also Freedman, 'Flowering', pp. 166-74, who dates this period from 165 BCE to 135 CE.

5. Hanson, 'Apocalyptic Consciousness', p. 31.

6. Hanson, 'Apocalyptic Consciousness', p. 32.

7. Hanson, 'Apocalyptic Consciousness', p. 32. Grabbe, 'Social Setting', p. 30, cautions that 'Apocalypticism does not necessarily arise in times of crisis nor is it always a product of the oppressed, the marginalized, and the powerless'.

The Themes of Job

Retribution

Job rejects the effectiveness of the theology of retribution in part because this theology represents the order of the known world. This theme is commonly referred to as the 'doctrine of divine retribution', and some consider it 'the most important theme' in the book.[8] Murphy disagrees, stating, 'it is not the main point of the Book of Job'.[9] To reject this doctrine as central to Job entails a theological challenge. How can one state that the rejection of divine retribution prevails in Job when God seemingly rewards Job for apparently recanting of his railings against God? In order to accommodate this theological problem, scholars are seemingly forced to posit various stages in the story. Such exercises may seem workable but do not fit the final form of the text.

In my reading then, divine retribution functions as the 'weapon of war' in the hands of the friends. As agents of the Satan, the friends use this universally accepted doctrine in an attempt to defeat Job, which would be signaled by his willingness to repent for a sin he knows he did not commit. Though he realizes that he is sinful (7.21), and though he too acknowledges the validity of the doctrine (21.7-8),[10] it is more the friends' twisted use of the doctrine that bothers Job than the doctrine itself. Understood in this way, the interpreter is not hampered by the fact that God rewards Job in the end. The doctrine of retribution plays an important role in the story, but it does not drive the story of Job. Instead, it is a prominent strand in the story's apocalyptic rope.

Wisdom

A second theme, wisdom, though also commonly considered the major one, is used to combat the very prominence of retribution. For example, John F.A. Sawyer argues that the author originally intended to dismiss 'the claims of human wisdom' and uphold the infinite wisdom of God.[11] As mentioned in Chapter 1, wisdom is simply insufficient as an interpretive tool. Wisdom's primary role in Job arrives in ch. 28 where it serves to assist Job in moving past the friends' misuse of worldly retribution.

---

8. Gregory W. Parsons, 'The Structure and Purpose of the Book of Job', *Bibliotheca Sacra* 138 (1981), pp. 139-57 (143).

9. Murphy, *A Short Reading of the Book of Job*, p. 122.

10. Good concurs: 'Job's assumptions about how the world works do not differ significantly from those of the friends' ('The Problem of Evil', p. 61).

11. John F.A. Sawyer, 'The Authorship and Structure of the Book of Job', in E.A. Livingstone (ed.), *Studia Biblica* (JSOTSup, 11; Sheffield: JSOT Press, 1979), pp. 253-57 (256).

As Hanson unpacks the content of the apocalyptic consciousness, he points to another continuing thread that seems to pervade all apocalyptic expressions. He argues that 'a basic truth in the apocalyptic vision' is that 'in a deep sense, our earth and its inhabitants *are* being torn between opposing worlds'.[12] This struggle is nothing short of 'a world caught in an awesome struggle between good and evil'.[13]

From the outset, Job's story introduces this struggle. It is perhaps too strong to say that it is a struggle between good and evil. Nevertheless, in this nascent form of apocalypse, the reader can easily identify the cosmic opposition between God and the Satan. The plain scenario has led many to believe that the story of Job therefore revolves around 'the problem of evil'.

The Problem of Evil
Edwin M. Good champions this position, asserting, 'I am convinced that the purpose of the book of Job is to solve the problem of evil', which Good encapsulates as 'the question of whether the creator of the universe is really in charge or not'.[14] There are two significant reasons that this cannot be the central theme of Job. First, God is clearly shown to be 'in charge'. While he allows the Satan some latitude to test Job, in each instance, God has the power to limit the extent of the Satan's endeavors. Furthermore, God clearly demonstrates his own sovereignty in the tempest speeches to Job.

Second, Good himself admits that the search for the solution to the problem of evil fails.[15] Would the author of the story seek to solve the problem, only to fail? Unless one argues that God in fact is the author of evil, which is inferred in at least Job 42.11—'Then there came to him all his brothers and sisters and all who had known him before…they showed him sympathy and comforted him for all the evil that the Lord had brought upon him'—this argumentation fails. Even with that, Job 42.11 places only Job's suffering at the foot of God, not necessarily humanity's collective suffering. Thus, I am not convinced that the author actively sought to solve the problem of evil, though he seems to have clearly intended to address it.

Suffering
Related to the problem of evil is the issue of suffering, which some conclude is the primary theme of Job.[16] Alan Cooper writes, 'the theme of the Book of

12. Hanson, 'Apocalyptic Consciousness', p. 38.
13. Hanson, 'Apocalyptic Consciousness', p. 35.
14. Good, 'Problem of Evil', pp. 50-51.
15. Good, 'Problem of Evil', pp. 50, 69.
16. Robert Gordis, *Poets Prophets and Sages: Essays in Biblical Interpretation* (Bloomington, IN: Indiana University Press, 1971), p. 280, conflates the two into one conundrum, remarking that Job 'addresses itself to the most agonizing mystery in the world—the problem of evil and human suffering'.

Job is man's response to suffering; only in that theme is literary integrity of the book manifest'.[17] J.T.E. Renner considers the entirety of Job a book 'born out of misery and suffering'.[18] However, few scholars appeal to suffering with greater passion than Gustavo Gutiérrez, who argues that the central theme of Job is 'how are we to talk about God from within a specific situation—namely, the suffering of the innocent'.[19]

That Job suffers is indisputable, but designating it as the encompassing theme of the book is simply not persuasive. Presupposing 'innocent suffering' as the interpretive grid does not adequately account for the Wisdom chapter, and it fails truly to address the plot of the story, which is whether or not Job will curse God to his face. In my reading, Job's suffering simply establishes his condition in order to provide a forum from which to present the author's larger concern of perseverance. After all, perseverance is not something that will occur without some degree of assumed suffering.[20]

Integrity

Two recent efforts that also seek to subsume all of the disparate features of Job can be mentioned briefly because they each come closer to my effort, but for different reasons. Ellen F. Davis argues that the central question of Job is 'the matter of Job's תמה'.[21] Comparing Job to Jacob, who is also considered תם, Davis interprets the two figures with regard to integrity.[22]

17. Alan Cooper, 'Narrative Theory and the Book of Job', *Studies in Religion* 11 (1982), pp. 35-44 (41).
18. J.T.E. Renner, 'Aspects of Pain and Suffering in the Old Testament', *The Australian and New Zealand Theological Review* 15 (1982), pp. 32-42 (32).
19. Gustavo Gutiérrez, *On Job: God-Talk and the Suffering of the Innocent* (trans. Matthew J. O'Connell; Maryknoll, NY: Orbis, 1987), p. xviii.
20. Webster's dictionary defines 'persevere' as 'to persist in a state, enterprise, or undertaking in spite of counter influences, opposition, or discouragement' (*Merriam-Webster's Ninth New Collegiate Dictionary* [ed. Frederick C. Mish; Springfield, MA: Merriam-Webster], 1989).
21. Ellen F. Davis, 'Job and Jacob: The Integrity of Faith', in Cook, Patton and Watts (eds.), *The Whirlwind: Essays on Job*, pp. 100-20 (101). Davis credits two other studies for elevating the issue of Job's integrity: R.D. Moore, 'The Integrity of Job', *CBQ* 45 (1983), pp. 17-31, and Walter Brueggemann, 'A Neglected Sapiential Word Pair', *ZAW* 89 (1977), pp. 234-58.
22. Davis, 'Job and Jacob', p. 113, limits those who are blameless to Job and Jacob. Though she acknowledges that Abraham and Noah also have תמים in their stories, they are thematically different enough to be excluded. However, Davis is wrong to exclude Noah in my view because his integrity similarly emerges when his character is first introduced, unlike Abraham, and, the integrity attributed to him describes his character, like Job and Jacob. By contrast, Abraham's connection with the word is a command from God to 'be blameless'. Thus, the use of תמים in Noah agrees semantically and dramatically with both Job's and Jacob's uses. Only the form of the word is different.

Her characterization of integrity is dense with meaning. Ultimately it is 'a constant awareness of God' or a 'disposition toward God'.[23] Both characters undergo a transformation of 'ego' that allows them to identify fully with God's creation.[24] The story of Job, according to Davis, seems to concentrate on Job's personal struggle to develop into a more worthy man of integrity, and while Job is the individual struggling, he is also 'Israel in exile: radically alienated from God, and yet unable to separate himself from this God who seems bent on destroying him'.[25]

Davis has done Joban scholars a great service. She has correctly elevated the status of תמה in Job to its rightful place in the narrative, though I find her application in the Yahweh speeches unconvincing. Furthermore, she has probed into the exilic setting as an obvious place for Job's composition, which is an area of Joban scholarship that could use additionally incisive studies such as hers. I will broach this topic shortly. Still, I find Davis's study incomplete because it is unable to capture key nuances to the story.

First, Davis has brilliantly defended a 'communal' notion of integrity, that is, how one functions in relationship. Understood in this way, Job then has some room for 'growth' in the Yahweh speeches, and this helps to explain why he repents. However, I am not convinced that this is how the word תמה was intended. Davis, it seems, has concentrated her efforts on one aspect of the man who was 'blameless and upright, one who feared God and turned away from evil' (1.1). In doing so, Davis fails to account for how her treatment of integrity contributes to the dialogue speeches. The friends are judged wrong and Job is judged favorably because he stubbornly maintained his integrity.

A better reading is that Job's commitment to his integrity refers mostly to his unwillingness to repent of something he did not do in the first place. To do so would be to turn toward evil, not away from it, as the narrative's definition of תמה suggests. In resisting the friends, Job is actually resisting the Satan's machinations. Davis's analysis does not adequately address how Job's transformation of integrity affects the Satan, or respond to the many other unanswered questions posed by scholars. For example, how does Job's transformation of integrity address the mysterious ch. 28? How does Elihu contribute to this transformation? Answers to these questions require a solution that is beyond the mere earthly realm that Job abides in. Thus, while Davis is correct to shed light on this important theme of integrity, it is not a sufficient governing theme because, at a minimum, it is limited to the earthly struggle, which is only the battleground for the larger cosmic struggle.

---

23. Davis, 'Job and Jacob', pp. 108-109.
24. Davis, 'Job and Jacob', p. 118.
25. Davis, 'Job and Jacob', p. 108.

Can a Mortal Love God during Suffering?
Like Davis, Christopher Seitz treats the text as it is received.[26] Dismissing the popular notion that Job is about suffering, Seitz wonders what one can say about God theologically through Job.[27] The one question that 'hovers over all that follows in the Job story' is whether a mortal can 'love and serve God under an extraordinary set of circumstances'.[28] This question resembles the question I ask in my reading of Job, namely: Can a mortal persevere in their faith under persecution? That is the cosmological context that the prologue unveils for the reader, and it lingers throughout the story.

Seitz's burden is to defend a full-structure reading of Job over against the developmental model that emerges from historical-critical research. I share his commitment to a full-structure reading because only then can one discern a coherent message that allows the final text to speak on its own terms.

Like many others, Seitz correctly identifies the cosmic storyline, but his analysis does not connect the cosmic to Job's earth, and then ultimately to the reader's world. In other words, Seitz misses the apocalyptic aspect of the story and does not identify the forces influencing the friends. The only explicit question that is posed to the reader is whether or not Job will persevere and refuse to curse God to his face, and Seitz draws one's attention to this conspicuous pattern.[29] However, he does not connect this cosmic current with Job's earthly battlefield, where the majority of the action occurs.

Thus, in newer, creative ways, Davis and Seitz repeat a common oversight in Joban studies, which is to focus on either the earthly or heavenly aspects of the story to the exclusion of the other. If one assumes wisdom as the starting point for interpreting Job, one is almost forced down one path or the other because wisdom seems to presuppose that a problem exists. So, either the problem is with God, which leads one down the cosmological path, or the problem is with Job, which directs one to the earthly realm. The former concentrates on the ancient tale and Yahweh speeches, while the latter concentrates on chs. 3–27. In the case of Job, wisdom is unsatisfactory, then, for bridging the gap between the cosmological and earthly.

An apocalypse, by contrast, flourishes under such conditions. The reader, who is outside of the story, yet able to discern both spheres, has the advantage. The reader does not have this advantage in typical wisdom texts, nor, for that matter, does the reader have an advantage in any other biblical

26. Seitz adheres to a canonical interpretation. For a selection of his studies, see *Word without End: The Old Testament as Abiding Theological Witness* (Grand Rapids: Eerdmans, 1998).
27. Christopher R. Seitz, 'Job: Full-Structure, Movement, and Interpretation', *Interpretation* 43 (1989), pp. 5-17 (5).
28. Seitz, 'Job: Full-Structure', p. 9.
29. Seitz, 'Job: Full-Structure', p. 6.

genre. Only apocalypse allows the reader to see and understand both the heavenly and the earthly.

Scholarship offers several other themes, or variations of those just discussed, and many of these may deserve greater treatment.[30] I believe that my reading of Job is fully capable of incorporating these traditional themes under the theme of hopeful perseverance in the face of trial. Each sub-theme contributes greatly to the overall trajectory of the book, but they are subordinate to perseverance.

What remains, then, is to ascertain when this amazing book was put together. Accepting that the book of Job contains various stages that probably came together over time, Seitz astutely points out that, 'if one could determine the actual sequence in which these various constituent parts came together, one could say a good deal about the theology of Job'.[31]

The Setting of Job

Lester L. Grabbe noted that the search for apocalypticism's sociological setting has not been as aggressive as other biblical genres, such as prophecy.[32] This brief discussion seeks merely to whet the appetite, or at least suggest a possible trajectory for future research into the setting of proto-apocalyptic Job.

Attempting to establish a setting for Job necessarily involves dating Job, which is an enterprise that is notoriously uneven. For example, Andersen posits a seventh-century date, though he suggests the substance of the book took form during Solomon's reign.[33] Pope also holds to a seventh-century date for the dialogues, though not enthusiastically.[34] Hartley supports a sixth-century date because the Babylonian Captivity could have provided the necessary milieu for the book's content, and because of the literary affinities Job shares with Second Isaiah and Jeremiah.[35] On the other hand, Habel,

---

30. Clines, *Job 1–20*, p. xxxvii, claims that the chief issue of Job is 'the problem of the moral order of the world, the principles on which it is governed'. John Baker Austin, 'The Book of Job: Unity and Meaning', in Livingstone (ed.), *Studia Biblica*, pp. 17-26 (25), calls attention to moral choices, remarking, 'Life is morally random; but this randomness has within it the greatest of all possibilities for us, the opportunity to do what is right and good whether or not it is for our advantage. This is the supreme moral achievement; and it is what the book of *Job* is ultimately about.'

31. Seitz, 'Job: Full-Structure', p. 8.

32. Grabbe, 'Social Setting', p. 27.

33. Andersen, *Job*, p. 63. Andersen confesses that this date is offered without substantiation.

34. Pope, *Job*, p. xxxvii.

35. Hartley, *The Book of Job*, p. 18.

5. *Implications for Apocalyptic Job*

who advances no date, rightly cautions against appealing to literary connections because they are simply not demonstrable.[36] Gordis, by contrast, holds to a date as late as the third century.[37] If there is a general consensus, it is that the date of Job is either exilic or postexilic.

Considering the final form of Job as at least exilic, and no earlier, the context of the Babylonian Captivity surely serves as a possibly major influence on the author(s). As noted, Hartley argues that the captivity functions as a 'trauma for Judah' and thereby stimulated the need for the book.[38] However, Hartley presumes a conventional wisdom context in which humans are able to serve God faithfully even during suffering.[39]

Davis's remark that 'Job is Israel in exile' is intriguing.[40] Blenkinsopp seems to share her position and also considers the Captivity as a probable setting. 'The likelihood is increased that the book deals with the crisis not just of an individual but of the nation'.[41] Cross also holds this position, first by establishing that the sixth century BCE served as the origin for apocalyptic because of the 'catastrophe of the exile where the crisis led to the collapse or transformation of Israel's institution'.[42] With this background Cross points out that Job was a new voice that 'attacked the central theme of Israel's religion', and ultimately 'brings the ancient religion of Israel to an end'.[43] The catastrophe led 'proto-apocalyptists' to 'salvage the ancient faith, but in new forms', where 'Job was a major force in the evolution of Israel's religion'.[44] It is at this point in Cross's argument that he expresses his intrigue with the fact that 'Job's importance was not forgotten in apocalyptic circles'.[45]

Cross does not explicitly label Job an apocalypse, but the intersection of all of these features, especially the emergence of 'proto-apocalyptists' and the employment of eclectic approaches to newer forms of transmitting Israel's faith, substantially favors my argument that Job is rightly considered a nascent form of apocalypse.

If the Babylonian Captivity can be considered the appropriate setting, one could argue that the scribes in exile were no doubt engaged with more than self-lamentation. Most now agree that the origin of the apocalypses seems to

---

36. Habel, *The Book of Job*, p. 41.
37. Robert Gordis, *The Book of God and Man: A Study of Job* (Chicago: University of Chicago Press, 1965), p. 216.
38. Hartley, *The Book of Job*, p. 18.
39. Hartley, *The Book of Job*, p. 50.
40. Davis, 'Job and Jacob', p. 108.
41. Blenkinsopp, *Wisdom and Law in the Old Testament*, p. 57.
42. Cross, 'New Directions', p. 161.
43. Cross, 'New Directions', p. 162.
44. Cross, 'New Directions', p. 163.
45. Cross, 'New Directions', p. 163

be scribal in that they were literary works instead of oral traditions.[46] Perhaps they were besieged and ridiculed by their Babylonian counterparts, who sought to convince them that surely Israel's God did not exist if he could not have spared them from Babylonian aggression. Blenkinsopp argues that Job fits this scenario because the exiles were also questioning God and because there was a 'shift towards a more transcendental and universalist understanding of Yahweh to which the national disasters of the sixth century certainly contributed'.[47] It is not hard to imagine a situation whereby the practitioners of Babylonian cults exhorted Judah's exiled priests and scribes to consider embracing the worship of Babylonian gods since the god of Judah was clearly weak and unable to save either Jerusalem or his own temple!

It could be that the exiled scribes appropriated the story of the Babylonian Job and created a parable whereby Job represents Israel in exile, and the friends are Israel's tormentors. Many of the exiles were likely challenged in their faith and would have needed this story, couched in non-Israelite terms, to encourage them to endure in their faith in the God of Israel through this terrible time of suffering. The scribe(s) who wrote Job probably recognized that many of the people less familiar with the prophetic books felt that the Judahites did not deserve their degree of suffering. Whatever the exact circumstances, the exile seems as likely a time for at least the initial compilation of the story of Job.

It is worth repeating Cross's suggestion that this time in Israel's development may have produced the 'Proto-apocalyptists' who would 'salvage the ancient faith, but in new forms. History and myth, the wisdom tradition and the prophet tradition, coalesced in the late sixth century never fully to separate again.'[48] Thus, the temporal setting of the exile, in which exiled scribes would become exposed to vast amounts of Babylonian literature, including the various versions of the righteous sufferer, seems to represent a logically fertile arena for the production of new 'genres'. Grabbe also considers the social and literary roles as intermingling: 'apocalypticism, prophecy, mantic wisdom, and the priesthood may be and often are closely related'.[49] Furthermore, Grabbe counsels that apocalyptic communities, or individual scribes, were not limited to producing apocalypses. A wide variety of expressions, both oral and written, must be accepted from the environment where the message is superior to the medium.[50] Thus, one could imagine some nascent form of the story of Job that contains certain 'wisdom' features gleaned from their captors' literature, which were tailored into an embryonic form of apocalypse.

46. Grabbe, 'Social Setting', p. 32.
47. Blenkinsopp, *Wisdom and Law*, p. 60.
48. Cross, 'New Directions', p. 163.
49. Grabbe, 'Social Setting', p. 33.
50. Grabbe, 'Social Setting', pp. 38-39.

Such theorizing about Job's possible setting is necessary according to Hans Dieter Betz, who declared the search for apocalypse's origins a 'primary task'.[51] Betz was also convinced that apocalypticism's origins should not be limited to prophecy, stating:

> We have to free ourselves from the idea of treating apocalypticism as an isolated and purely inner-Jewish phenomenon. Rather, we must learn to understand apocalypticism as a peculiar manifestation within the entire course of Hellenistic–oriental syncretism.[52]

Since Betz's comments, apocalyptic research has advanced significantly in the area of genre distinction. Grabbe is not convinced, however, that Betz's charge to find the literary origins of apocalypse has progressed as urgently.[53] Thus, my suggestion that the earliest story of Job represented a new form of writing whose crucible was the exile and perhaps drew from a Babylonian 'wisdom' tale, may serve as a small effort to locate the primordial apocalyptic origins from which Job emerged. That only Ezekiel refers to Job supports the contention that the form of Job was perhaps a new literary expression in the exile.

I argued in Chapter 3 that tradition from LXX Job to Christian pseudepigrapha viewed Job along apocalyptic contours and that Job lent itself to such interpretation. It may be that Job's earliest form stimulated such a development. Though working with far later apocalypses, Grabbe has noted that an 'apocalypse or related form, once in existence (however it originated), may serve to fuel and drive a movement'.[54] Given tradition's persistent apocalyptic tailoring of Job, and given the possible reliance on Job from other classic apocalypses, it is more than possible that Job does represent a kind of prototype of apocalypse. As a 'new' genre, perhaps the book of Job functioned as the pattern upon which later apocalyptic writings were based.

If Job's setting is the scribal community of the exile, was there a parent genre from which Job's new genre, that is, nascent apocalypse, was born? I will now turn to that heavily debated issue.

---

51. Hans Dieter Betz, 'On the Problem of the Religio-Historical Understanding of Apocalypticism', *JTC* 6 (1969), pp. 134-56 (155).
52. Betz, 'On the Problem', p. 138.
53. Grabbe, 'Social Setting', p. 27, noting the lack of research into the social context of apocalypticism, seems to testify that little has been done some 20 years after Dieter Betz's charge. This is not to say that no progress has been made, however. The essays in Hellholm (ed.), *Apocalypticism in the Mediterranean World and the Near East*, indicate interest in the setting of apocalypses. For example, see Anders Hultgård, 'Forms and Origins of Iranian Apocalypticism', pp. 387-412, where the issues of setting are explored.
54. Grabbe, 'Social Setting', p. 37.

Wisdom and Apocalypse

At a minimum, it seems clear that Job exemplifies one of the few works where wisdom and apocalypse converge. Due in part to von Rad's claim that apocalypse emerged from wisdom, a great many studies have explored such a convergence. Commonly, several biblical and pseudepigraphal works are cited as examples, but I have yet to find Job considered among them. Such a designation would open the way for new streams of thought concerning Job's setting, date, composition and interpretation.

One of the key stumbling blocks to von Rad's thesis was that he did not offer a sacred work that exemplified his ideas. Job is such a book, especially when one considers the possible 'layering' of traditions found in Job, an idea at home with von Rad's tradition-critical approach.

What follows here is a brief review of the scholarship pertaining to the convergence of wisdom and apocalypse with an emphasis on von Rad. Much of the terrain relating to this area of study has already been covered in E. Elizabeth Johnson's exceptional summary, from which I will draw.[55] I will then discuss the several biblical and extra-biblical works that exhibit the confluence of wisdom and apocalypse. Finally, I will endeavor to make the cases both that Job should be considered part of the 'wisdom/apocalypse' corpus, essentially, and that Job may serve as the model von Rad needed in order to embolden his thesis.

According to Johnson, the first discussion regarding the intersection of wisdom and apocalypse occurred in the early nineteenth century by Nowack and Ewald.[56] In 1919, Gerhard Hölscher was more explicit about apocalyptic thought's reliance on wisdom,[57] and finally von Rad took up the issue in both his *Old Testament Theology* and *Wisdom in Israel*.[58] It was von Rad's more contemporary expression of the issue that stimulated further interest, much of which persists today.

In general, von Rad dispensed with the conventional view that apocalyptic thought emerged from prophecy. Von Rad writes:

---

55. E. Johnson, *The Function of Apocalyptic and Wisdom Traditions in Romans 9–11* (SBLDS, 109; Atlanta: Scholars Press, 1989). Her second chapter is dedicated to a survey of scholarship on the convergence of wisdom and apocalypse.

56. Johnson (*The Function of Apocalyptic*, p. 56) directs the reader to J.M. Schmidt, *Die jüdische Apokalyptik: Die Geschichte ihrer Erforschung von den Anfängen bis zu den Textfunden von Qumran* (Neukirchen–Vluyn: Neukirchener Verlag, 1976), pp. 13-21.

57. G. Hölscher, 'Die Entstehung des Buches Daniel', *Theologische Studien und Kritiken* 92 (1919), pp. 113-38.

58. G. von Rad, *Old Testament Theology* (2 vols.; trans. D.M.G. Stalker; New York: Harper & Row, 1965), II, pp. 301-15, and *Wisdom in Israel* (trans. J.D. Martin; Nashville: Abingdon Press, 1972), pp. 263-83.

> The decisive factor, as I see it, is the incompatibility between apocalyptic literature's view of history and that of the prophets. The prophetic message is specifically rooted in the saving history, that is to say, it is rooted in definite election traditions. But there is no way which leads from this to the apocalyptic view of history.[59]

According to von Rad, since the tradition could only add material to what was already present, and since apocalyptic does not refer to Israel's saving history, wisdom is a more likely candidate as the source for apocalypse.[60]

Saving history, so central to von Rad's theology, is also abandoned in apocalyptic thought and he questions whether any 'existential relationship with history' existed in Apocalyptic Literature.[61] Furthermore, the prophets allegorized specific historical events whereas Apocalyptic Literature tends to represent the whole historical process, 'by the allegory of an upright human figure'.[62] Though von Rad does not suggest it, 'blameless' Job, in my view, immediately comes to mind as an example of another biblical figure, like Daniel, whom the Hebrew Bible portrays as an 'upright human figure'.

The prophets, according to von Rad, 'had always openly taken their standpoint in their own day and age', while 'the apocalyptic writers veiled their own standpoint in time'.[63] Von Rad concludes:

> Once it is realized, however, that knowledge is thus the nerve-centre of apocalyptic literature, knowledge based on a universal Jahwism, surprisingly divorced from the saving history, it should not be difficult to determine the real matrix from which apocalyptic literature originates. This is Wisdom...[64]

Emphasizing the significance of knowledge, von Rad elevates the role of 'secret' in apocalyptic material, describing it as 'absolutely fundamental' to apocalyptic, yet wholly lacking in prophecy. Accepting that the role of prophecy, not surprisingly, was to be 'interpreted' by the apocalypticists, von Rad does not discount the role that prophecy played in influencing the apocalyptic authors.[65]

Johnson points out that von Rad's proposal met with resistance, which led to nuances and defenses of it in later editions of his *Old Testament Theology*. Curiously, though, she does not engage with von Rad's expression of his thesis in his latest and most mature discussion of wisdom, which is found in

---

59. Von Rad, *Old Testament Theology*, II, p. 303.
60. Gordis, *Poets, Prophets, and Sages*, p. 295, concurs, saying, 'Tradition finds it much easier to supplement, modify and reinterpret older elements than to discard them when they proved inadequate'.
61. Von Rad, *Old Testament Theology*, II, p. 304.
62. Von Rad, *Old Testament Theology*, II, p. 305.
63. Von Rad, *Old Testament Theology*, II, p. 305
64. Von Rad, *Old Testament Theology*, II, p. 306.
65. Von Rad, *Old Testament Theology*, II, p. 308.

Wisdom in Israel. In this work, von Rad includes an excursus entitled, 'The Divine Determination of Times', where he focuses on the place of 'determinism'.[66] For von Rad, divine determination influences several questions, such as salvation, life and death—all of which are fundamental to later 'didactic writings, especially the apocalyptic ones'.[67]

The prophets, by contrast, operated under a far more historical framework. God's intervention into worldly affairs is 'an unexpected event...both for the prophet and for his hearers'.[68] Indeed, since the prophet perceived God's actions as constantly fluctuating, von Rad suggests that the 'gulf between this conception of history and the deterministic–apocalyptic one seems unbridgeable'.[69]

History came under the jurisdiction of divine determination, which was manifested most clearly in the 'apocalyptic historical summaries', that is, God knew everything in advance.[70] In this new conception of history, salvation is no longer contained within the realm of history, but is reserved for both the primeval election and the eschaton. Hope rests on a salvation that must make its appearance in a new way, but the recipient is not Israel renewed. It is, rather, a selected group or individual. As the predominance of a theology of individualism increased with regard to salvation, 'even the concept of "Israel" begins to disintegrate'.[71] This new view of history is undoubtedly focused on consolation and the exhortation to persevere.[72]

While von Rad insists that determinism 'was absolutely constitutive for all apocalyptic', he recognizes that the determination of time was not limited to apocalyptic works. For example, Sirach was not an apocalyptist, but the apocalyptist was considered a wise man.[73] At this point von Rad makes his ultimate claim: 'The attempt, convincingly to derive the essential characteristics of apocalyptic from another tradition (such as the prophetic) has not hitherto been successful'.[74]

In what might be his most developed statement challenging the notion that eschatology must play a central role in apocalypses, as his early critics maintained, von Rad affirms:

66. Von Rad, *Wisdom*, p. 263.
67. Von Rad, *Wisdom*, p. 263.
68. Von Rad, *Wisdom*, p. 269.
69. Von Rad, *Wisdom*, p. 270.
70. Von Rad, *Wisdom*, pp. 271-72.
71. Von Rad, *Wisdom*, p. 273.
72. Von Rad, *Wisdom*, p. 274.
73. Von Rad, *Wisdom*, p. 277.
74. Von Rad, *Wisdom*, p. 278.

5. Implications for Apocalyptic Job

Of absolutely central significance for apocalyptic is the looking to an end to the present course of events, to a judgment and the dawning of a time of salvation, that is, its thoroughgoing eschatological orientation. One can, of course, scarcely describe as eschatological the idea that events which are predetermined happen in due course, nor the prediction of specific times, nor the division of history into periods. It is, rather, the expectation of a great culmination of history which is already fixed in the divine scheme of determination and in which, as we have seen, the salvation event is realized. But even this idea is not so entirely new that it could be described as the specifically apocalyptic factor.[75]

In a footnote, von Rad responds to one of his earliest critics, P. Vielhauer, in these terms:

Vielhauer considers the eschatological element to be the fundamental one in apocalyptic, with the wisdom elements as an outer layer. This impression may indeed be given by individual apocalypses; from a tradition-historical point of view, the situation is very probably the opposite: the wisdom element is the fundamental one.[76]

In the end, for von Rad, a strong sense of determinism, especially as yielded in a determination of times, is more fundamental to apocalyptic than eschatology. Accordingly, one might propose that Sirach could best serve as the prototype for von Rad's hypothesis. Sirach does represent a form of didactic teachings whereby the 'theologization' of the determination of times becomes clearer, which is also the case in Ecclesiastes.[77] However, von Rad observes that Sirach is not easily compared to the great apocalypses.[78] Thus, in his most convincing expression of wisdom as the source for apocalypse, von Rad maintains that determinism is the regnant element bridging wisdom and apocalypse, though he does not utilize a work that explicitly manifests the phenomenon.

Others attempted to fill the void. For example, H.P. Müller suggested that apocalyptic thought emerged from *mantic* wisdom as opposed to conventional Jewish wisdom, and he considered the book of Daniel the primary representative of his theory. For Müller, Daniel is portrayed as the mantic sage in Daniel 1–6 who is then transformed into the apocalyptic sage in the latter part of the book. Several features that do not exist in traditional wisdom, such as eschatology, pseudepigraphy and special enlightenment, can be understood to co-exist with apocalypse by recourse to Daniel.[79] However,

---

75. Von Rad, *Wisdom*, p. 278.
76. Von Rad, *Wisdom*, p. 278 n. 23. See P. Vielhauer, 'Apocalyptic in Early Christianity', in *New Testament Apocrypha*, II, pp. 597-600.
77. Von Rad, *Wisdom*, p. 264.
78. Von Rad, *Wisdom*, p. 279.
79. H.P. Müller, 'Mantische Weisheit und Apokalyptik', in *Congress Volume, Uppsala 1971* (VTSup, 22; Leiden: Brill, 1972), pp. 268-93. For a critique of Müller, see

many consider Daniel a late book with its first chapters (1–6) likely dating from the mid-third century BCE, and its latter chapters (7–12) from the second century BCE. Thus, Müller's appeal to Daniel does not satisfactorily detail what earlier 'developments led up to the apocalyptic wisdom found in Daniel'.[80] It is certainly possible that von Rad may have regarded Müller's hypothesis as plausible, but von Rad seemed intent on tracing the apocalyptic connection to the kind of wisdom expressed in typical Jewish traditions, not mantic strands that derived from the ancient Near East.

However, the tradition-historical paradigm does allow for Job as a possible witness to his theory, since the book of Job seems to display possible layers of interpretation.[81] Von Rad underscores this use: 'Apocalyptic literature could only alter the form of the traditional material available to it. Thus, by means of allegory it could put the tradition into code.'[82]

Newer research tends to validate von Rad's proposal.[83] For example, Michael E. Stone has catalogued various 'lists' of revelatory subject matter related to 'apocalyptic speculation'.[84] The lists studied by Stone all have in common their tendency to appear at the 'high point of a revelation'.[85] Two apocalyptic works studied by Stone are *2 Baruch* 59 and *4 Ezra* 4, which, according to Stone, exhibit familiarity with Job. Stone remarks, 'It is clear that many of the elements mentioned in the lists in IV Ezra and in II Baruch are drawn from the important Job chaps. 28 and 38'.[86]

Three valuable points can be made here. First, Stone demonstrates that the accepted apocalypse of *4 Ezra* and *2 Baruch* derive value in their 'apocalyptic' lists from two areas in Job that I have argued are laden with revelatory material, namely, the Wisdom chapter and the Yahweh speeches.[87] Second, Stone concluded that these lists seem to occur at the high point of the revelation, and there can be no argument that the Yahweh speeches represent the apex of Job's story. Finally, the fact that Job is seen as a book that

---

James C. VanderKam, *Enoch and the Growth of an Apocalyptic Tradition* (CBQMS, 16; Washington, DC: The Catholic Biblical Association of America, 1984), pp. 6-8.

80. Lester L. Grabbe, *Priests, Prophets, Diviners, Sages: A Socio-Historical Study of Religious Specialists in Ancient Israel* (Valley Forge, PA: Trinity Press International, 1995), p. 177.

81. For example, scholarship tends to agree that the prologue and epilogue represent one layer, the dialogues another, the wisdom hymn another and the Elihu speeches yet another. Pope suggests that the whole book 'suggests a sort of piecemeal composition' (*Job*, p. xxi), and treats issues of Job's literary integrity well (pp. xxi-xxviii).

82. Von Rad, *Old Testament Theology*, II, p. 304.

83. Grabbe, *Priests*, p. 177.

84. Stone, 'Lists', p. 414.

85. Stone, 'Lists', p. 418.

86. Stone, 'Lists', p. 421.

87. Stone ('Lists', p. 422) also identifies Job 11.7 as an important example.

5. Implications for Apocalyptic Job

influenced later apocalypses perhaps supports my contention that Job as 'proto-apocalyptic' was fairly well accepted in the scribal guild.

In view of my suggestion that Job could have served as a model for von Rad's theory on the origins of apocalypse, it is somewhat ironic that von Rad felt that the 'list' of Job 38 'follows an established pattern, which derives ultimately from Egyptian wisdom-literature...'[88] On this point, Stone cautions that von Rad's conclusion might be challenged by further scholarly research, and Stone even directs the reader to Cross's 'suggestive comments' regarding Job's association with apocalypse.[89] Stone contends that there existed a 'general movement in the apocalyptic writings toward reinterpretation and reuse of Wisdom language. "Wisdom" is invested, therefore, with a new meaning'.[90] In either case, the tension between von Rad's wisdom assessment and Stone's apocalyptic perspective points to a text that does not resist either, but is open to the latter.

Von Rad's commitment to Job as wisdom may have prevented him from seeing the possibility that Job could serve as a possible paradigm for his theory on apocalypse and wisdom. However, von Rad may have come closer to the notion of Job's apocalyptic nature with his statement that Job 'points mysteriously to the future'.[91] Thus, it seems that von Rad touched on various characteristics of Job that intersect with apocalypse, and yet he did not recognize Job's formal affiliation with apocalypse because of his commitment to Job as wisdom.

Conclusion

George W.E. Nickelsburg understands this tendency towards generic compartmentalization and determines that 'Jewish wisdom and apocalypticism cannot be cleanly separated from one another'.[92] However, he argues that apocalyptic thought is a product of 'wisdom circles that are becoming increasingly diverse in the Greco-Roman period'.[93] For him, Apocalyptic Literature relies on 'language, genres, and motifs of Israel's wisdom literature'.[94] Like Stone, Nickelsburg points out affinities between Job to both

---

88. Gerhard von Rad, 'Job xxxviii and Ancient Egyptian Wisdom', in *The Problem of the Hexateuch and Other Essays* (trans. E.W. Trueman Dicken; New York: McGraw-Hill, 1966), pp. 281-91 (289).
89. Stone, 'Lists', p. 421 n. 14.
90. Stone, 'Lists', p. 426.
91. Von Rad, *Old Testament Theology*, II, p. 320.
92. Nickelsburg, 'Wisdom and Apocalypticism', p. 717. Collins also shares this view; see his 'Wisdom, Apocalypticism, and Generic Compatibility', in L. Perdue (ed.), *In Search of Wisdom* (Philadelphia: Westminster Press, 1993), pp. 165-86.
93. Nickelsburg, 'Wisdom and Apocalypticism', p. 717.
94. Nickelsburg, 'Wisdom and Apocalypticism', p. 718.

2 *Baruch* and *4 Ezra*, but instead of associating them with revealed lists, he marks their relationship with a shared concern over theodicy by way of argumentative dialogues.[95] Thus, Nickelsburg handily derails those who would limit Job to wisdom, or any genre, including apocalypse:

> The history of scholarship also attests the ways in which our categories have become hermetically sealed compartments that give the impression that each refers to, or contains something totally different from the other. Thus 'wisdom' or 'sapiential' is distinct from 'apocalyptic'. By focusing intently on one or the other, as the thing itself, we fail to see that in the world from which they have come to us, they were related parts of an organic whole, each with some of the same genes as the other.[96]

Thus, contemporary scholarship may be inclined to recognize that Job might very well emerge from an era whereby apocalyptic features were intended from the outset. As Nickelsburg concludes, a major difficulty for scholarship is that it treats texts in the abstract 'apart from the real worlds that created the texts'.[97]

That said, a continued search for Job's setting is quite important. In my interpretation of Job, it seems reasonable to locate Job in the time of the exile where the story represents a completely new form of writing that was intended to encourage the captives to persevere in their faith. At a minimum, the prologue, epilogue, dialogue speeches and whirlwind speeches comprised the original story. Later developments may have occurred, namely, the Wisdom chapter and the Elihu speeches. However, any additions would simply complement, if not emphasize, the already existing apocalyptic trajectory.

---

95. Nickelsburg, 'Wisdom and Apocalypticism', p. 721.
96. Nickelsburg, 'Wisdom and Apocalypticism', p. 729.
97. Nickelsburg, 'Wisdom and Apocalypticism', p. 730.

Conclusion

Around the world, the story of Job continues to be one of the most recognizable of all biblical books. In recent years, a leading contender for the office of President of the United States erred by claiming that the book of Job was his favorite New Testament book of the Bible. Such a gaffe by a leading cultural figure indicates that while Job is widely known, it is not necessarily known for the reasons that it should be.

Above all, Job offers encouragement to those in distress. In the new, post-9/11 world order where fear is routinely employed for political gain, the reverence that Job receives in all three of the great Abrahamic faiths might serve to remind us that the more traditionally peaceful expressions of Judaism, Christianity and Islam are better ways to ground our mutual desire to live in harmony with one another. For that matter, as a decidedly non-Israelite figure, the story of Job is capable of crossing many other religious and cultural barriers as well. In this universal context, the book of Job will always be relevant and mined for the endless lessons it holds.

This study has presented arguments demonstrating that the governing genre for the book of Job is closer to apocalypse than to wisdom, which is usually the more common description for the book. I have claimed that Job contains sufficient evidence to warrant a new designation of 'proto-apocalyptic'. Recently, Ben Witherington III acknowledged as much:

> [Job] also shares something of the apocalyptic perspective we find in books of the Bible like Ezekiel and Daniel. This worldview in essence asserts—there are many things wrong with the world, which humans themselves cannot remedy, but God still cares for his people and in the end God will personally intervene and set things right. This seems to be the perspective of the author of Job.[1]

I have pursued what Witherington and several other prominent scholars such as John J. Collins, Christopher Rowland and Frank Moore Cross have hitherto only intimated.

---

1. Ben Witherington III refers to Howard Dean in 'Long Suffering Job: Does the Book of Job Have a Happy Ending?', n.p. (cited 8 Jan 2004). Online: http://www.beliefnet.org/story/138/story_13817.html.

By reviewing numerous alternative proposals concerning Job's genre, I have shown that scholarship is actually further away from consensus than one might expect. Many who assert that Job is most aligned with wisdom do so with reservations. The primary reason that wisdom is a less than satisfying label is that Job's style deviates so drastically from those works that are usually accepted as wisdom, such as Proverbs and Sirach. Job simply is not a collection of aphorisms and maxims, though these forms exist in the book. Additionally, the story does not explicitly claim to be didactic, though certainly much is taught. Furthermore, a wisdom paradigm is not able to account for all of the disparate elements in Job. For example, wisdom is not generally associated with narrative, though the story of Job is framed by narrative. In short, I have offered that 'wisdom' simply does not function as the best interpretive paradigm for Job.

With recourse to the Master Paradigm developed by the SBL's Apocalyptic Study Group, I then showed that a large number of features found in the book of Job conform to the elements contained in the paradigm. The most important point of intersection between Job and apocalypse is the existence of three revelations within the book of Job. I argued that revelations are found in Job 4.17-21, 28.23-28, and the Yahweh speeches in chs. 38–41. Since revelations are central to an apocalypse, I concentrated much of my study in these areas.

However, I also pointed to several other features of Job that accord nicely with an apocalypse, such as the place of narrative, the use of protology, the role of otherworldly mediators and the use of otherworldly journeys. I also argued that while MT Job does not explicitly refer to eschatological activity, the book of Job parallels many of the eschatological formulas found in the paradigm. For example, while Job does not refer to eschatological salvation as a reward for faithfulness, Job's double reward in the epilogue clearly functions in a similar way.

Recognizing that Job's lack of overt eschatology needed further discussion, I presented a brief survey of the later tradition of interpretation about Job. I showed that tradition clearly understood Job's story as possessing basic apocalyptic tendencies. The premier example of tradition's appreciation for Job's apocalyptic character is LXX Job, where Job is depicted as resurrected in the epilogue. During this discussion, I attempted to dispel the notion that LXX Job must have been a Christian translation designed to align with the Early Christian belief in resurrection. I showed that it is just as likely, if not more likely, that LXX Job emerged from a completely Jewish context.

Other clearly apocalyptic interpretations of Job are found in the *Testament of Job*, the letter of James and the Christian *Apocalypse of Paul*. I also suggested that the reason the Qumran community preserved Job in paleo-Hebrew script was that their apocalyptic community recognized and honored the inherent apocalyptic characteristics associated with the story of Job. In the end, I argued that tradition understood that Job was a nascent form of what later become known as apocalypse, and that, as such, the design of the story reveals itself as apocalyptic. Thus, what some might claim as the major challenge to my thesis becomes a major strength.

I then presented an apocalyptic reading of Job. I began by proposing a new literary structure for Job that divides along the cleavages of three revelations that are given, and I showed that this new structure was strikingly similar to conventional structures. I argued that the Satan's prediction that Job would curse God to his face is the primary plotline that drives the entire story. The Satan's self-curse indicates that he has a greater stake in the story than previously recognized and he cleverly uses Job's various antagonists for his own preservation. The reader is therefore always wondering whether or not Job will actually curse God to his face, if given the chance.

I concentrated on the revelations to demonstrate their integral nature in understanding Job as apocalypse, and I showed that the story of Job is subsumed under an apocalyptic rubric because one must recognize the pivotal place that endurance holds as the underlying theological message of Job. I also sought to explain how traditionally enigmatic verses in Job might be more easily understood in this apocalyptic interpretation. For example, I argued that God's first words from the whirlwind were directed to Elihu and not Job. In this way, God intervenes on Job's behalf and judges Elihu. This judgment explains why Elihu receives no attention in the epilogue. Similarly, I demonstrated why Job's wife and the Satan are not heard from or about after their brief appearances in the prologue.

Finally, I addressed two natural implications that result from my thesis. First, I discussed how the many other themes of Job are not neglected in my proposal, though they are subservient to the overall theme of endurance. For example, the book of Job's critique of retribution theology plays a significant role in an apocalyptic reading. It was the tool that the friends used in attempting to force Job to admit that he had done something to deserve his punishment. Other themes such as 'the problem of evil' were also addressed, and I showed how inclusive the 'proto-apocalyptic' understanding proves to be.

I concluded with a survey of proposed settings for the book of Job, and I suggested that the most likely setting is that of the Babylonian captivity. It is here that Israel in exile likely experienced the kind of anguish and self-reflection so apparent in Job. In captivity, Israel would be exposed to new styles of writing, perhaps even to 'Babylonian Job'. It was in exile that Israel would most likely yearn for an end of the world order as they then knew it.

I then proposed that Job exhibits sufficient wisdom and apocalyptic features to serve perhaps as the example that Gerhard von Rad needed to demonstrate his theory that Apocalyptic Literature is the child of wisdom. I thus offer a unique approach to identifying Job's literary roots.

This research has clearly demonstrated that Job exhibits far more apocalyptic features than hitherto recognized. The book of Job should be classified with those works that evidence both wisdom and apocalyptic characteristics. The Society of Biblical Literature has dedicated sections at its Annual Meeting to exploring the intersection of Wisdom and Apocalypse. In my view, the section would do well to dedicate some energy into examining Job's rightful place in this increasingly popular area of study.[2]

The form and content of Job simply resists a strictly wisdom label. While some have argued that *sui generis* should therefore be the alternative, such a rendering is merely thin gruel when fresh interpretations of Job require a more substantive and hermeneutically vital generic assumption. None of the various alternative genres offered to date can subsume all of the seemingly unconnected features of Job as well as the apocalyptic paradigm does. I am convinced that Job should no longer be classified as part of the so-called wisdom corpus. Instead, Job should be treated as an early form of apocalypse that is designed to promote endurance during suffering and persecution.

The practice of interpretation presupposes genre assumptions, and John Gammie reminds us that the intention of genre analysis is to provide heuristic value by yielding fresh interpretations of the author's theological aims.[3] For those who handle the book of Job regularly in either formal or informal settings, I hope that my thesis has stimulated an interest in reading the entirety of Job as an early form of apocalypse, and that such a reading will lead to new exegetical and theological discoveries centered on the idea that hope for God's intervention in a world gone bad provides the necessary condition to persevere in the midst of suffering.

---

2. A recent volume containing essays read at the Fifty-first Colloquium biblicum lovaniense in 2002 does indeed discuss this intersection of wisdom and apocalypse. See the essays appearing in F. García Martínez (ed.), *Wisdom and Apocalypticism in the Dead Sea Scrolls and in the Biblical Tradition* (Leuven: Leuven University Press, 2003).

3. Gammie, 'Paraenetic Literature', p. 42.

BIBLIOGRAPHY

Adamson, James B., *The Epistle of James* (NICNT; Grand Rapids: Eerdmans, 1976).
—, L., *A Manual of Hebrew Poetics* (Subsidia biblica, 11; Rome: Pontifical Biblical Institute, 1988).
—'Toward a Dramatic Reading of the Book of Job', in Polzin and Robertson (eds.), *Studies in the Book of Job*, pp. 45-61.
Alter, R., 'The Voice from the Whirlwind', *Commentary* 77 (1984), pp. 33-41.
Andersen, F.I., *Job* (TOTC; Leicester: Inter-Varsity Press, 1976).
Andrews, C. (ed.), *The Ancient Egyptian Book of the Dead* (Austin, TX: University of Texas Press, 1985).
Aquinas, T., *The Literal Exposition on Job: A Scriptural Commentary concerning Providence* (ed. A. Domico; Atlanta: Scholars Press, 1989).
Are, T., 'Job 38:1-7', *Interpretation* 53 (1999), pp. 294-98.
Augustine, *The City of God against the Pagans* (ed. and trans. R.W. Tyson; Cambridge: Cambridge University Press, 1998).
Austin, J.B., 'The Book of Job: Unity and Meaning', in E.A. Livingstone (ed.), *Studia Biblica* (JSOTSup, 11; Sheffield: JSOT Press, 1979), pp. 17-26.
Balentine, S., *Job* (Macon, GA: Smith & Helwys, 2006).
Barton, J., 'Form Criticism: Old Testament', in *ABD*, II, pp. 838-41.
Baskin, J., *Pharaoh's Counsellors: Job, Jethro, and Balaam in Rabbinic and Patristic Tradition* (Brown Judaic Studies, 47; Chico, CA: Scholars Press, 1983).
Benoit, P., 'L'inspiration des Septante d'après les pères', in *Exégèse et théologie* (Paris: Les Editions du Cerf, 1968), pp. 69-89.
—'The Inspiration of the Septuagint', in *Jesus and the Gospel*, I (trans. Benet Weatherhead; London: Darton, Longman, & Todd, 1973).
Bentzen, A., *Introduction to the Old Testament*, II (Copenhagen: G.E.C. Gad, 1952).
Besserman, L.L., *The Legend of Job in the Middle Ages* (Cambridge, MA: Harvard University Press, 1979).
Betz, H.D., 'On the Problem of the Religio-Historical Understanding of Apocalyptic', *JTC* 6 (1969), pp. 134-56.
Bimson, J.J., 'Who is "this" in "Who is this…?" (Job 38.2)? A Response to Karl G. Wilcox', *JSOT* 87 (2000), pp. 125-28.
Blake, N.F. (ed.), *The Phoenix* (Manchester: Manchester University Press, 1964).
Blake, W., *The Book of Job* (New York: Paddington Press, 1976).
Blenkinsopp, J., *Ezekiel* (Interpretation; Louisville: John Knox Press, 1990).
—*Wisdom and Law in the Old Testament: The Ordering of Life in Israel and Early Judaism* (OBS; Oxford: Oxford University Press, 1983).
Boer, R. (ed.), *Bakhtin and Genre Theory in Biblical Studies* (SBLSS, 63; Atlanta: SBL, 2007).
Brenton, C.L., *The Septuagint Version of the Old Testament and Apocrypha* (London: Samuel Bagster & Sons, 1851).

Brown, R., *An Introduction to the New Testament* (New York: Doubleday, 1997).
Brownlee, W.H., *Ezekiel 1–19* (WBC, 28; Waco, TX: Word Books, 1986).
—*The Meaning of the Qumran Scrolls for the Bible* (New York: Oxford University Press, 1964).
Brueggemann, W., *In Man We Trust: The Neglected Side of Biblical Faith* (Atlanta: John Knox Press, 1972).
—'A Neglected Sapiential Word Pair', *ZAW* 89 (1977), pp. 234-58.
—'Resurrection', in *Reverberations of Faith: A Theological Handbook of Old Testament Themes* (Louisville: Westminster/John Knox Press, 2002), pp. 173-74.
Buccellati, G., 'Wisdom and Not: The Case of Mesopotamia', *JAOS* 101 (1981), pp. 35-47.
Carey, G., 'Apocalyptic Ethos', in *Society of Biblical Literature Seminar Papers, 1998* (SBLSP, 37; 2 vols.; Atlanta: Scholars Press, 1998), II, pp. 731-61.
Childs, B.S., *Introduction to the Old Testament as Scripture* (Philadelphia: Fortress Press, 1979).
Clines, D.J.A., *Job 1–20* (WBC, 17; Dallas: Word Books, 1989).
Coats, G.W., *Saga, Legend, Tale, Novella, Fable: Narrative Forms in Old Testament Literature* (JSOTSup, 35; Sheffield: JSOT Press, 1985).
Collins, A.Y., 'Apocalyptic Themes in Biblical Literature', *Interpretation* 53 (1999), pp. 117-30.
—'Introduction: Early Christian Apocalypticism', *Semeia* 36 (1986), pp. 1-12.
Collins, J., 'Apocalyptic Eschatology as the Transcendence of Death', *CBQ* 36 (1974), pp. 21-43.
—*The Apocalyptic Imagination: An Introduction to Jewish Apocalyptic Literature* (Grand Rapids: Eerdmans, 2nd edn, 1998).
—'Cosmos and Salvation: Jewish Wisdom and Apocalyptic in the Hellenistic Age', *History of Religions* 17 (1977), pp. 121-42.
—'Introduction: Towards the Morphology of a Genre', *Semeia* 14 (1979), pp. 1-20.
—'Structure and Meaning in the Testament of Job', in G. MacRae (ed.), *Society of Biblical Literature Seminar Papers, 1974* (SBLSP; 2 vols.; Cambridge, MA: Scholars Press, 1974), I, pp. 35-52.
—'Wisdom, Apocalypticism, and Generic Compatibility', in L. Perdue, B.B. Scott and W.J. Wiseman (eds.), *In Search of Wisdom: Essays in Memory of John G. Gammie* (Louisville: Westminster/John Knox Press, 1993), pp. 165-86.
Cook, A.S. (ed.), *The Christ of Cynewulf: A Poem in Three Parts* (Boston: Ginn & Company, 1900).
Cook, S.L., C.L. Patton and J.W. Watts (eds.), *The Whirlwind: Essays on Job, Hermeneutics and Theology in Memory of Jane Morse* (JSOTSup, 336; Sheffield: Sheffield Academic Press, 2001).
Cooper, A., 'Narrative Theory and the Book of Job', *Studies in Religion* 11 (1982), pp. 35-44.
Crenshaw, J.L., *Old Testament Wisdom: An Introduction* (Atlanta: John Knox Press, 1981).
—*Story and Faith: A Guide to the Old Testament* (New York: Macmillan, 1986).
—'The Twofold Search: A Response to Luis Alonso Schökel', in Polzin and Robertson (eds.), *Studies in the Book of Job*, pp. 63-69.
—'Wisdom', in Hayes (ed.), *Old Testament Form Criticism*, pp. 225-64.

Cross, F.M., 'The Development of the Jewish Scripts', in *The Bible and the Ancient Near East* (London: Routledge & Kegan Paul, 1961), pp. 133-202.
—'New Directions in the Study of Apocalyptic', *JTC* 6 (1969), pp. 157-65.
Curtis, J.B., 'On Job's Response to Yahweh', *JBL* 98 (1979), pp. 497-511.
Dailey, T.F., 'And Yet He Repents—On Job 42,6', *ZAW* 105 (1993), pp. 205-209.
—'Theophanic Bluster: Job and the Wind of Change', *Studies in Religion* 22 (1993), pp. 187-95.
Damon, S.F., *Blake's Job: William Blake's Illustrations of the Book of Job* (Hanover: University Press of New England, 1982).
Davids, P.H., *The Epistle of James: A Commentary on the Greek Text* (Grand Rapids: Eerdmans, 1982).
Davis, E.F., 'Job and Jacob: The Integrity of Faith', in Cook, Patton and Watts (eds.), *The Whirlwind*, pp. 100-20.
Day, J., 'The Daniel of Ugarit and Ezekiel and the Hero of the Book of Daniel', *VT* 30 (1980), pp. 174-84.
Dell, K.J., *The Book of Job as Sceptical Literature* (BZAW, 197; Berlin: Walter de Gruyter, 1991).
—*'Get Wisdom, Get Insight': An Introduction to Israel's Wisdom Literature* (Macon, GA: Smyth & Helwys, 2000).
Dhorme, E., *A Commentary on the Book of Job* (trans. Harold Knight; London: Nelson, 1967).
Dressler, H., 'The Identification of the Ugaritic DNIL with the Daniel of Ezekiel', *VT* 29 (1979), pp. 152-61.
Dreyfus, F.G., 'L'inspiration de la Septante: quelques difficultés à surmonter', *Revue des sciences philosophiques et théologiques* 49 (1965), pp. 210-20.
Driver, S.R., and G.B. Gray, *A Critical and Exegetical Commentary on the Book of Job* (ICC; Edinburgh: T. & T. Clark, 1921).
Duensing, H., 'Apocalypse of Paul', in Hennecke and Schneemelcher (eds.), *New Testament Apocrypha*, II, pp. 755-98.
Duff, D., *Modern Genre Theory* (Harlow, Essex: Longman, 2000).
Essick, R.N., *William Blake, Printmaker* (Princeton, NJ: Princeton University Press, 1980).
Fohrer, G., *Das Buch Hiob* (Kommentar zum Alten Testament; Gütersloh: Gerd Mohn, 1963).
—'The Righteous Man in Job 31', in J.L. Crenshaw and J.T. Willis (eds.), *Essays in Old Testament Ethics* (New York: Ktav, 1974), pp. 3-22.
Fontaine, C., 'Folktale Structure in the Book of Job: A Formalist Reading', in E.R. Follis (ed.), *Directions in Biblical Hebrew Poetry* (JSOTSup, 40; Sheffield: JSOT Press, 1987), pp. 205-32.
—'Wounded Hero on a Shaman's Quest: Job in the Context of Folk Literature', in Perdue and Gilpin (eds.), *The Voice from the Whirlwind*, pp. 70-85.
Fowler, A., *Kinds of Literature: An Introduction to the Theory of Genres and Modes* (Cambridge, MA: Harvard University Press, 1982).
Freedman, D.N., 'The Flowering of Apocalyptic', *JTC* 6 (1969), pp. 166-74.
Freedman, D.N. (ed.), *Eerdmans Dictionary of the Bible* (Grand Rapids: Eerdmans, 2000).
Gammie, J.G., 'Paraenetic Literature: Toward the Morphology of a Secondary Genre', *Semeia* 50 (1990), pp. 41-71.

García Martínez, F., 'Encore l'apocalyptique', *JSJ* 17 (1986), pp. 224-32.
Gard, D., 'The Concept of the Future Life according to the Greek Translator of the Book of Job', *JBL* 74 (1953), pp. 137-43.
Geller, S.A., '"Where is Wisdom?" A Literary Study of Job 28 in its Settings', in J. Neusner, B.A. Levine and E.S. Frerichs (eds.), *Judaic Perspectives on Ancient Israel* (Philadelphia: Fortress Press, 1987), pp. 155-88.
Gerhart, M., 'Generic Competence in Biblical Hermeneutics', *Semeia* 43 (1988), pp. 29-44.
Gerstenberger, E., 'Psalms', in Hayes (ed.), *Old Testament Form Criticism*, pp. 179-224.
Gibson, J.C.L., *Job* (The Daily Study Bible; Philadelphia: Westminster Press, 1985).
Ginzberg, L., *The Legends of the Jews* (7 vols.; Philadelphia: The Jewish Publication Society of America, 1928, repr. 1968).
Glasson, T.F., 'What is Apocalyptic?', *NTS* 27 (1980), pp. 98-105.
Good, E.M., *In Turns of Tempest: A Reading of Job with a Translation* (Stanford: Stanford University Press, 1990).
—'The Problem of Evil in the Book of Job', in Perdue and Gilpin (eds.), *The Voice from the Whirlwind*, pp. 50-69.
Gordis, R., *The Book of God and Man: A Study of Job* (Chicago: University of Chicago Press, 1965).
—*Poets, Prophets and Sages: Essays in Biblical Interpretation* (Bloomington, IN: Indiana University Press, 1971).
Gottwald, N., *The Hebrew Bible: A Socio-Literary Introduction* (Philadelphia: Fortress Press, 1985).
Gowan, D., 'God's Answer to Job: How is it an Answer?', *HBT* 8 (1986), pp. 85-102.
—'Reading Job as Wisdom Script', *JSOT* 55 (1992), pp. 85-96.
—'Wisdom and Endurance in James', *HBT* 15 (1993), pp. 145-53.
Grabbe, L.L., *Priests, Prophets, Diviners, Sages: A Socio-Historical Study of Religious Specialists in Ancient Israel* (Valley Forge, PA: Trinity Press International, 1995).
—'The Social Setting of Early Jewish Apocalypticism', *JSP* 4 (1989), pp. 27-47.
Gray, G.B., 'The Additions in the Ancient Greek Version of Job', *The Expositor* 19 (1920), pp. 422-38.
Gray, J., 'The Book of Job in the Context of Near Eastern Literature', *ZAW* 82 (1970), pp. 251-69.
Greer, R.A., *Theodore of Mopsuestia: Exegete and Theologian* (London: The Faith Press, 1961).
Gruenwald, I., *Apocalyptic and Merkavah Mysticism* (Leiden: E.J. Brill, 1980).
Gutiérrez, G., *On Job: God-Talk and the Suffering of the Innocent* (trans. Matthew J. O'Connell; Maryknoll, NY: Orbis, 1987).
Haas, C., 'Job's Perseverance in the Testament of Job', in *Studies on the Testament of Job* (SNTSMS; ed. Michael A. Knibb and Pieter W. van der Horst; Cambridge: Cambridge University Press, 1989).
Habel, N., *The Book of Job* (Philadelphia: Westminster Press, 1985).
—'In Defense of God the Sage', in Perdue and Gilpin (eds.), *The Voice from the Whirlwind*, pp. 21-38.
Hamerton-Kelly, R.G., 'The Temple and the Origins of Jewish Apocalyptic', *VT* 20 (1970), pp. 1-15.
Hanson, P.D., 'Apocalypse, Genre', and 'Apocalypticism', in *IDBSup*, pp. 27-34.
—'Apocalyptic Consciousness', *Quarterly Review* 4 (1984), pp. 28-39.

—*The Dawn of Apocalyptic: The Historical and Sociological Roots of Jewish Apocalyptic Eschatology* (Philadelphia: Fortress Press, rev. edn, 1979).
—*Old Testament Apocalyptic* (IBT; Nashville: Abingdon Press, 1987).
Hanson, R.P.C., 'St Paul's Quotations of the Book of Job', *Theology* 53 (1950), pp. 250-53.
Hartin, P.J., *A Spirituality of Perfection: Faith in Action in the Letter of James* (Collegeville, MN: Liturgical Press, 1999).
—'"Who is Wise and Understanding among You?' (James 3:13): An Analysis of Wisdom, Eschatology, and Apocalypticism in the Epistle of James', in *Society of Biblical Literature Seminar Papers, 1996* (SBLSP, 35; Atlanta: Scholars Press, 1996), pp. 483-503.
Hartley, J., *The Book of Job* (NICOT; Grand Rapids: Eerdmans, 1988).
Hayes, J.H. (ed.), *Old Testament Form Criticism* (TUMSR, 2; San Antonio: Trinity University Press, 1974).
Hellholm, D., 'The Problem of Apocalyptic Genre and the Apocalypse of John', *Semeia* 36 (1986), pp. 13-64.
Hellholm, D. (ed.), *Apocalypticism in the Mediterranean World and the Near East: Proceedings of the International Colloquium on Apocalypticism Uppsala, August 12-17, 1979* (Tübingen: J.C.B Mohr [Paul Siebeck], 1983).
Hengel, M., *The Septuagint as Christian Scripture: Its Prehistory and the Problem of its Canon* (trans. M.E. Biddle; Edinburgh: T. & T. Clark, 2002).
Hennecke, E., and W. Schneemelcher (eds.), *New Testament Apocrypha* (2 vols.; trans. R.McL. Wilson; Philadelphia: Westminster Press, 1965).
Hirsch, E.D., Jr, *Validity in Interpretation* (New Haven: Yale University Press, 1967).
Hölscher, G., 'Die Entstehung des Buches Daniel', *Theologische Studien und Kritiken* 92 (1919), pp. 113-38.
Hultgård, A., 'Forms and Origins of Iranian Apocalypticism', in Hellholm (ed.), *Apocalypticism in the Mediterranean World and the Near East*, pp. 387-412.
Hunter, A., *Wisdom Literature* (London: SCM Press, 2006).
Hurvitz, A., 'The Date of the Prose Tale of Job Linguistically Reconsidered', *HTR* 67 (1974), pp. 17 34.
Jackson-McCabe, M.A., 'A Letter to the Twelve Tribes in the Diaspora: Wisdom and "Apocalyptic" Eschatology in the Letter of James', in *Society of Biblical Literature Seminar Papers, 1996* (SBLSP, 35; Atlanta: Scholars Press, 1996), pp. 504-17.
Jacobs, I., 'Literary Motifs in the Testament of Job', *JJS* 21 (1970), pp. 1-10.
Jobes, K.H., and M. Silva, *Invitation to the Septuagint* (Grand Rapids: Baker, 2000).
Johnson, E., *The Function of Apocalyptic and Wisdom Traditions in Romans 9–11* (SBLDS, 109; Atlanta: Scholars Press, 1989).
Johnson, T.J., 'Critical Note on Job 2:8', *BIOSCS* 36 (2003), pp. 87-92.
—'Implied Antecedents in Job xl 2B and Proverbs iii 6A', *VT* 52 (2002), pp. 278-84.
—'Paleo-Hebrew and Qumran: With an Analysis of 4QpaleoJob(c)', unpublished paper, Marquette University, 1999.
Kaiser, O., *Introduction to the Old Testament: A Presentation of its Results and Problems* (trans. J. Sturdy; Minneapolis: Augsburg, 1977).
Kallen, H.M., *The Book of Job as Greek Tragedy* (New York: Hill & Want, 1958).
Kaplan, L.J., 'Maimonides, Dale Patrick, and Job xlii 6', *VT* 28 (1978), pp. 356-58.
Koch, K., *The Rediscovery of Apocalyptic* (trans. M. Kohl; London: SCM Press, 1972).

Köhler, L., *Hebrew Man* (trans. P.R. Ackroyd; New York: Abingdon Press, 1956).
Kraft, R.A. (ed.), *The Testament of Job according to the SV Text* (Missoula, MT: Scholars Press, 1974).
Lapointe, R., 'Les traductions de la Bible sont-elles inspirées?', *Science et esprit* 23 (1971), pp. 69-83.
LaSor, W.S., D.A. Hubbard and F.W. Bush, *Old Testament Survey: The Message, Form, and Background of the Old Testament* (Grand Rapids: Eerdmans, 2nd edn, 1996).
Lemaire, A., 'L'épigraphie paléo-hébraïque et la Bible', in W. Zimmerli (ed.), *Congress Volume: Göttingen 1977* (VTSup, 29; Leiden: Brill, 1978), pp. 165-76.
Linafelt, T., 'The Undecidability of ברך in the Prologue to Job and Beyond', *Biblical Interpretation* 4 (1996), pp. 154-72.
Livingstone, E.A. (ed.), *Studia Biblica* (JSOTSup, 11; Sheffield: JSOT Press, 1979).
Longman, Tremper, III, 'Form Criticism, Recent Developments in Genre Theory, and the Evangelical', *WTJ* 47 (1985), pp. 46-67.
Lunceford, J.E., 'Whirlwind', in Freedman (ed.), *Eerdmans Dictionary of the Bible*, p. 1377.
MacLeish, A., *J.B. A Play in Verse* (Boston: Houghton Mifflin, 1959).
Magdalene, F.R., 'Curse', in Freedman (ed.), *Eerdmans Dictionary of the Bible*, pp. 301-302.
Magnan, C., *The Targum of Job* (The Aramaic Bible; Collegeville, MN: The Liturgical Press, 1987).
Martin, Ralph P., *James* (WBC, 48; Waco, TX: Word Books, 1988).
Martinez, F.G. 'Encore l'apocalyptique', *JSJ* 17 (1986), pp. 224-32.
—*Wisdom and Apocalypticism in the Dead Sea Scrolls and in the Biblical Tradition* (Leuven: Leuven University Press, 2003).
Matthews, V.H., and D.C. Benjamin (eds.), *Old Testament Parallels: Laws and Stories From the Ancient Near East* (New York: Paulist Press, 2nd edn, 1997).
McGinnis, C.M., 'Playing the Devil's Advocate in Job: On Job's Wife', in Cook, Patton and Watts (eds.), *The Whirlwind*, pp. 121-41.
McLean, M.D., 'The Use and Development of Palaeo-Hebrew in the Hellenistic and Roman Periods' (PhD dissertation, Harvard University, 1982).
Milik, J.T. '4QtgJob' (DJD, 6; Oxford: Clarendon Press, 1977), pp. 86-90.
Mitchell, C., 'Power, *Eros*, and Biblical Genres', in Boer (ed.), *Bakhtin and Genre Theory in Biblical Studies*, pp. 31-42.
Molino, J., 'Les genres littéraires', *Poétique* 24 (1993), pp. 3-28.
Moo, D.J., *James* (TNTC; Grand Rapids: Eerdmans, 1986).
Moore, G.F., 'Introduction', in H.M. Kallen, *The Book of Job as Greek Tragedy* (New York: Moffat, Yard & Company, 1918).
Moore, R.D., 'The Integrity of Job', *CBQ* 45 (1983), pp. 17-31.
Morrow, W. 'Consolation, Rejection, and Repentance in Job 42:6', *JBL* (1986), pp. 211-25.
Muller, H.P., 'Mantische Weisheit und Apokalyptik', in P.A.H. de Boer (ed.), *Congress Volume, Uppsala 1971* (VTSup, 22; Leiden: Brill, 1972), pp. 268-93.
Müller, M., *The First Bible of the Church: A Plea for the Septuagint* (JSOTSup, 206; Sheffield: Sheffield Academic Press, 1996).
—'The Septuagint as the Bible of the New Testament Church: Some Reflections', *Scandinavian Journal of the Old Testament* 7 (1993), pp. 194-207.

Murphy, R.E., *The Book of Job: A Short Reading* (New York: Paulist Press, 1999).
—*The Tree of Life: An Exploration of Biblical Wisdom Literature* (Grand Rapids: Eerdmans, 2nd edn, 1996).
—*Wisdom Literature: Job, Proverbs, Ruth, Canticles, Ecclesiastes, and Esther* (FOTL, 13; Grand Rapids: Eerdmans, 1981).
Murtagh, J., 'The Book of Job and The Book of the Dead', *Irish Theological Quarterly* 35 (1968), pp. 166-73.
Neusner, J. (trans.), *The Talmud of the Land of Israel* (35 vols.; Chicago: The University of Chicago Press, 1984).
Newsom, C., *The Book of Job: A Contest of Moral Imaginations* (Oxford: Oxford University Press, 2003).
—'Spying out the Land: A Report from Genology', in Boer (ed.), *Bakhtin and Genre Theory in Biblical Studies*, pp. 19-30.
Nickelsburg, G., 'Wisdom and Apocalypticism in Early Judaism: Some Points for Discussion', in E.H. Lovering (ed.), *Society of Biblical Literature Seminar Papers, 1994* (SBLSP, 33; Atlanta: Scholars Press, 1994), pp. 715-32.
Noah, M.M. (trans.), *The Book of Jashar, Referred to in Joshua and Second Samuel* (New York: Noah & Gould, 1840).
Noth, M., 'Noah, Daniel und Hiob in Ezechiel xiv', *VT* 1 (1951), pp. 251-60.
Ohlander, U. (ed.), *A Middle English Metrical Paraphrase of the Old Testament* (5 vols.; Gothenburg: Acta Universitatis Gothoburgensis, 1963).
Origen, 'Letter to Africanus', in *Ante-Nicene Christian Library* (trans. F. Crombie; Edinburgh: T. & T. Clark, 1869), X.
Orlinsky, H., 'The Septuagint as Holy Writ and the Philosophy of the Translators', *HUCA* 46 (1975), pp. 89-114.
—'Studies in the Septuagint of the Book of Job', *HUCA* 28 (1957), pp. 53-74; 29 (1958), pp. 229-71; 30 (1959); pp. 153-67; 32 (1961), pp. 239-68; 33 (1962), pp. 119-51; 35 (1964), pp. 57-78; 36 (1965), pp. 37-47.
Osborne, G., 'Genre Criticism—Sensus Literalis', *Trinity Journal* 4 (1983), pp. 1-27.
Oswalt, J.N., 'Recent Studies in Old Testament Apocalyptic', in D. Baker and B. Arnold (eds.), *The Face of Old Testament Studies: A Survey of Contemporary Approaches* (Grand Rapids: Baker, 1999), 369-90.
Parsons, G.W., 'The Structure and Purpose of the Book of Job', *Bibliotheca Sacra* 138 (1981), pp. 139-57.
Patrick, D., 'The Translation of Job xlii 6', *VT* 26 (1976), pp 369-71.
Penchansky, D., *The Betrayal of God: Ideological Conflict in Job* (Louisville: Westminster Press, 1990).
—'Job's Wife: The Satan's Handmaid', in D. Penchansky and P.L. Redditt (eds.), *Shall Not the Judge of All the Earth Do What is Right? Studies on the Nature of God in Tribute to James L. Crenshaw* (Winona Lake, IN: Eisenbrauns, 2000), pp. 223-38.
Penner, T.C., *The Epistle of James and Eschatology: Re-reading an Ancient Christian Letter* (JSNTSup, 121; Sheffield: Sheffield Academic Press, 1996).
Perdue, L.G., *Wisdom in Revolt: Metaphorical Theology in the Book of Job* (JSOTSup, 112; Sheffield: Sheffield Academic Press, 1991).
Perdue, L.G., and W.C. Gilpin (eds.), *The Voice from the Whirlwind: Interpreting the Book of Job* (Nashville: Abingdon Press, 1992).

Perrot, C. 'L'inspiration des Septante et le pouvoir scripturaire', in G. Dorival and O. Munnich (eds.), *KATA TOUS O' Selon les Septante: trente études sur la Bible grecque des Septante, en hommage à Marguerite Harl* (Paris: Cerf, 1995), pp. 169-83.

Pfeiffer, R.H., *History of New Testament Times* (London: A. & C. Black, 1949).

Pietersma, A., and B. Wright (eds.), *A New English Translation of the Septuagint* (New York: Oxford University Press, 2007).

Ploeg, J. van der, *et al.*, *Le Targum de Job de la grotte XI de Qumran* (Leiden: Brill, 1971).

Polzin, R., and D.A. Robertson (eds.), *Studies in the Book of Job* (Semeia, 7; Missoula, MT: Scholars Press, 1977).

Pope, M., *Job* (AB, 15; Garden City, NY: Doubleday, 1965).

Pritchard, J.B. (ed.), *The Ancient Near East: A New Anthology of Texts and Pictures* (Princeton: Princeton University Press, 1975).

Rad, G. von, 'Job 38 and Ancient Egyptian Wisdom', in *The Problem of the Hexateuch and Other Essays* (New York: McGraw–Hill, 1966), pp. 281-91.

—*Old Testament Theology* (2 vols.; trans. D.M.G. Stalker; New York: Harper & Row, 1965).

—*Wisdom in Israel* (trans. J.D. Martin; Nashville: Abingdon Press, 1972).

Reicke, B., *The Epistle of James, Peter, and Jude* (AB, 37; Garden City, NY: Doubleday, 1964).

Renner, J.T.E., 'Aspects of Pain and Suffering in the Old Testament', *The Australian and New Zealand Theological Review* 15 (1982), pp. 32-42.

Rex, R., 'St John Fisher's Treatise on the Authority of the Septuagint', *JTS* 43 (1992), pp. 55-72.

Richter, H., *Studien zu Hiob: Der Aufbau des Hiobbuches, dargestellt an den Gattungen des Rechtslebens* (Theologische Arbeiten, 11; Berlin: Evangelische Verlagsanstalt, 1959).

Robertson, D.A., 'The Comedy of Job: A Response', in Polzin and Robertson (eds.), *Studies in the Book of Job*, pp. 41-44.

Rodd, C., *The Book of Job* (Philadelphia: Trinity Press International, 1990).

Rowland, C., *The Open Heaven: A Study of Apocalyptic in Judaism and Early Christianity* (New York: Crossroad, 1982).

Rowley, H.H., *Job* (NCB; Grand Rapids: Eerdmans, 1970).

Russell, D.S., *The Method and Message of Jewish Apocalyptic* (OTL; Philadelphia: Westminster Press, 1964).

Sacchi, P., *Jewish Apocalyptic and its History* (trans. William J. Short; JSPSup, 20; Sheffield: Sheffield Academic Press, 1997).

Sanders, E.P., 'The Genre of Palestinian Jewish Apocalypses', in Hellholm (ed.), *Apocalypticism in the Mediterranean World and the Near East*, pp. 447-59.

Sarna, N.M., 'Epic Substratum in the Prose of Job', *JBL* 76 (1957), pp. 13-25.

Sawyer, J.F.A., 'The Authorship and Structure of the Book of Job', in Livingstone (ed.), *Studia Biblica*, pp. 253-57.

Schmidt, J.M., *Die jüdische Apokalyptik: Die Geschichte ihrer Erforschung von den Anfängen bis zu den Textfunden von Qumran* (Neukirchen–Vluyn: Neukirchener Verlag, 1976).

Schmithals, W., *The Apocalyptic Movement: Introduction and Interpretation* (trans. J.E. Steely; Nashville: Abingdon Press, 1975).

Segal, A., 'The Sacrifice of Isaac in Early Judaism and Christianity', in *The Other Judaisms of Late Antiquity* (Atlanta: Scholars Press, 1987), pp. 109-30.
Seitz, C., 'Job: Full-Structure, Movement, and Interpretation', *Interpretation* 43 (1989), pp. 5-17.
Sewall, R.B., *The Vision of Tragedy* (enlarged edn; New Haven: Yale University Press, 1980).
Siegel, J., 'The Employment of Palaeo-Hebrew Characters for Divine Names at Qumran in Light of Tannaitic Sources', *HUCA* 52 (1971), pp. 159-71.
Simonetti, M., and M. Conti (eds.), *Job* (ACCS, 6; Downer's Grove, IL: InterVarsity Press, 2006).
Skehan, P.W., 'Exodus in the Samaritan Recension from Qumran', *JBL* 74 (1955), pp. 182-87.
Skehan, P.W., E. Ulrich, and J. Sanderson, *Qumran Cave 4: Palaeo-Hebrew and Greek Biblical Manuscripts* (DJD, 9; Oxford: Clarendon Press, 1992).
Sokoloff, M., *The Targum to Job from Qumran Cave XI* (Ramat-Gan: Bar-Ilan University, 1974).
Smith, G., 'Job iv 12-21: Is it Eliphaz's Vision?', *VT* 40 (1990), pp. 453-63.
Soulen, R.N., *Handbook of Biblical Criticism* (Atlanta: John Knox Press, 2nd edn, 1981).
Spiegel, S., *The Last Trial: On the Legends and Lore of the Command to Abraham to Offer Isaac as a Sacrifice: The Akedah* (trans. Judah Goldin; New York: Behrman House, 1979).
—'Noah, Danel, and Job', in *Louis Ginzberg Jubilee Volume* (2 vols.; New York: American Academy for Jewish Research, 1945), I, pp. 305-55.
Spittler, R., 'Testament of Job', in *OTP*, I, pp. 829-68.
Steiner, G., 'Tragedy: Remorse and Justice', *The Listener* 18 (1979), pp. 508-11.
Steinmann, A.E., 'The Graded Numerical Saying in Job', in A.B. Beck, A.H. Bartelt, P.R. Raabe and C.A. Franke (eds.), *Fortunate the Eyes that See: Essays in Honor of David Noel Freedman in Celebration of his Seventieth Birthday* (Grand Rapids: Eerdmans, 1995), pp. 288-97.
Stone, M.E., 'List of the Revealed Things in Apocalyptic Literature', in F.M. Cross, W.E. Lemke and P.D. Miller (eds.), *Magnalia Dei: The Mighty Acts of God* (Garden City, NY: Doubleday, 1976), pp. 414-52.
Swete, H.B., *An Introduction to the Old Testament in Greek* (New York: Ktav, 1968).
Tigchelaar, E.J.C., 'More on Apocalyptic and Apocalypses', *JSJ* 18 (1987), pp. 137-44.
Tiller, P., 'The Rich and Poor in James: An Apocalyptic Proclamation', in *Society of Biblical Literature Seminar Papers, 1996* (SBLSP, 37; Atlanta: Scholars Press, 1996), pp. 909-20.
Ulrich, E., 'Our Sharper Focus on the Bible and Theology Thanks to the Dead Sea Scrolls', *CBQ* 66 (2004), pp. 1-24.
Urbrock, W.J., 'Job as Drama: Tragedy or Comedy?', *Currents in Theology and Mission* 8 (1981), pp. 35-40.
—'Reconciliation of Opposites in the Dramatic Ordeal of Job', in Polzin and Robertson (eds.), *Studies in the Book of Job*, pp. 147-53.
VanderKam, J.C., *Enoch and the Growth of an Apocalyptic Tradition* (CBQMS, 16; Washington, DC: Catholic Biblical Quarterly, 1984).
Vermes, G., *The Complete Dead Sea Scrolls in English* (New York: Penguin, 1997).
Vielhauer, P., 'Apocalyptic in Early Christianity', in Hennecke and Schneemelcher (eds.), *New Testament Apocrypha*, II, pp. 597-600.

Vines, M.E., 'The Apocalyptic Chronotype', in Boer (ed.), *Bakhtin and Genre Theory in Biblical Studies*, pp. 109-18.
Volz, P., *Das Buch Hiob* (Göttingen: Vandenhoeck & Ruprecht, 1911).
Waltke, B., and M. O'Connor, *An Introduction to Biblical Hebrew Syntax* (Winona Lake, IN: Eisenbrauns, 1990).
Webb, R.L., 'Apocalyptic: Observations on a Slippery Term', *JNES* 49 (1990), pp. 115-26.
Weeks, S., *Early Israelite Wisdom* (OTM; Oxford: Clarendon Press, 1994).
Weinfeld, M., 'Job and its Mesopotamian Parallels: A Typological Analysis', in W. Claassen (ed.), *Text and Context: Old Testament and Semitic Studies for F.C. Fensham* (JSOTSup, 48; Sheffield: JSOT Press, 1988), pp. 217-26.
Weiser, A., *Das Buch Hiob übersetzt und erklärt* (Göttingen: Vandenhoeck & Ruprecht, 1951).
Westermann, C., *Roots of Wisdom: The Oldest Proverbs of Israel and Other Peoples* (trans. J.D. Charles; Louisville: Westminster/John Knox Press, 1995).
—*The Structure of the Book of Job: A Form-Critical Analysis* (trans. C.A. Muenchow. Philadelphia: Fortress Press, 1981).
Whedbee, J.W., 'The Comedy of Job', in Polzin and Robertson (eds.), *Studies in the Book of Job*, pp. 1-39.
Whybray, R.N., *The Intellectual Tradition in the Old Testament* (BZAW, 135; Berlin: Walter de Gruyter, 1974).
Wilcox, K.G., '"Who is this...?" A Reading of Job 38.2', *JSOT* 78 (1998), pp. 85-95.
Williams, J.G., 'Comedy, Irony, Intercession: A Few Notes in Response', in Polzin and Robertson (eds.), *Studies in the Book of Job*, pp. 135-45.
Wise, M., M. Abegg Jr and E. Cook, *The Dead Sea Scrolls: A New Translation* (San Francisco: HarperSanFrancisco, 1996).
Witherington, B., 'Long Suffering Job: Does the Book of Job Have a Happy Ending?', n.p. (cited 8 January 2004), http://www.beliefnet.org/story/138/story_13817.html.
Würthwein, E., *The Text of the Old Testament* (rev. and enlarged edn; trans. E.F. Rhodes; Grand Rapids: Eerdmans, 1995).
Zaharopolous, D.Z., *Theodore of Mopsuestia on the Bible: A Study of his Old Testament Exegesis* (New York: Paulist Press, 1989).
Ziegler, J., *Iob* (Septuaginta Vetus Testamentum graecum; Göttingen: Vandenhoeck & Ruprecht, 1982).
Zimmerli, W., *Ezekiel* (Hermeneia; Philadelphia: Fortress Press, 1979).
Zuckerman, B., 'The Date of 11Q Targum Job: A Paleographic Consideration of its Vorlage', *JSP* 1 (1987), pp. 57-78.
—'Job, Targums of', in *ABD*, III, pp. 868-69.
—*Job the Silent: A Study in Historical Counterpoint* (New York: Oxford University Press, 1991).

INDEXES

INDEX OF REFERENCES

OLD TESTAMENT		1.6	91, 111	3.11-26	114
Genesis		1.8	115, 121	3.17	91, 114
1.2-3	114	1.11	108, 109,	3.20-21	68
1.3	113		111	3.20	114
2.1-3	114	1.12	96, 110	4–27	23, 33, 48,
2.7	53	1.13-22	111		106
16.13	123	1.21	91, 111	4–14	26, 106
20.31	94	1.22	111	4	47, 49, 52,
22	80	2	109, 111-		63, 69, 74,
22.12	80		13, 115,		115, 118,
22.16	80		129, 131		130
22.19	80	2.1	91	4.1-11	115
32.30	123	2.3	111	4.3-4	129
36.33	51	2.4-5	111	4.3	156
46.13	81	2.9-10	111	4.4	129
46.15	94	2.9	57, 99,	4.6-11	115
			109-12	4.6	115, 120
Exodus		2.10	58, 71,	4.7-11	115
22.4	157		111, 156	4.8	115
22.28	108	2.11-13	112	4.12–28.22	107, 116
		2.11	113	4.12-21	46, 49, 116
Deuteronomy		3–31	106	4.12-16	116
6.4-5	62	3–27	165	4.14	47
		3	23, 48, 52,	4.15	48
1 Kings			53, 106,	4.16	47
8.31-32	109		113, 114,	4.17-21	47, 50, 63,
			118-20,		117, 120,
Job			122-24,		178
1–2	79, 106-		142, 146,	4.17	49, 53,
	108		154, 156		117-19
1	129	3.1–42.7	35	4.19-21	118
1.1–4.11	107	3.3-10	114	4.21	118
1.1-5	107	3.3	57	5	52, 56,
1.1	112, 164	3.4	113		119, 120,
1.5	108, 112	3.5-9	91		152

Job (cont.)		12.16-22	135	19.27	126
5.1-8	116	12.22	123	19.28	127
5.1	118	12.23	123	19.29	127
5.2	118	13.3	123	20.3	128
5.4	91	13.4	53	20.5	128
5.8	118, 119	13.7	123	21	128
5.9–14.35	119	13.8	123	21.7-8	161
5.11	84	13.15	123	21.7	57
5.17-27	151	13.18-20	86	21.22	91
5.17	119	13.23-27	86	21.27	128, 132
5.19-26	55, 82, 120	13.23	123	22–27	106, 128
5.24-26	30	14	123	22.2	119
5.27	120	14.5	68	22.6	129
6.8-9	120	14.13-18	86	22.7	129
6.10	122	14.13	68	22.9	129
6.13	120	14.14	68, 69, 71,	22.15	129
6.24-25	120		84, 87, 91	22.23	129
7	120	15–31	26	22.30	129
7.14	117	15–21	106, 124	23.3	129
7.20-21	144	15.4	124	24	27
7.21	121, 161	15.8	117	24.1	130
8	121	15.9	124	24.13	129
8.3-4	121	15.11	117	24.14	129
8.5	121	15.13	124	24.15	129
8.6	121	15.15-16	119	24.24	130
8.13	121	15.21	91	25.1-6	130
8.20	121	15.25	124	25.2	91
9	121, 126	15.35	124	25.4	130
9.11	117	16	124, 126	26	130, 132
9.13-24	26	16.17	124	26.1-4	130
9.15	121, 122	16.19	124, 154	26.2	130
9.16	123	16.21	124	26.4	130, 151
9.17	57	17	124	26.5-14	130
9.33	122, 154	17.13	68	26.6	135
10	121, 122	18.3	125	27	131-33,
10.7	121, 122	18.13	91		139
10.8-17	122	18.21	125	27.1-12	130
10.16	91	19	125	27.3-4	130
10.18-22	68, 122	19.1-12	26	27.4	131
11	122	19.7	68	27.11-12	131
11.4	122	19.25-29	125	27.11	130, 135
11.7	61, 174	19.25-27	84, 126	27.12	137
11.10	91	19.25	58, 125-27,	27.13-23	130
11.17	91		154	27.16	134
12–14	123	19.26-27	28	27.20-21	134
12.13	135	19.26	126	27.20	134

28	1, 15, 17, 22, 25-32, 34, 35, 37, 47-56, 58, 60-62, 69, 74, 106, 131-40, 142, 150, 152, 161, 164, 174, 175	29	49, 55, 132, 133, 139, 140	34.4	144
				34.7	144
				34.8	144
		29.1	132, 139	34.15	146
		29.2	139	34.35	144
		29.4	55	35	144
		29.5	55	35.13-14	144
		29.7-10	156	35.14	68
		29.14	139	35.16	146
		29.17	156	36	145
		29.21-22	156	36.7	91
28.1-22	132	30	49, 139, 140	36.27	61
28.1-21	134			37	145
28.1	133, 134	30.15	139	37.9	149
28.6	134	30.20	68, 139	37.19-20	145
28.7	91	30.21	139	38–41	19, 22, 47-50, 53, 55, 178
28.11	133	30.25	140		
28.12	133, 136	31	49, 53, 98, 129, 138, 140-42, 144, 145	38	148, 174
28.13	60, 133			38.1–42.7	146
28.14	133			38.1–42.6	26, 106, 107
28.15	134				
28.17	134	31.5-6	140		
28.19	134	31.13-14	141	38.1	149
28.20	134, 136	31.16-17	141	38.2	58, 146-49, 152
28.22	60, 91, 134, 135	31.16	140		
		31.24	140	38.3	147
28.23–37.24	107	31.26	140	38.4	149
28.23-28	54, 136, 137, 178	31.35-37	144	38.7	61
		31.35	56, 68, 140, 142	38.16	61
28.23-27	55, 137			38.18	61
28.23-26	61	31.37	140	38.19	61
28.23	48, 50, 60, 136, 139	32–37	15, 25, 34, 106, 142	38.33	55
				39.30	149
28.25	136	32.1	141	40.1-7	148
28.26	136	32.2	142	40.2	62, 150, 151
28.27	54, 91	32.3	143, 144		
28.28	34, 50, 54, 60, 62, 132, 137, 139, 141	32.8	143	40.3-5	151, 152, 154
		33	144		
		33.9	144	40.7	147
		33.13-22	151, 152	40.8-14	150
29–31	23, 106, 138, 139, 152, 154	33.13	144	40.15–41.26	27
		33.15-16	144	40.19	151
		33.23	91	41.26	151
29–30	53	33.29-30	152	42	145
		34	144	42.1-6	69, 152

Job (cont.)		Ezekiel		2 Corinthians	
42.3	152	14	82, 83	12	99
42.5	70, 153, 155	14.12-23	82		
		14.14	51, 74, 81-83	Colossians	
42.6	53, 153, 155			2.14	95
		14.20	51, 74, 81-83	2 Thessalonians	
42.7–42.17	106, 107				
42.7-17	79, 156	14.21	120	2	96
42.7-9	57	28.3	83		
42.7	116, 120, 156	38–39	83	James	
		38.1–39.16	82	2.19	96
42.8	62, 63			5.1-11	95, 96, 98
42.10	58	Daniel		5.5	96
42.11	70, 89, 162	1–6	107	5.9	96
42.13-15	58	1.1	107	5.10	96
42.17	71, 84-86, 94	2.4	107	5.11	51, 95, 96, 100
		2.19-23	135		
43	145	2.31-45	134		
		7–12	107	Revelation	
Psalms		7.15	53	1.1-3	106
41	24	7.28	107	1.4–3.22	106
50.3	57	12.10	96	2.10	160
51	24	12.12-13	157	4.1–11.19	106
58.10	57			12.1–22.5	106
72	97	Hosea		22.6-21	106
74	55	13.3	57		
104	55			Pseudepigrapha	
111.10	54	Amos		1 Enoch	
		1.14	57	24	135
Proverbs		8.4	97		
1–9	133			2 Baruch	
1.7	54	Nahum		59	174
8.1-21	62	1.3	57	59.5	61
8.32-36	62				
9.10	54	Zechariah		4 Ezra	
		7.14	57	4	174
Isaiah				5.6	61
24–27	160	New Testament			
29.6	57	Matthew		Jubilees	
40.24	57	24–25	96	23	64
Jeremiah		Mark		Testament of Job	
4.19-26	52	13	96	4.9	93
23.19	57			33.3-4	93
25.32	57	Romans		33.3	93
		11.33-35	95	33.8	93

41.5	145	TALMUD		Cynewulf	
42.1-2	147	*t. Shabbat*		*Ascension*	
43.5	147	13.2		633-58	100
47.3	93				
52.1-12	93	CLASSICAL		*Phoenix*	
		Augustine		546-75a	100
Testament of Levi		*City of God*			
2–5	64	18.43	102		
MIDRASH		OTHER SOURCES			
Sefer Yashar Wa-Yera		*Book of Jashar*			
42b	80	66.15-22	155		
		67.42-43	155		

INDEX OF AUTHORS

Abegg, M., Jr 87
Adamson, J.B. 96
Alonso Schökel, L. 13, 28, 29, 116, 149
Alter, R. 146, 149
Andersen, F.I. 50, 59, 71, 108, 115, 117, 120, 126, 127, 130, 132, 147, 151, 156, 166
Andrews, C. 141
Are, T. 149
Austin, J.B. 166

Balentine, S. 97
Barton, J. 4
Baskin, J. 86
Benjamin, D.C. 141, 142
Benoit, P. 102
Bentzen, A. 24
Besserman, L.L. 79, 84, 99-102, 147
Betz, H.D. 169
Bimson, J.J. 147
Blake, N.F. 100
Blenkinsopp, J. 17, 83, 89, 106, 137, 167, 168
Boer, R. 4
Brenton, C.L. 87, 88
Brown, R. 106
Brownlee, W.H. 82, 83, 87
Brueggemann, W. 18, 85, 163
Buccellati, G. 15, 16
Bush, F.W. 3, 48, 107, 110

Carey, G. 52
Childs, B.S. 82
Clines, D.J.A. 15, 59, 78, 79, 117, 125, 126, 166
Coats, G.W. 9, 10
Collins, A.Y. 13, 39-41, 45, 108, 131, 150, 151, 158
Collins, J. 2, 42-46, 49, 51, 56, 58, 62-64, 89, 92-94, 105, 110, 114, 175

Conti, M. 97
Cook, A.S. 100
Cook, E. 87
Cooper, A. 163
Crenshaw, J.L. 17, 19, 29, 38, 82
Cross, F.M. 2, 86, 89, 167, 168
Curtis, J.B. 154

Dailey, T.F. 146, 148, 149, 153
Damon, S.F. 2
Davids, P.H. 97
Davis, E.F. 163, 164, 167
Day, J. 83
Dell, K.J. 5, 16-18, 22-24, 26, 28, 31, 32, 38, 46, 47, 100, 156
Dhorme, E. 50
Dressler, H. 83
Dreyfus, F.G. 102
Driver, S.R. 59, 60, 84
Duensing, H. 99, 156
Duff, D. 3, 4, 6

Essick, R.N. 2

Fohrer, G. 40, 142
Fontaine, C. 3, 36, 37, 138
Fowler, A. 6
Freedman, D.N. 159, 160

Gammie, J.G. 76, 77, 180
Gard, D. 85
Geller, S.A. 48, 134-39
Gerhart, M. 9, 11
Gerstenberger, E. 22
Gibson, J.C.L. 22
Gilpin, W.C. 3
Ginzberg, L. 80
Glasson, T.F. 42
Good, E.M. 58, 109, 110, 161, 162
Gordis, R. 38, 155, 162, 167, 171

Gottwald, N. 82
Gowan, D. 21, 22, 96, 146, 148
Grabbe, L.L. 160, 166, 168, 169, 174
Gray, G.B. 59, 60, 84, 85
Gray, J. 16
Greer, R.A. 102
Gruenwald, I. 2, 46
Gutiérrez, G. 163

Haas, C. 93
Habel, N. 38, 53, 54, 59, 70, 79, 108, 112, 114, 119, 126, 127, 129, 132, 148, 151, 152, 167
Hamerton-Kelly, R.G. 82
Hanson, P.D. 42, 49, 75, 82, 160, 162
Hanson, R.P.C. 95
Hartin, P.J. 96
Hartley, J. 53, 54, 71, 78, 114, 117, 120, 130, 133, 134, 140, 142, 166, 167
Hellholm, D. 45, 169
Hengel, M. 102
Hirsch, E.D. 9, 10, 39
Hölscher, G. 170
Hubbard, D.A. 3, 48, 107, 110
Hultgård, A. 169
Hunter, A. 19-21
Hurvitz, A. 79

Jackson-McCabe, M.A. 96
Jacobs, I. 52, 92, 93, 155
Jobes, K.H. 84, 102, 104
Johnson, E. 170
Johnson, T.J. 62, 87, 111, 150

Kaiser, O. 17, 79, 82
Kallen, H.M. 27, 28
Kaplan, L.J. 153
Koch, K. 42, 66, 70
Köhler, L. 25
Kraft, R.A. 100

LaSor, W.S. 3, 48, 107, 110
Lapointe, R. 102
Lemaire, A. 86
Linafelt, T. 109, 112
Longman, T., III 5
Lunceford, J.E. 149

MacLeish, A. 29
Magdalene, F.R. 109
Magnan, C. 90, 91, 134
Martínez, F.G. 64, 180
Martin, R.P. 96
Matthews, V.H. 16, 141, 142
McGinnis, C.M. 112
McLean, M.D. 88
Milik, J.T. 88
Mitchell, C. 5
Molino, J. 6, 8
Moo, D.J. 96
Moore, G.F. 27, 28
Moore, R.D. 163
Morrow, W. 154
Muller, H.P. 173
Müller, M. 103, 104, 173
Murphy, R.E. 5, 15, 17, 18, 23, 24, 26, 33, 50, 51, 55, 61, 69, 71, 106, 113-16, 122, 126, 130, 132, 136, 137, 140, 148, 151, 153, 161
Murtagh, J. 141

Neusner, J. 148
Newsom, C. 4-8, 35, 36, 72
Nickelsburg, G. 77, 175, 176
Noth, M. 83

O'Connor, M. 59
Ohlander, U. 100
Orlinsky, H. 85, 102
Osborne, G. 10
Oswalt, J.N. 41

Parsons, G.W. 161
Patrick, D. 153
Penchansky, D. 12, 16, 112
Penner, T.C. 95
Perdue, L.G. 3, 40, 55, 57, 58, 150
Perrot, C. 102, 103
Pfeiffer, R.H. 92
Ploeg, J. van der 88
Polzin, R. 28
Pope, M. 16, 38, 50, 51, 59, 60, 71, 78, 112, 119, 126, 127, 132, 134, 142, 143, 166
Pritchard, J.B. 16

Rad, G. von 19, 41, 170-75
Reicke, B. 96, 97
Renner, J.T.E. 163
Rex, R. 103
Richter, H. 25, 26
Robertson, D. 12, 28
Rodd, C. 50, 60, 114
Rowland, C. 2, 42, 46-48, 50, 52, 65, 108
Rowley, H.H. 147
Russell, D.S. 65

Sacchi, P. 65-67, 69, 78
Sanders, E.P. 43
Sanderson, J. 86
Sarna, N.M. 79
Sawyer, J.F.A. 161
Schmidt, J.M. 170
Schmithals, W. 65
Segal, A. 80
Seitz, C. 165, 166
Sewall, R.B. 28, 46
Siegel, J. 87
Silva, M. 84, 102, 104
Simonetti, M. 97
Skehan, P.W. 86, 87
Smith, G. 117, 118
Sokoloff, M. 88, 89
Soulen, R.N. 62
Spiegel, S. 79-81, 83
Spittler, R. 92, 94, 147, 148
Steiner, G. 28
Steinmann, A.E. 82, 120, 151, 152
Stone, M.E. 42, 60, 61, 174, 175
Swete, H.B. 84, 85, 102

Tigchelaar, E.J.C. 64, 67
Tiller, P. 97, 98

Ulrich, E. 86, 103, 104
Urbrock, W.J. 29

VanderKam, J.C. 174
Vermes, G. 86, 88, 90, 147
Vielhauer, P. 173
Vines, M.E. 72-75
Volz, P. 23

Waltke, B. 59
Webb, R.L. 41, 42
Weeks, S. 15
Weinfeld, M. 16
Weiser, A. 23
Westermann, C. 9, 17, 23-25, 38, 51, 114, 138, 146, 149
Whedbee, J.W. 13, 28-30
Whybray, R.N. 17
Wilcox, K.G. 147
Williams, J.G. 30
Wise, M. 87
Witherington, B. 177
Würthwein, E. 102, 108

Zaharopolous, D.Z. 102
Ziegler, J. 84, 127, 143
Zimmerli, W. 82, 83
Zuckerman, B. 16, 33, 34, 79, 81, 84, 88, 90, 97, 137

www.ingramcontent.com/pod-product-compliance
Lightning Source LLC
Chambersburg PA
CBHW071416160426
43195CB00013B/1715